A SEAT AT THE TABLE

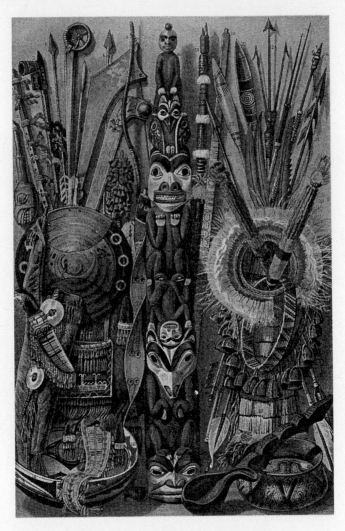

Nineteenth-century German lithograph of
North American Indian ceremonial objects.

A SEAT AT THE TABLE

HUSTON SMITH
IN CONVERSATION WITH
NATIVE AMERICANS
ON RELIGIOUS FREEDOM

EDITED AND WITH A PREFACE BY

PHIL COUSINEAU

WITH ASSISTANCE FROM
GARY RHINE

UNIVERSITY OF CALIFORNIA PRESS
BERKELEY   LOS ANGELES   LONDON

University of California Press, one of the most
distinguished university presses in the United
States, enriches lives around the world by
advancing scholarship in the humanities, social
sciences, and natural sciences. Its activities are
supported by the UC Press Foundation and by
philanthropic contributions from individuals
and institutions. For more information, visit
www.ucpress.edu.

University of California Press
Berkeley and Los Angeles, California

University of California Press, Ltd.
London, England

Library of Congress Cataloging-in-Publication Data

Smith, Huston.
    A seat at the table : Huston Smith in conversation
with Native Americans on religious freedom / edited
and with a preface by Phil Cousineau ; with assistance
from Gary Rhine.
        p.   cm.
    Includes bibliographical references and index.
    ISBN 978-0-520-25169-4 (alk. paper)
    1. Indians of North America—Religion.
2. Freedom of religion—United States.
I. Cousineau, Phil.   II. Rhine, Gary.   III. Title.
E98.R3556   2006
323.44'2'08997073—dc22   2005005290

Manufactured in the United States of America

13 12 11 10 09 08
10 9 8 7 6 5 4 3

This book is printed on New Leaf EcoBook 60,
containing 60% postconsumer waste, processed
chlorine free; 30% de-inked recycled fiber, elemental
chlorine free; and 10% FSC-certified virgin fiber,
totally chlorine free. EcoBook 60 is acid-free and meets
the minimum requirements of ANSI/ASTM D5634-01
(*Permanence of Paper*).♾

THIS BOOK IS DEDICATED TO THE MEMORY OF
REUBEN SNAKE (WINNEBAGO) AND VINCENT PARKER (COMANCHE)

Our religion is the traditions of our ancestors—the dreams of our old men, given to them in solemn hours of night by the Great Spirit; and the visions of our sachems (medicine people); and it is written in the hearts of the people.

CHIEF SEATTLE (DWAMISH), 1786-1866

A very great vision is needed, and the man who has it must follow it as the eagle seeks the deepest blue of the sky.

CRAZY HORSE (LAKOTA), 1849-1877

If we don't change directions, we're going to end up where we're headed.

REUBEN SNAKE (WINNEBAGO), 1943-1993

CONTENTS

ILLUSTRATIONS

PREFACE

A long time ago the Creator came to Turtle Island and said to the Red People: "You will be the keepers of Mother Earth. Among you I will give the wisdom about Nature, about the interconnectedness of all things, about balance and about living in harmony. You Red People will see the secrets of Nature. . . . The day will come when you will need to share the secrets with other people of the Earth because they will stray from their Spiritual ways. The time to start sharing is today."

MOHICAN PROPHECY

In December 1999 over seven thousand religious leaders, academics, and practitioners of every color and creed gathered in Cape Town, South Africa, for the Third Parliament of World Religions. The Parliament was held at the Good Hope Center in District Six, the symbol of apartheid for decades but now a potent symbol of reconciliation. During the eight-day Parliament hundreds of workshops, seminars, and performances exploring issues such as religious diversity, understanding sacred practices, practicing tolerance, and community activism were offered.

As the *Cape Town Argus* reported, a multitude of speakers shared the teachings of Bahai, Hinduism, Islam, Buddhism, Zoroastrianism, Judaism, Christianity, and African tribal religions, turning the city into a "crucible for believers." Among the presenting groups was a delegation of eight American Indian leaders and the world-renowned historian of religions Huston Smith. Under the title "America's Shadow Struggle," the delegation offered a series of panel discussions that covered a wide range of religious freedom issues of pressing concern to Native Americans. As if evoking the Mohican prophecy, as rendered by Don Coyhis, about sharing tribal wisdom in a time of spiritual crisis, the delegation inspired the gathering with their impassioned testimony. But they were also determined to present the seldom-heard Indian side of the story about America's much-vaunted religious freedom.

In Professor Smith they had the consummate interlocutor, to use one of his favorite terms for an interviewer. Not only is he one of the most widely respected scholars of religion in the world, he has also been a tireless advocate for Native Americans for the last twenty-five years. His lifelong search for what is ultimately true in the world's religions is reminiscent of the passion the Irish writer James Stephens once described in one of his short story characters: "All desires save one are fleeting, but that one lasts forever . . . he would go anywhere and forsake anything for wisdom."

Go anywhere and everywhere Huston has, traveling the world for the last fifty years to "winnow the wisdom from the world's great religious traditions." At the Parliament of World Religions, in Cape Town, Professor Smith, a strong proponent of interfaith dialogue, had the chance of a lifetime to express his deepening concern over the "fate of the human spirit," especially as it relates to the primal religions of the world. "Tribal peoples," Smith told the Cape Town press, "have religions which are fully deserving of the world's attention. Unfortunately, these traditions have suffered from noncomprehending governments." Inspired by the trickster advice of his friend Reuben Snake, "Listen, or your tongue will keep you deaf," Smith urged the audience to learn how to *listen* to native people. Only then, he said, will we have the *nuanced* view of world religions on which our future depends.

His sage advice was in accord with the unusually realistic goals laid out in the Parliament's official program: "Very few religious and spiritual communities can reach consensus with one another on an extensive religious, moral, ethical, or social agenda. . . . [But] there are points of convergence—of shared interest, common purpose, or common cause—that can provide a basis for dialogue and cooperation."[1] For the duration of the conference the American Indian forums on religious freedom unfolded in just that spirit of common cause. The participants revealed not only the hidden history of Anglo-Indian relations but also the enduring tensions within contemporary Indian life, what Navajo author Simon Ortiz once described as the "real struggle" for Native Americans: "You have to fight it, to keep what you have, what you are, because they are trying to steal your soul, your spirit, as well as your land, your children."

Though "no one voice speaks for all," as Lakota writer Joseph Bruchac writes, sometimes many speak as one.

What Ortiz describes as the *real struggle* was evoked throughout the delegation's presentations, in which nine voices spoke as one about one of the strangest paradoxes in history. With the traditional eloquence of Indian orators going back to Tecumseh, Black Hawk, and Chief Joseph, the delegation described how the United States, founded on the ideal of freedom of expression, had routinely denied religious and political freedom to its native people. This refusal has forced the land's original inhabitants—its "First People"—to struggle again and again for an equal voice in the religious and political debates that have determined their destiny.

With this legacy of disregard for Indian participation in mind, Pawnee lawyer and author Walter Echo-Hawk set the theme for the panels that followed: "An important reason that our delegation came here," he said, "was to try to get *a seat at the table* with the recognized religions on the planet. If we hadn't come to represent the religions of the New World this wouldn't be a real *world* Parliament. We want a seat at the table to make this gathering real and complete."

In the final session sacred lands activist Anthony Guy Lopez told Professor Smith that the real reason the Apaches are banding together is to fight against the latest seizure of their land in Arizona: *"We can't allow this to happen anymore."* The causes motivating Echo-Hawk and Lopez and so many other American Indian leaders to carry forth the fiery message about their struggle for religious freedom, like the long-distance Indian runners who used to carry messages from village to village, were the inspiration for this book.

My longtime filmmaking partner, Gary Rhine, and I were privileged to accompany Professor Smith and the Indian delegation to the Parliament in Cape Town and to film all nine sessions there. Over the next few years we augmented those conversations by taping Huston's interviews with all the participants in their own countries, as well as new interviews with two other eminent Native American leaders, Vine Deloria Jr. and Oren Lyons. Our documentary film premiered at the Amnesty International Film Festival in March 2004, under the title inspired by Echo-Hawk's cri de coeur at the Parliament in Cape Town: *A Seat at the Table: Struggling for American Indian Religious Freedom.*

These forums, follow-up interviews, and archival footage reveal more than just a litany of grievances. They are lively conversations that offer a unique record of contemporary American Indian voices speaking out on both history and current events. What emerges here is a terrific resolve to transform "crisis into challenge," as Iroquois journalist Douglas George-

Kanentiio says of his own nation's response to modern times. These remarkable dialogues also show a deep respect for the form itself, much in
the manner described by the great Oglala Sioux medicine man Luther
Standing Bear (1904–1939) as the speaking style of the old orators:

> Conversation was never begun at once, nor in a hurried manner. No one
> was quick with a question, no matter how important, and no one was
> pressed for an answer. A pause giving time for thought was the truly
> courteous way of beginning and conducting a conversation. Silence was
> meaningful with the Lakota, and his granting a space of silence to the
> speech-maker and his own moment of silence before talking was done
> in the practice of true politeness and regard for the rule that, "Thought
> comes before speech."[2]

The spirit of deliberation and respect for religious freedom for everyone permeates the first two chapters, featuring conversations with Vine
Deloria Jr. and Walter Echo-Hawk. Together, they reveal what poet Joy
Harjo calls "a heart for justice," while giving an unflinching view of the
roots of religious intolerance in the New World. Chapters 3 and 4, with
Winona LaDuke and Charlotte Black Elk, eloquently portray the inextri-
cably connected relationship between human beings, nature, and religion—
or what Peter Matthiessen calls "the religion before religion," nature itself as the "Great Mysterious." In chapter 5 Douglas George-Kanentiio
explores another aspect of the indigenous idea of the web of life, the intimate relationship between language and religion, and in chapter 6 Frank
Dayish Jr. offers a humble and triumphant view of one of Indian country's
most dramatic success stories, the regaining of legal rights to worship in
the Native American Church.

Chapters 7 and 8 concern two of the harsher struggles for religious
freedom: prisoners' rights, as represented by the courageous spiritual
counselor Lenny Foster, and the protection of indigenous peoples' rights
to "informed consent" with scientific researchers, as presented by lawyer
Tonya Frichner. In chapter 9 sacred lands activist Anthony Guy Lopez
shares his impassioned ideas about the enduring Indian struggle for access to sacred lands, the vital connection between ecology and spirituality, and healing ceremony. The final two chapters of the book feature tribal
leader and college professor Oren Lyons and Vine Deloria Jr., who reveal their strong convictions about the depredations of the past, and
where we can look for signs of the spiritual and cultural renaissance that
is under way in Indian country.

Each conversation with Professor Smith displays the grit of those engaged in the "good fight," not only the struggle against religious injustice

but also the fight to achieve a very valuable goal: it is exceedingly difficult to reach understanding with a culture whose understanding of you is either nonexistent or heavily influenced by the gauzy world of stereotypes, archetypes, old movies, or modern advertising. As Walter Echo-Hawk explained it at a question-and-answer session at the end of the Parliament, the problem is that "most Americans have never even met a native person and wouldn't even recognize one if they saw one." The forums at the Parliament, and this book, are an effort on the part of contemporary Native Americans to resist the double bind of romanticism and racism that endures in Indian country.

THE TRAIL OF BROKEN PROMISES

When the hulls of the first European ships scraped the shores of Arawak Island in the Caribbean, they were landing in a vast New World several times larger than the one they had left behind. This land, called Turtle Island by its original inhabitants, was populated by an estimated 12 million people who comprised some five hundred nations. The People, as most tribes referred to themselves, spoke over six hundred languages, as distinct from one another as Icelandic and Tibetan.[3] They created imaginative artworks and beautiful crafts, built complex cities, and explored the land from coast to coast. They knew more about the healing properties of the native herbs and plants than most Europeans knew about theirs. Many of their foods—tomatoes, squash, potatoes, chocolate, and tobacco—are now a part of everyday life around the world.

By the end of the nineteenth century, the combination of war, famine, conversion at sword point, the appearance of railroads, and Indian removal programs had conspired to destroy entire tribes and to decimate the rest. The mosaic of proudly independent tribes was reduced to less than 300,000 people surviving on a crazy quilt of reservations. To many contemporary Americans and Europeans, the bathetic statue *The End of the Trail,* featured at the 1893 Chicago World's Fair, was not symbolic art; it was the literal truth, proof that the Indians had been conquered and removed from the land—and from sight. The Plains Indian slumped over his horse represented the inevitable result of a "century of progress," as the Fair proclaimed. And though the World's Fair also featured the First Parliament of World Religion, not one group of indigenous people was invited, though millions of visitors filed past Sitting Bull's log cabin, which had been installed as a tourist attraction.

Yet despite the trail of over eight hundred treaties broken by the U.S.

government and all the "broken promises" reported by the U.S. Commission on Civil Rights, Native Americans are living in a time of tremendous transition and vitality. According to the 2000 Census Bureau report, there are now 567 federally recognized tribes in thirty-three states (Alaska alone has 226 tribes), with 1,300,000 living on reservations, out of a total Indian population of 2,476,000. Indians are the youngest and fastest-growing minority in the United States. While America's indigenous people still confront serious levels of diabetes, cancer, and heart disease, and many still struggle under what the Commission on Civil Rights called the "quiet crisis of discrimination and poverty," many believe that the corner has been turned.

Dramatic reversals have been won in areas such as health, education, and the recovery of lost land. Great social strides have been made with the passing of the Repatriation Act, protection for the Native American Church, and the Native Land trust. And the efforts continue at an electrifying pace. Moreover, according to an editorial in the *New York Times* in September 2004, some $3 billion dollars of restitution are at stake for the "profound cultural and symbolic legacy of America's indigenous peoples":

> [There is] a continuing lawsuit, whose purpose is to restore to the Indians assets and revenues that are rightfully theirs. Specifically, the suit seeks a proper accounting of a huge trust established more than a century ago when Congress broke up reservation lands into individual allotments. The trust was intended to manage the revenues owed to individual Indians from oil, timber leases and other activities. Yet a century of disarray and dishonesty by the federal government, particularly the Interior Department, whose job it is to administer the trust, has shortchanged generations of Indians and threatens to shortchange some half million more—the present beneficiaries of the trust.[4]

Along with the recovery of lost land and revenues comes the revitalizing of what many elders call the "Good Red Road," the spiritual path that emphasizes the community and the great web of life. The return to this ancient way of life, the way of native ceremony and oratory, of ethics and morality, has helped build a sense of hope about a future that weaves together the best of the two worlds in which native people find themselves. But even this effort to walk in both worlds, Indian and Anglo, is difficult if the inhabitants of these worlds don't share a language. "The fundamental factor that keeps Indians and non-Indians from communicating," wrote Vine Deloria Jr. in 1979, "is that they are speaking about two entirely different perceptions of the world."

NO WORD FOR RELIGION

In the eleven conversations that comprise this book it becomes evident that no Native American language has a word for "religion," at least the way that Westerners conceive of it, as institutionalized spirituality. Traditionally, Indians had no institutions, no dogma, no commandments, and no one idea about how to worship, or even what to call the great force at the heart of all life that was perceived by all the tribes in their own way. Instead, there was what sociologist Duane Champagne (Chippewa) calls "religiousness," rather than a belief system, a *way of life* that encompassed a rich variety of ceremonies, a mosaic of myths, legends, and poetry, together forming a complex heritage and a deep spiritual force.

In this animating spirit revered medicine man Lame Deer spent his life resisting claims of superiority made by organized religion, writing later, "I carried church within me . . . and wanted to see with the eye of the heart. . . . All nature is within us and all of us is in nature." Likewise, Ohiyesa (Charles Alexander Eastman) wrote a hundred years ago, in *The Soul of the Indian,* "We believed that the spirit pervades all creation and that every creature possesses a soul in some degree, though not necessarily a soul conscious of itself. The tree, the waterfall, the grizzly bear, each is an embodied force and as such an object of reverence."[5]

Although there was never one word for God, for art, for the spiritual path, and most assuredly no one voice for all Indian people, there was what Huston Smith calls a "wisdom tradition" that is recognizable among primal cultures the world over. No one word for God, but many for the Great Mystery—*Wakan-Tanka, Awoawilonas, Tirawa, May Wah-Kon-Tah, Tatanga Mani, Usen, the Great Spirit, Grandfather, the Creator*—sacred names for the great force in the universe that connects all living beings in the circle of life. And for the Hopis, ultimate reality is simply, numinously, *a'nehimu,* "a mighty something."

No word for "religion," but innumerable metaphors for the spiritual path, luminous expressions for the right road to take in life, such as Oglala Sioux holy man Nicholas Black Elk's description of his Great Vision: "Behold the circle of the nations' hoop, for it is holy, being endless, and thus all powers shall be one power in the people without end. Now they shall break camp and go forth upon the Red Road, and your Grandfathers shall walk among them."[6] This earnest search has been echoed for generations in ceremonial songs, such as this one: "Wacho ney ney ney ney wacho ney, ney," "I am searching for the road of life." And this one, from the singers of Laguna Pueblo, who beautifully echo the Creator's call down the Good Red Road, the path with heart, the journey where we look for one another:

> I add my breath to your breath
> That our days may be long on the Earth;
> That the days of our people may be long;
> That we shall be one person;
> That we may finish our roads together.
> May Oshrats [God] bless you with life;
> May our life roads be completed.

The common thread running through these conversations, philosophies, ceremonies, ways of being, and calls to action is this one unconquerable belief in the spiritual road that keeps individuals and their communities intact. This belief binds them to the land, to the whole, to the Creator, to the sacred truth behind the illusion of separateness that marks the institutionalized religions of the world. It imbued all Creation with meaning and was reinforced by a complex web of worship, ceremonies, songs, and storytelling, so that there was no boundary between the individual, Mother Earth, and what Luther Standing Bear called the "Big Holy."

In her conversation with Professor Smith, Winona LaDuke vigorously described this way of conducting oneself in the world when she remarked how wearying it was for indigenous people to be charged with always wanting to go back to an idealized past: "It's not about looking back—it's about being on your path—staying on the path the Creator gave you."

That plangent note of timeless wisdom and inspired optimism was echoed at the recent grand opening, in September 2004, of the new National Museum for the American Indian on the National Mall in Washington, D.C., when Director W. Richard West remarked, "We were here before, we're here after, and we'll be here into the future far beyond."[7]
Aho!

Phil Cousineau
March 2005

THE INDIAN WAY OF STORY

To the questions, "Why do you write? Who do you write for?" Simon Ortiz replies: "Because Indians always tell a story. The only way to continue is to tell a story and that's what Coyote says. The only way to continue is to tell a story and there is no other way. Your children will not survive unless you tell something about them—how they were born, how they came to this certain place, how they continued." And to the further question, "Who do you write for besides yourself?": "For my children, for my wife, for my mother and my father and my grandparents and then in reverse order so that I may have a good journey on my way back home."

Simon Ortiz, A Good Journey, *1977*

INTRODUCTION

THE PRIMAL RELIGIONS

HUSTON SMITH

Among the languages of American Indians there is no word for
"art," because for Indians everything is art. Equally, everything
is, in its way, religious. This means that to learn of primal religion,
we can start anywhere.

HUSTON SMITH, *THE WORLD'S RELIGIONS*, 1989

Huston Smith speaking at the Parliament of World Religions,
Cape Town, South Africa, 1999. Photograph by Phil Cousineau.
Used by permission of Phil Cousineau.

The Third Parliament of World Religions exceeded my expectations in a number of ways. The attendance was far beyond what I imagined it would be, more than seven thousand people paying what was required in time and money to make a kind of pilgrimage to South Africa. It was amazing for sheer numbers. But the objective and the quality of the presentations were even more important. In this time of so much ethnic conflict, with religion involved in people's antagonism toward one another, to have them come together was a very important statement to the world that conflict is not the bottom line of religion. Working together is a higher priority.

I think the conveners of the Parliament were brilliant in their choice of location, Cape Town, South Africa, because if there is any geographical spot in the world that stands as a kind of symbol of oppression—especially racial oppression—it is Cape Town. To hold the Parliament there underscored a leading problem of our time, and maybe through much of history. Nelson Mandela, former president of South Africa, gave one of the most moving addresses I have ever heard, with its climactic line, "There can be no future without forgiveness." All this came together to make Cape Town an unexpectedly important event.

The Parliament vividly brought back to me a string of memories relating to my discovery of the place of Native Americans (and through them indigenous religions generally) in the history of religions. The discovery took place during the 1970s, the decade when I taught at Syracuse University, in upstate New York. When I accepted the invitation to teach there I didn't even know that the Onondaga Reservation is only five miles from the university. As the decade progressed, I found myself spending more and more of my weekends hanging out with the chiefs. Up until then I had dismissed the whole family of indigenous religions—namely, the tribal and the oral—as unimportant. I blame my teachers for this, for *they* dismissed them. After all, they said, they can't (or until recently couldn't) even write, so what did they know? I was young and impressionable. I simply accepted what they said until my Onondaga friends set me straight, and I will never be able to adequately repay the gift they gave me.

Three moments in that decade with them stand out. The first occurred early on. I had spent a Saturday afternoon talking with Chief Leon Shenandoah and current Onondaga Wisdomkeeper Oren Lyons, and was beginning to sense the importance of what only came through to me later. My excitement—that would not be too strong a word—mounted as the afternoon progressed, until it detonated as I was driving home. I can remember my exact words.

"My God, Huston," I heard myself saying in the car. "For three decades you have been circling the globe trying to understand the metaphysics and religions of worlds different from your own, and here's one that has been right under your feet the entire time—and you haven't even noticed it!" That was the moment when the significance of this totally new area of world religions, supposedly my field of study, just clicked.

The second moment came later. On one of the many splendid afternoons I spent with them, Chief Leon Shenandoah and Oren Lyons informed me that the following Saturday the annual gathering of the Six Nations Iroquois was scheduled to begin. Their chiefs would be trickling in from 9 A.M. on, and if I would like to meet representatives from the other Iroquois nations I would be welcome. I readily accepted and spent a lovely morning with them, sitting around, drinking coffee, with no agenda. At one point Oren looked at his watch and said, "Well, it's 11:00, time for us to begin." Then looking me square in the eye, he said, "And, Huston, that means that we are going into the longhouse, and you are not."

Then Oren, being Oren, assuaged my disappointment by saying, "You know we love you to pieces, and we know you're totally on our side. But this is sacred material for us, and we will be meeting in a place that is sacred for us, and we believe it's not a time for the profane to come in."

What I still find amazing is that rather than feeling rejected, I felt a surge of exultation rising and coursing through me. The reason was immediately clear to me. It was simply thrilling that there were still people on our planet who think that there are things sacred enough that the profane—meaning those for whom these things are not equally sacred—would desecrate the substance itself with their presence.

The third moment occurred when I had arranged for two carloads of Onondaga youths to be taken to a park near New York City for an event that would open the International Youth Program, a gathering of students who were setting off on a summer-long round-the-world trip. There were about a hundred young members of various faiths, representatives of the world's religions. As an advisor to that project, I proposed that since this pilgrimage to the major religious sites of the world was beginning in America, it would be appropriate for Native Americans to conduct the opening ceremony.

The proposal was accepted, and the afternoon was turned over to them. A young Onondaga man in his late twenties stood under a large oak tree and assumed the leadership position by announcing that the ceremony would begin with a prayer.

My eyes automatically closed, and I bowed my head. But after a minute or two I opened them and looked at the young leader. His head was not bowed, nor were his eyes closed. Instead, he was actively looking around in the four sacred directions, up at the sky, and down at the ground. His opening prayer, said in his native tongue, lasted more than forty minutes. I always regard chaplain's prayers at presidential inaugurations as tediously long, but this was something else. After concluding his prayer, he walked back to his people, signaling that the ceremony was over. I made my way over to him and asked what he had said.

The young man responded, "I needed to call upon every living thing in the area that came into my line of vision—the trees, the birds, the stones, the clouds, and the Earth—to invite their participation. I asked their spirits to bless what is to follow in our journey and our International Youth Program."

Together, these moments, along with innumerable others, were major factors in inducing me to bring out a second edition of my book *The World's Religions*. So thirty-five years after the first edition had appeared, I added a chapter about the primal religions, making it eight, instead of seven, religions covered in the book. There are still other important religions, such as Sikhism and Shinto, not included, but I didn't want to make the book just a catalog. I wanted to provide space to go more deeply. I knew I had to do that because the religions I had dealt with in the first edition were all part of the field we call "historical religions," which have sacred text and histories recorded in writing. But these religions are only the tip of the iceberg. They are only about four thousand years old, whereas the primal, tribal, oral religions can be traced back archeologically into the twilight zone of prehistory, perhaps forty or fifty thousand years ago. To omit them from the first edition of my book was inexcusable, and I am glad I will not go my grave with that mistake uncorrected. The added chapter honors the primal religions as fully equal to the historical ones.

But why include them? Is there anything in the primal religions that is uniquely important? I would say yes. They correct our modern assumption that *later is better*. That illusion is contained in this word *progress,* and progress has been, pardon the language, the bitch goddess of the twentieth-century West. Even today's stand-up comics get into the act. Recently I heard one of them say, "I like even my antiques to be of the latest genre!" From a traditional perspective, and with regard to the things that matter most, this kind of reductionism is a flat mistake. Some commentators in the Middle Ages said St. Paul understood Moses far better than we can. The point is that from a traditional standpoint, the closer to the source you are, the more sacred the ground is, and that's why many tribal people honor animals over human beings: they're closer to the source.

We can imagine a Darwinist's horrified response to the notion that earlier is better. And yet I think that there is a great deal of truth in that view, because it recognizes what is ultimately important. I was taught that tribal religions were "primitive," with a pejorative built solidly into that word. I went into the first fifty-five years of my teaching with that prejudice instilled in me. Students are young and impressionable; they just believe what their teachers tell them. Great danger! I might have stayed in that mode if I hadn't moved to Syracuse. Those ten years in the shade of the Onondaga Reservation absolutely transformed my view of indigenous religions.

I am grateful to Phil Cousineau and Gary Rhine for gathering and editing these conversations so that others may have their perceptions about indigenous religions as transformed and deepened as mine have been over the course of these past two decades.

1

THE SPIRITUAL MALAISE IN AMERICA

THE CONFLUENCE OF RELIGION, LAW, AND COMMUNITY

Vine Deloria Jr., 2000. Photograph by Mankato State University. Used by permission of Vine Deloria Jr.

Vine Deloria Jr. is from the Standing Rock Sioux Agency, in Fort Yates, North Dakota, and a leading Native American scholar whose research, writings, and teachings have encompassed history, law, religious studies, and political science. He is the former executive director of the National Congress of American Indians and a professor emeritus of history at the University of Colorado. In January 2005 *Indian Country Today* chose him for the American Indian Visionary Award. He has written many acclaimed books, including *Evolution, Creationism, and other Modern Myths; Spirit and Reason; God Is Red; Red Earth, White Lies; Power and Place: Indian Education in America; Custer Died for Your Sins; Behind the Trail of Broken Treaties;* and *For This Land.*

This dialogue between Deloria and Huston Smith was recorded in two parts, at Deloria's home in Tucson, Arizona, in February 2000, six weeks after the Parliament of World Religions. Along with the interview with Oren Lyons, these conversations augment and enrich the themes that emerged in the Cape Town forums.

In this first chapter, Deloria expands on one of the central themes of his life's work, what he calls the "spiritual malaise" of contemporary America, especially how it relates to the Indian struggle for religious freedom. Another theme that emerges here is his impassioned concern for the vital connection between Indian spirituality and the natural world. He insists that any religion not intimately rooted in this world is delusional: "The lands of the planet call to humankind for redemption," he wrote in *God Is Red.* "Religion cannot be kept within the bounds of sermons and scriptures. It is a force in and of itself and it calls for an integration of lands and peoples in harmonious unity. . . . The peculiar geniuses of each continent all call for relief from the burden of exploitation."[1]

For Professor Smith, the conversation was an extraordinary opportunity to explore several of his favorite topics, such as the epistemology of religion, the difference between symbolism and literalism, and what native people consider natural law. Smith is particularly enlivened by Deloria's insight about the roots of our current spiritual crisis—which Deloria believes is based on our overreliance on the mythology of the lone individual—and our undervaluing the tribal belief in religion as an expression of community. What emerges in the exchange is Smith's extension of his discovery that "at the center of the religious life is a particular kind of joy, the prospect of a happy ending that blossoms from necessarily painful beginnings, the promise of human difficulties embraced and overcome."[2] On the edge of meaning here rests an ardent belief in the modern need to return to some semblance of tradition, which is, Deloria has written, "a renewal of meaning, not a flight from reality,"[3] and to an intimate connection with the land.

In an indication of his respect and of his ability to challenge and listen, moments before the interview began, Professor Smith turned to me off camera and confided, "What a privilege to spend a morning with a mind, a man, like this."

We believed in one God, the Great Spirit, we believed in our own kind of Ten Commandments. And we behaved as though we believed in them.

VINE DELORIA SR. (STANDING ROCK SIOUX), 1901–1990

HOUSTON SMITH: Vine, I can't begin this conversation without first expressing that I feel greatly honored by this opportunity, and I also feel extremely happy. It's a great good fortune that has fallen into my lap. I have followed your words from afar, and once I have been in your *presence,* as the Indians from Asia would say. I've had your *darshan,* an infusion of spiritual power that comes from a disciple listening to a master, if you look directly "eye to eye."

Two or three years ago, at an annual meeting of the American Association of Religion conference, you delivered the most remarkable plenary address I've heard in my fifty years of indentured service to that organization. You told us what we needed to hear, and you told us without mincing words, but your words were totally free of cant and bitterness. I remember your conclusion, which, I will have to confess, I have stolen many times for my own talks. After you had us all in the palm of your hand, you concluded by saying, "If I have offended anyone, I wish to apologize, and if there are any of you who feel lonesome because I have not offended you, my apologies to you also."

It was a remarkable occasion, and now it is equally remarkable to be with you again. Let me start with the big picture. In your writings you often come back to the point that here in America we are living in a time of a great spiritual malaise. You say that our problems exceed the particulars, such as population explosion, environmental danger, and the peculiar economic arrangements that allow the rich to keep getting richer. Underlying this, you say, is this immense spiritual malaise, which is caused by the decline of the sacred certainty that you say has been common to traditional or primal religions all over the world. I would like to hear you expand on that point so that it might serve as a basis for our discussion about the native struggle for religious freedom.

VINE DELORIA: Boy, that's a tough question.

SMITH: You've written about it as if it were glibly rolling off your tongue!

DELORIA: I think we have one basic problem we haven't defined yet. It's a problem we don't know how to deal with, which is the structure of the world's great religions, the institutional religions. They cannot provide religious experiences. We go out and search for religious experiences, but we have no framework to put them in. So we need some theological or metaphysical view that has not yet emerged. We're all experimenting by crossing, synthesizing, syncretizing, and trying frantically to find some way to express ourselves. But the community and the religions that are based on Western institutions are based on the solitary individual—not on the group. So we don't really have any communities to bring anything back *to*. The reason you find people interested in tribal groups is that the community is there. Religion is the expression of the community and its history, and not of individual searches, or of more precise renditions of religious belief.

SMITH: The *community* is the focus of the tribal religion. I think you've made your point, and you escalate it to a superlative. The entire focus of Native American religion, and indigenous religions, generally speaking, is the community. I thought when I read that sentence in one of your books that you didn't mention the land because you probably took the connection for granted. So would you say that the focus is on the community and the land on which the community lives?

DELORIA: Well, the land is part of the community and the animals and the spirits.

SMITH: Oh, well, here I am making a white distinction between the animate and the inanimate, as we Westerners tend to think of things.

DELORIA: If you look at the sacred pipe ceremonies or the sand paint-ings, you see that the whole universe is part of the community and must be represented in that ceremony.

SMITH: You said it right out front—the whole universe is alive. Now, Vine, when I put that against the Western picture of the universe being 15 billion light years of dead matter, I mean, what a contrast. It goes without saying that the effect of living with a belief that the whole uni-verse is alive is deeply humanizing, as opposed to the other, more West-ern outlook, in which most of the universe is dead, which leads to a kind of spiritual deadening. And as you know, I have always believed this hu-manizing aspect of religion to be one of its greatest attributes.

So I know I don't have to tell you that the dominant scientific out-look is changing every week. Every Tuesday the *New York Times* has a science section whose reports are sort of turned over the following week. In the latest report scientists are withdrawing their previous surmise that with the hugeness of the universe there must be life in innumerable other galaxies. The evidence now points to our being on this little planet called Earth that is surrounded by a moat, which is outer space, and it's the only place where there is *consciousness*, awareness.

I'm glad you are laughing!

DELORIA: Most science *is* speculation. The problem with the United States today is we take these speculations as some kind of reality, as some kind of concreteness. In one of his essays, philosopher Alfred North Whitehead calls it "misplaced concreteness." We get into it and think it is real, when they're revising things all the time. They don't know what they're doing.

SMITH: In his book *The End of Science* John Horgan argues that the age of great discoveries in foundational empirical science, physics, has come to a close. Isaac Newton—on through Albert Einstein, Werner Heis-enberg, Niels Bohr, and their likes—revolutionized our understanding of the physical universe, and DNA was a genuine biological break-through, but it doesn't look like there are going to be any more revolu-tionary discoveries about the material world.

DELORIA: Not only that, but what scientists are saying is that life, all life, has physical underpinnings. Life grows out of matter and is completely dependent on it—no matter, no life. We don't *know* that's the case. For all we know, there may be immaterial forms of life, like shamans' allies.

SMITH: Yes, yes. In fact, it's becoming clear that the opposite is the case. Matter isn't the fundamental reality; consciousness is.

DELORIA: Right. We do not know that this is the only form of life. Our individual experiences tell us that there is a nonphysical realm that we have to come to grips with.

SMITH: Oh, you're stirring up all kinds of opinions in me! Let me run this one by you. In the indigenous view, spirit is first and, if anything, matter is a kind of "spin-off" from spirit, whereas in the modern scientific view, matter is fundamental, and spirit is like the foam on top of the beer. You can have beer without the foam—spirit—but you can't have foam without the beer—matter.

DELORIA: Yes, well, many tribes reverse that and agree with modern physics that the universe is essentially an *idea*. But the analogy I like to use is that of an architect who draws up a beautiful plan. That's an expression of spirit, the concept of how shapes go together, places and livability. But you don't know if it's going to work, unless you build it. Once you build it, then you have to deal with it as a concrete expression. So if you view the world as primarily *spirit* having all these ideas manifesting themselves materially to see if it actually works, well, that's the *reverse* of saying that you start with inner matter and evolve it to the point where it has intelligence and personality. That's why we're always so at odds with science and mainstream thinking. We're the reverse.

Huston, all this connects again with the point I brought in at the beginning, which is the spiritual malaise of our time. I guess T. S. Eliot's poem "The Rock" gives us a document of the spiritual denouement: "Here were decent godless people . . ." That's what we have today!

RECONCILING LAW AND THEOLOGY

SMITH: I know that one of the thrusts among your people is to really speak to the white European community, because you feel there are things they need to hear, things that will probe the spiritual basis of this malaise in which people are living. Do you make a point in your writing to speak to two audiences?

DELORIA: Yes. I've always viewed myself as standing between the two and trying to find the points where they touch. Then I try to figure out how to translate ideas from one context to another. You see, that's the tough part. I don't think you can take concepts straight across, from one culture to another; you've got to find out the substance of that idea in one context and then how it would be expressed in another.

For some years I taught a seminar called Law and Theology. Now, the idea was that this is one world we experience, so we don't have subgroup experiences. When the disciplines of law and theology are speaking to the condition of humanity, you must have concepts that are equivalent but which have to be translated back and forth. If you look at all this modern social legislation and you take out the word *eligible* and put in the word *worthy,* you have Protestant theology. If you take "equality before the law" and translate it, you've got "brotherhood of man" theology. So you can take law and theology and trace out what they are expressions of, but how do you move them back and forth? That's why the civil rights movement starts with religion but is essentially political. Now you have the conservative right wing, which is essentially political, trying to express itself as religion. You have to watch those things all the time.

SMITH: When you first said that law and theology are the same, it seemed like such an oxymoron, but as I think about it Judaism says virtually the same thing. In religious studies, Judaism is said to center on orthodoxy, but it is a religion of *orthopraxis,* or right practice.

DELORIA: Now, Huston, if you go to the tribal traditions you see they don't separate the two. They say, "This is our way." Religion and law are the same thing, except you present them in different contexts. Someone was telling me last night that when the Navajo went to the Parliament of World Religions in Cape Town last year, one of their elders said, "We don't have a religion, but we do have a 'way.'" That's why you didn't have religious conflict between tribes. You might have fought over everything else—women, horses, or buffalo—but not over religion. Each person, each group, had to do what their tradition told them to do. So it's very difficult now to keep the Indians focused on their own tradition. We continually want to syncretize, and now we've got Indian missionaries going out and trying to convert whites to Indian religion!

SMITH: There is always this gnawing around the edges by the dominant culture. It's very difficult to keep the focus clear. But when you say that law and religion are the same, my first reaction is alarm because law is going to be the dominant word, the way the law is moving in and dictating what can and cannot go on in the region of religion. Of course, the Al Smith case picked on the most powerless group of the land to strip them of their right to practice their religion. [See chapter 5.] They targeted them so as to deprive them of their constitutional rights to their sacrament peyote, a harmless cactus. On the other hand, when we look at the sacrament of the dominant religion—alcohol—the situation, as you said in the film *The Peyote Road,* is "surrealistic." That is precisely the right word!

DELORIA: If it just acts in its brute force, it's not law in its better expression.

SMITH: Hm, "better expression."

DELORIA: I was told when I was studying in the seminary that the original Hebrew concept of law was meant to point the way, but then it degenerated into all those rules and regulations.

SMITH: Vine, I've learned something in an area I thought was my turf, but it is really your turf! I recall the epigraph for your book *For This Land.* It is only one sentence long: "While America has produced great businessmen and scientists, it has been unable to produce one great philosopher, one great theologian." You may be lying through your teeth in saying that! I mean, you may be he!

DELORIA: No, no, no. I'm a very practical philosopher.

SMITH: I mean this very seriously. You just referred to Whitehead, and he is a great philosopher, but he did not have the indigenous experience that you have.

DELORIA: He was not Native American, native in the sense of being born here.

SMITH: That's right!

DELORIA: I'm not a political tactician. You're giving me far too much credit.

THE ROLE OF ELDERS IN INDIAN COUNTRY

SMITH: Let me ask you something. With your astonishing life work and productivity, do you feel you are getting anywhere?

DELORIA: I'm getting older.

SMITH: Well, so am I! But I know you're doing your best. It's just that you're swimming against the tide. I know it's hard to ask about the weather system of our culture as a whole. Do you feel your message getting through to any degree?

DELORIA: Many of the things I write about start from the grass roots and move up. That's the way I want it, because I want to communicate with ordinary people, put questions in their minds, give them questions they can take to more intellectual people and force them to confront reality. And so I write very simple books and try to cover simple themes. I try to answer all the questions I've had whenever I've seen inconsistencies in the way we believe or the way we act. I write about *why* we are doing these things. I'm not really writing for American intellectuals at all. I am writing to kind of erode the social foundations and get people to look at change in that way. Americans are too prone to grab fads and run down the road with them, and if your message becomes a fad, you may just as well not have sent it.

I do have a very complex manuscript about Jungian psychology and Sioux religion, and I've had it, I think, about fourteen years. But I don't want to release it while the emphasis is on this "delicatessen Christianity" that all the people like the New Agers are dining on. I think there is a sincere effort to find things in the New Age, but Americans are too flip. So I'm just going to keep refining the manuscript and eventually, I'll find the right audience and then publish it.

SMITH: So this book is on Native American psychology?

DELORIA: No, what I'm doing is looking at Jungian psychology and what it tried to do. Of course, it had great outreaches, as you know, to the world religions and European paths. But what I find in Jung is that when he's a scientist he says terrible things about "primitives," like they can't distinguish themselves from the environment, or they have no families. These are his offhand remarks when he's got his class in front of him. But then he says the closest you can get to wisdom is with the chief of the Taos Pueblo or with an African medicine man. So the so-called primitive, the wise old man, becomes the goal for Jungian psychology.

Then I ask myself, "Why does this guy have this schizophrenia?"

SMITH: Hm, perhaps this search for the wise old man, the elder, is an offshoot of our fascination with kinship—or our lack of it—in the modern world.

DELORIA: What I think is that the Indian concept of family is very inclusive. It's a concept of responsibilities, not rights! So the European concept of the nuclear family is one in which they have rights against each other, but they don't articulate responsibilities. It's the difference between zero being conceived as the fullness of things and zero being conceived of as nothing, and so once again you have that reversal.

Now, if you have psychic energy in individuals they have to express it in some way, and if you keep that psychic energy within the nuclear family you have all these complexes, Oedipus, Electra, and so forth.

SMITH: A real pressure cooker, right?

DELORIA: Right! Go to the Indian tribes, and you've got sixteen possible relationships within the family. Grandma and grandpa, uncle and

---

CARL JUNG'S REFLECTIONS ON NATIVE AMERICANS

On my next trip to the United States [in 1925] I went with a group of American friends to visit the Indians of New Mexico, the city-building Pueblos. . . . There for the first time I had the good fortune to talk with a non-European, that is, to a non-white. He was a chief of the Taos pueblos, an intelligent man between the ages of forty and fifty. His name was Ochwiay Biano (Mountain Lake). I was able to talk with him as I have rarely been able to talk with a European. . . . It was astonishing to me to see how the Indian's emotions change when he speaks of his religious ideas. In ordinary life he shows a degree of self-control and dignity that borders on fatalistic equanimity. But when he speaks of things that pertain to his mysteries, he is in the grip of a surprising emotion, which he cannot conceal—a fact which greatly helped to satisfy my curiosity. . . . Their religious conceptions are not theories to them (which, indeed, would have to be very curious theories to evoke tears from a man), but facts, as important and moving as the corresponding external realities. . . . "Why," Mountain Lake said, "do the Americans not let us alone? Why do they want to forbid our dances? Why do they make difficulties when we want to take our young people from school in order to lead them to the kiva [ceremonial site], and instruct them in our religion? We do nothing to harm the Americans." After a prolonged silence he continued, "The Americans want to stamp out our religion. Why can they not let us alone? What we do, we do not only for ourselves but for the Americans also. Yes, we do it for the whole world. Everyone benefits by it. . . . "

I then realized on what the "dignity," the tranquil composure of the individual Indian, was founded. It springs from his being a son of the sun; his life is cosmologically meaningful for he helps the father and preserver of all life in his daily rise and descent. . . . Knowledge does not enrich us; it removes us more and more from the mythic world in which we were once at home by right of birth. . . .

Such a man is in the fullest sense of the word in his proper place.

FROM CARL JUNG, *MEMORIES, DREAMS, REFLECTIONS,* 1961

aunt, cousin and cousin; you multiply them on both sides, and you go through life with responsibilities to each of these people. So you never have a confusion of roles, such as who is supposed to teach whom, and who is supposed to discipline whom. The elder is supposed to set an example. Kinship is a very complex thing. But what it allows you to do is to take individual psychic energies and distribute them over a field or a community rather than a small group.

SMITH: That's powerful! That's wonderful! I grew up in China, where my parents were missionaries. So I think East Asians are midway between our individualistic Western society and the indigenous view. When I came to this country I was comparing the two with a Western view, not with an indigenous view. China certainly was feeling-oriented, in terms of the extended family, and as you pointed out, the indigenous people probably just take that further.

DELORIA: With Indian people you always have responsibilities toward your grandfather, your grandmother, your grandson, uncle, or son-in-law. What does Christianity tell you? "Love your neighbor as yourself." You don't get the identity of the neighbors: Are they young, old, or middle aged? What gender is the neighbor? The neighbor remains nebulous. So you end up liking only those qualities in your neighbor that are the same qualities you see in yourself. Anything different becomes alien, and then you feel the compulsion to change that person to conform to who you think you are. There's the source of our conflict.

SMITH: For a moment let me put on my historian of religions cap. The urge to comment just bubbles up so powerfully here. I have concluded in my studies that religious history goes through three stages.

First, there's the archaic stage, and we take the Australian aboriginal as an example. Then you get to the historical religions that have texts, such as Christianity, Judaism, and Islam. Third, there's the indigenous prewriting civilizations in which I have found a very interesting, distinctive feature. There's not much about ethics with regard to them. That puzzled me until I realized that these are religions of the primary group, where they are really an extended family. In an extended family you don't have to pound down on the virtues to do this or not to do that, because empathy, to a very large degree, spreads over to the group.

I have heard that there is an Indian tribe in which there is no word for "disobedient." Now, to a Western parent that is mind-boggling! How could I have raised my children without drawing that line? But my imagination has been so stretched by the notion of this feeling-centered sense of the human self, rather than the isolated, perpendicular "I" obtruding everywhere, that I now can imagine this possibility.

DELORIA: See how you just brought up responsibility to the family? Instead of setting rules: "You can do this or you can't do that," people can grow up, or they can go back and forth from the group. The older members say you mustn't do that because that will bring shame on *everyone*. So you share that sense that you have to represent something definite— your family or your tribe—and *that* becomes the standard.

If you want to go further, there's a book on the Creeks that goes through this method of training children. It's just fascinating how they do it. They teach you to make up errands for the kids to do, like fetching a bucket of water. So the little boy goes to get a bucket of water, and everybody in the village praises him. They say, "Look at that fine young man getting water for his parents." So he learns that his job is to make the rest of the community feel proud and his relatives feel proud.

SMITH: Oh, my. When one contrasts that behavior with switchblades in the schools, I mean, it's enough to make one just weep with longing for our young people to lead a different way of life.

DELORIA: Yes, yes, it does.

THE CONFLICT BETWEEN SCIENCE AND RELIGION

SMITH: This modern view, with the changes wrought by modern science and its individualism, has really taken over.

DELORIA: But modern science is really a very confused version of Western religion, isn't it?

SMITH: Hm, I need to get my mind around that. I think of the distinctive feature of science as being the controlled-experiment laboratory where knowledge can be proven. But you don't get any controlled experiments in Christianity.

DELORIA: No, but what you do have is a whole set of concepts, beginning with the possibility of isolating the individual. So when Jesus comes along and says, "Leave father and mother and follow me," you're destroying the family there, and you're pulling together a group that has in common only that they all believe in Jesus. You get to modern science, and the proposition is that you can set up an experiment. You pretend all other things don't count except the concepts of your experiment. You run the experiment and report, "This is reality," but of course we know it isn't. All the great physicists are saying, "We're not telling you about nature; we're telling you about what we were able to find out when we asked nature certain questions."

SMITH: As Francis Bacon, the leading publicist for modern science, put it, "We need to put nature on the rack!" It's a powerful quote, and it says something to us even today.

DELORIA: Yes, Bacon and Heisenberg both say this. What they're saying is there's no subjective knowledge. That's what I think Christianity turns into. The question is, How are we going to get people to follow these creeds, to follow the sacraments, to perform everything we want them to do? There you've got this force entering, and that's when law becomes demonic, when it becomes an expression of religion.

Lately, I've been reading an awful lot of science, and now I think these people could really use a good law school course. They don't make their point; they don't muster enough evidence. This is powder puff; it's not answering the questions. But I really trace the problem back to Christianity. We're having all these problems between science and fundamentalist Christianity because Christianity originally had the theory that God made everything. That put the concept of "monogenesis" into science, and Darwin figured he had to have an alternative to the fundamentalist version. But there's no missing links, no punctuation, there's nothing to it. So everything we've done in evolution—none of which works—is answering a question that was wrongly assumed to be valid many centuries ago.

If you look at other religions—and you're the expert here—you see the Earth has cycles, you have period-destruction. Things continue to go. They give a preliminary explanation and say this is what we think the world is, or that is what we think the world is. But then in their devotional life it all goes to another area, into all kinds of Creation stories. But then who do we deal with in our ceremonies? The thunders and animal spirits, the Earth spirits and the spirits of places? These have only a logical connection to the doctrine of Creation.

SMITH: Now, Vine, you mention that scientists need courses on law, which reminds me that probably the two most forceful critiques of evolution have been written by lawyers. The first one was written by Norman Macbeth after a newsman said to him, "Look, you're not a biologist, what right do you have to write about biology?"

DELORIA: Listen, Huston, that's the attitude of bishops when you start talking about religion. They'll say, "I am ordained of the Church of God— so you don't have the right to tell people what religion is."

SMITH: It's the same thing, but on the other foot. Macbeth answered the newsman saying, "I have a right to write about this because as a lawyer I am an expert on evidence, and I fault them on their use of evidence." Twenty years later, a harsh critique came from Phillip E. Johnston, the most voluble critic of Darwinism, and again coming out of the Boalt School of Law, at the University of California at Berkeley. You're a lawyer. Let me pick up on that and just ask you what you think of Darwinism.

DELORIA: I just finished reading Niles Eldredge's *Time Frames,* an explanation of the theory of punctuated equilibrium. If he were in the boxing ring, he wouldn't lay a glove on his opponent. He wouldn't be able to do a thing. If I had him on the stand in a courtroom, I would just cut him into tiny little bits. He offers no evidence, no logic. Every now and then he says, "Of course this is all valid because you have this assumption." Well, my God, can you imagine translating that attitude to criminal law? You could say there was a robbery down at the 7-Eleven this morning, at ten o'clock, and Huston Smith was six blocks away at ten thirty. We have no other suspects, so Huston did it!

I was involved in the Wounded Knee trials and gave some of the arguments. The judge wrote this opinion saying we've heard from traditional people, lawyers, and scholars. All of them say that the United States broke the treaty. But what about all the people who didn't appear here today? How do they feel? Then he writes this mushy opinion that's totally irrational and illogical, from a legal standpoint.

No, you take what you have and make the best use of it. You don't say all these people saw Huston do this, but there are millions of people who didn't see him do it. This is the kind of reasoning you get in Darwinism or in Stephen Jay Gould's "punctuated equilibrium," that says that all these species step offstage and evolve like mad and come back and are stable. You say, well, that's what the Creationists said. They were created, and now they're stable. So what's point there? There is none.

RELIGION AS EPISTEMOLOGY

SMITH: What my mind is going to from what you said is that according to the Darwinian point of view, this conflicting view of human origin, the view of indigenous people, and now the "scientific Darwinian view" really has built into it maybe a more fundamental question. Namely, not origins, but anthropology, the study of who we are. According to the Darwinian account we are organisms that over the eons have developed more sophisticated strategies for working out our survival within our environment. But all the subjective stuff is only this "foam on the beer" I referred to earlier. They use the word *emergent,* but that's not an explanatory concept at all. It's a descriptive. But let's move on. Let me ask you about the Great Spirit. Is that a personal God?

DELORIA: It's personal because the universe is personal. That's the way we say things. What I'm getting at is epistemology. If we just took an ordinary group of people, what can we reasonably know? See, I think a lot of religion is epistemology, a way to ask, "What can we reasonably know?" The philosophers and theologians stagger around the question and go through generations of experiences and then they come out and say, well there seems to be a personal energy underneath all this, which is what physics is saying now.

SMITH: But how is that personal? Scientists say the universe is energy, but they just haven't said it's personal because they're trying to be objective. How many religions start with that premise, as opposed to the pantheons of deities or the solitary deity who does all these miraculous things and now is keeping score on a blackboard of the things we're doing? We've been talking about this almost opposite conception of the "big picture," the whole shebang, between indigenous and modern, Western science. How does this difference between big pictures concern the dominant culture's allowing the indigenous culture religious freedom? Is there a connection? What I am reaching for is an understanding of the restrictions that have been placed on the indigenous point of view. In effect, how can we work out of this basic misunderstanding, this polarity between diametrically opposite points of view?

DELORIA: It's been very oppressive the whole time. It is simply a total lack of understanding of who the natives were and who they are today. But there is also a basic misunderstanding by non-Indians of who "they" are and what they really want because of this schizophrenia. They want to take everything the Indians have, and at the same time they want to have the Boy Scouts or the YMCA teach the Indian virtues. You say, now look, this doesn't fit together. They want to set aside beautiful lands for national parks for tourists to visit, but you can't get them to change a law to set aside land for people to simply go and pray on. So you're going to have schizophrenia all across. When you look at it as that kind of problem, then one, you identify where the problems are going to emerge in the future, and two, you begin to build a strategy for communicating and dealing with these things. The problem is that non-Indians have too much energy!

You try to set aside wilderness, which basically means you don't want logging roads and buildings and other things in there. But then they adopt a law that says wilderness should have *nothing* to do with humans. Now, there's never been a landscape on this planet that has had nothing to do with humans. There were plenty of landscapes that were revered, used sparingly, if at all, and they were given an integrity of their own. That's what a lot of tribes have got to communicate to the larger society. We must maintain the integrity of the place, which eliminates multiple use. Multiple use just says everybody can use it, and if you feel like praying over the ruins then go ahead. So that's no solution at all.

SMITH: Can I ask you to apply this situation to Mount Graham, which is sacred to the Apache, but where the Vatican and several universities are building telescopes?

DELORIA: An old Indian told me they want to put all those telescopes up to try to find God—but they're a long way away!

SMITH: Currently, the Indians have to have permits to go up onto the sacred mountaintop and pray. Is that right? That seems cruel, and opposed to the promise of religious freedom the United States was founded on.

DELORIA: This was true of Blue Lake, near Taos, New Mexico, until finally the circumstances came about so the laws could change, and Blue Lake was finally returned to the people of Taos in 1970. Whenever you confront one of these problems, these issues on religious freedom, you have to build a total context. Only then can you have a true expression of the Indian religion and say, "This is what it is and this is what it means." But then you have to find a way to translate it so it affects people who wouldn't ordinarily be involved in this and get them committed to help. There are a lot of good people out there who will help you—but it's a very tedious educational job.

SMITH: Oh, yes. But religious freedom has required eternal vigilance throughout history, even if it seems tedious at times. Think of the process we have of educating the world about the situation in Tibet. But the

Mount Graham case is particularly outrageous because it is so unnecessary to build the telescopes.

DELORIA: But what are they going to find? Tucson is growing so fast, Arizona is growing so fast, the smog and light pollution are going to cancel anything they might achieve there. Eventually those telescopes are going to fall into disuse. Then the tribes will have to come in and try to reconsecrate that area and to rededicate people to the land. They're going to lose a lot because there is so much economics involved. But mistakes can be rectified. In the long run the tribes are going to win.

SMITH: *Win*. That's a hopeful word to hear in this context. What popped into my head is that there are a lot of churches now empty, sort of like mausoleums. Maybe the observatory on Mount Graham may become, before too long, just another mausoleum.

DELORIA: I'm sure it will.

SMITH: The observatory project is just not fit for the ecology of the universe, and as you say, the Native Americans will have to reconsecrate it, which, in my understanding, means to make it sacred again. That's a marvelous concept.

DELORIA: After World War II, the government built all these dams on the Columbia River and the Snake River, which killed the salmon. Now they're taking the dams out. So you see, if you just kept fighting and you just kept educating people, like the Nisqually tribe, in western Washington State, did for the fishing rights on those rivers, you'll win in the long run. You'll win because what you're doing is right.

SMITH: This may not fit into your argument, but I just heard a joke about two beavers looking out at the Hoover Dam. The first beaver asks the second if he built the dam, and the second one says, "No, I didn't actually build it. They just picked up on one of my ideas."

DELORIA: Right! Beaver ideas are coming back everywhere, Huston, but not only from the animals. Ideas are coming back from indigenous people. The hope is that we can pick up some ideas that make a difference. What a joy! In the sixties we used to say, "We want this country completely cleaned up. You're leaving, and we want the holes in the golf course filled in; we don't want any buffalo with broken legs!"

SMITH: Did you say you knew nothing? Let me just make this connection. When we talk about a sustainable environment I hear the Native

Americans translating this idea into concrete terms like planning for seven generations. Longer than that is beyond the human ken, but we can preserve our planet if we plan for seven generations.

DELORIA: Oh, sure. That's what science does; if it's possible theoretically to do it, they'll do it. Then there are no brakes on them at all. We're basically saying we're gods. But do we have the right to make that statement? We're also saying human beings are nothing more than material, but we have plenty of evidence that that's not true.

If you look at traditional native healing, a lot of it can't be done today, because we're in an urban, mechanized context. Many of those old Indian healers were able to do things that modern science has not begun to do. They had to learn from the animals and the birds and all the other creatures how to get along in this world, rather than embracing the idea that we are just visitors on this Earth.

SMITH: As I see it, this is precisely the kind of wisdom we can learn from you. The wisdom traditions are perhaps the most enduring attempts to infer meaning to the whole, and they teach that things are more integrated than they seem.

2

FIVE HUNDRED NATIONS WITHIN ONE

THE SEARCH FOR
RELIGIOUS JUSTICE

Walter Echo-Hawk, 2000. Used by permission of Walter Echo-Hawk.

Walter Echo-Hawk, Pawnee, is a courtroom attorney, political activist, lobbyist, tribal judge, and scholar. As senior staff attorney of the Native American Rights Fund (NARF), he has been a powerful champion of human rights. Echo-Hawk has worked on cases involving Native American religious freedom, prisoner rights, water rights, treaty rights, and reburial and repatriation rights. He was a leader in the Indian civil rights campaign to obtain passage of the Native American Grave Protection and Repatriation Act, which required the return of ancestral remains to tribal descendants. In 1992–1994, Echo-Hawk joined Reuben Snake in leading NARF efforts to secure federal legislation to protect Native American religious freedom. Mr. Echo-Hawk is a member of the Carter Center's International Human Rights Council and has been profiled in *Notable Native Americans* (1995). A prolific writer, his publications include an award-winning book, *Battlefields and Burial Grounds* (1994). He has received various awards, including the American Bar Association's Spirit of Excellence Award for legal work in the face of adversity (1996).

In this forum at the Parliament, Echo-Hawk spoke with Huston Smith about the background of the five-century-long Native American search for religious freedom, which provided an important context for the entire presentation of the delegation. For Echo-Hawk, depriving indigenous people of their freedom of religion is not just a theological question but a "basic human rights issue."

Together, Echo-Hawk and Smith provide an important overview of what has been called the "American Holocaust," offering vital background on the roots of intolerance between the early European colonists and the native people they encountered, as well as an invaluable exchange about the complex reality of five hundred nations existing within one. Other themes explored in this chapter include Echo-Hawk's description of Native American religion as a "mark of humanity," "a way of life, and a way of prayer," in contrast to institutionalized worship. For his part, Smith explores "why religion matters" out of his deep concern over the suffocation of the human spirit by the materialism of modern times. Here he discusses the indigenous worldview that he now champions in books and lectures all over the world, a religion that permeates everyday life and offers a transcendent view of reality, but one whose survival he is deeply concerned about.

Let us see, is this real,
Let us see, is this real,
This life I am living?
You Spirits, you dwell everywhere,
Let us see, is this real,
This life I am living?

PAWNEE WAR SONG

HUSTON SMITH: Walter, I'm going to begin by telling you something you don't know. I have one sibling, and one only. He is a brother, and his name is Walter, and so perhaps I contribute somewhat to the feeling of being at home with you, which feels very nice. I also want to mention one other thing that I think is relevant. I was recently invited to a conference in India. But instead of describing it as a conference, the organizers used a unique word that I have never heard used before or since. They called it not a conference, but a "convivium." The distinction was that in a conference people come together to talk, whereas in the convivium they had mounted we were coming together to live together, which would, of course, include talking. I hope that we can import that idea into this Third Parliament of World Religions, that we can live and talk together for the next five days. We have convened not just to talk but to share the blessings of living together.

Now, as we settle into the agenda for this interview, I think it's important to ask why the Native American sessions at this Parliament—aptly titled "America's Shadow Struggle"—are being given prime billing, nine one-hour sessions at the best hour of the day.

I see two reasons. One is that the primal indigenous religions of the world are generally overlooked. I don't have to tell *you* that. At the First World Parliament, in Chicago in 1893, the world's indigenous people weren't even invited, though I'm sure that it wasn't deliberate. It just never occurred to the conveners that indigenous religions were advanced enough to warrant invitations. One hundred years later, in 1994, at the Second World Parliament of Religions, again in Chicago, indigenous peoples were

The First Parliament of World Religions, Chicago, 1893. Used by permission of the Parliament of World Religions.

included in a number of plenary sessions. Five years later you have been given prime time to bring the religious freedom concerns of Native Americans to the attention of the world. That's an encouraging development.

The second reason your people have been given prime billing, as I see it, is because of *where* this Parliament is being held. We all know that the reason it is convening in Cape Town is because its organizers wanted to highlight the issue of justice. There is no place on this planet that so graphically calls to mind the injustice human beings inflict on each other as South Africa. Turning the spotlight on South Africa could easily divert attention from injustices elsewhere, and you wanted to point out that not all the injustices occur here. There are injustices all over the world, including in the United States, the nation that initiates these Parliaments, which is why the title for our symposium refers to the "shadow struggle" within America. I have watched you nodding, so I assume that you agree with this.

WALTER ECHO-HAWK: Huston, I do agree with you. I think that all people have a religion. There are a lot of really good things about religion. It inspires humanity to the highest ideals and brings warmth to the human spirit; it actually reminds us that everyone has a spirit. Religion is a mark of humanity in all ages, in all corners of the world, and that includes Native Americans in the United States and the other indigenous peoples of the world. It's true that the native religions that have survived are vastly different from the Judeo-Christian religious traditions most of us are familiar with. They have survived, but they are overlooked and unprotected by the laws of their countries. An important reason our delegation came here was to try to get a "seat at the table" with the recognized religions on the planet. If we hadn't come to represent the native religions of the New World, this wouldn't be a real *world* Parliament. We want a seat at the table to make this gathering real and complete.

SMITH: Very well put. Now, I wonder if you would give us an overview of the genocide that newcomers to America inflicted on the natives. I'm sure *genocide* is not too strong a word here. Smallpox and syphilis were imported from the Old World, and they killed vastly more natives than muskets did. Smallpox is one of the most contagious diseases there is, and in trading with Indians whites pawned off on them infected blankets that they had used to keep their families warm while they were dying. They reasoned that it was an easier way to get rid of Indians than shooting them.[1] That's so horrendous it makes me shudder just to think of it. Can you give us an overview that will put all this in perspective?

ECHO-HAWK: Gladly. My own tribe, the Pawnee, once numbered 10,000 in the central United States, but we were hit by smallpox twice, and it drastically reduced our numbers. It was such a devastating disease. It has taken a century for us to recover. Today we number around 4,500.

In terms of an overview, I would like to share some information that I have as an attorney who has represented Native American practitioners in the United States. The present population of Indians is over 2 million in the United States and Alaska, and it's a growing population. But most of your average American citizens, as well as the government policy makers, know virtually nothing about Native American people, although Native Americans are famous worldwide. Everyone, including our taxi driver here in South Africa, is well aware of Native American people and their plight, which is very similar to their own plight here in South Africa. Yet at home the average American knows very little about us. The native indigenous peoples are virtually invisible. Other than those who live in areas near pueblos or reservations, most Americans have never met a Native American, have never spoken with one, have never been to their reservation homelands. All they know about native people is essentially the stereotypes that exist in the media, or the little that might be gleaned from public education, which is minimal. So I agree that before we get into the religious aspect it is helpful first to talk about the baseline information about Native Americans in the United States.

To begin with, there are over five hundred tribes that are federally recognized with which the federal government conducts political relationships. These tribes have reservations, which are permanent home-lands that were established by treaties between the various tribes and the federal government. The policy of the government was to obtain Indian lands and to put Indians onto small reservations, which represented just a small part of their original lands. The policy was very similar to the apartheid system that until recently existed here in South Africa. On these reservations the Indian tribal governments are the ruling bodies. They exercise sovereignty and jurisdiction over the land and natural resources, the water, and the people of those particular territories. So the United States is not just one nation; it is composed of over five hundred nations within one.

Our relationship to the federal government is that of trustee and ward, which basically means that the federal government owns all our property in trust. It is assumed to be the trustee or the fiduciary from the time we are born until the time we die. Under that system the Indian people are the poorest of the poor. We live at the bottom of every socioeconomic indicator, whether you're talking about education, life expectancy, or housing.

SMITH: Can you speak specifically about your religion and the five hundred tribes, their differences and similarities? Can you tell us in your own words why you want to continue your religion and what you feel would be lost if you were to be assimilated into a dominant religion? I am curious about religion as an integral part of your daily life. Tell us why religion *matters* to native people.

ECHO-HAWK: That's easy. As I touched on briefly earlier, religion is a mark of humanity. All people and races and cultures have religion. Religion matters because it's part of being human, part of the human spirit. No matter what race, what country, what culture, or what age, what makes us human is this recognition that we are part of a larger universe and that there is a spiritual side to it. Take that away, and you're no longer human.

However, I think many of the native people in the United States view their religion not as religion proper, but more as a spirituality, a *way of life*. The religious traditions of the indigenous tribes that have survived are based on centuries, or millennia, of close observation of the natural world. They are based on a way of looking at the natural world, including the animals, plant behavior, and the land itself. Our ties to the land have evolved a very unique set of diverse forms of worship among the tribes, and they are vastly different from the Judeo-Christian religions. Nonetheless, tribal religions survived, even though Christianity and other forms of Judeo-Christian religions have come into Indian country through the proselytizing process and other historical factors that attempted to suppress them.

SMITH: May I just interject something here from my perspective as a historian of religions? Anthropologists tell us that there is something about indigenous religions that separates them from historical religions, with their written text and cumulative history. They say that they can't point to anything in indigenous cultures that is distinctly religious because religion is their entire way of life. I gather that is what you were saying.

ECHO-HAWK: Yes. That is true. I guess the closest parallel would be to the Amish or the Mennonite faith, where religion is also a way of life. In traditional tribal communities religion is not compartmentalized; it really serves as a kind of glue that holds these groups together over the centuries, even through great adversity. It's hard to generalize, because the communities are so diverse and there are so many of them. They are oral traditions. Indigenous cultures do not reduce their traditions to holy books such as the Bible or the Koran. They hand their traditions down through elders and ceremonies and stories.

SMITH: I'm certain the refusal to commit them to writing is due to the traditional belief that writing things down sort of freezes them, whereas if they are in the memories of people, that weaves the tradition into everyday life and makes histories come alive. Is that correct? I'm thinking of the invisibility of their texts and their beliefs, which has left their eyes open to notice other ways the sacred is manifest in Creation. Also, oral traditions have the advantage of breathing new life into the familiar. I think of your ancestors as bands of blind Homers who gather each evening around the fire and retell the ancient tales.

ECHO-HAWK: I think that is partially true. The other part of the truth is that many of the tribal religions were forced to go underground. For a period of eighty years, from 1854 to 1934, it was illegal to practice tribal religions in the United States. So many of these tribes, for several generations, evolved a tactic of secrecy; they were not permitted to expose certain sacred knowledge to outsiders. A lot of the ceremonies of these tribes were done in secret, and it became a tenet of their faith that one could be punished or sanctioned for violating these tenets.

SMITH: Many scholars have speculated about why this tragic misunderstanding between the European colonists and the Native Americans they encountered came about. What do you think caused it, and how do you think native people can deal with it now?

ECHO-HAWK: This great cultural conflict over religion has gone on for five hundred years. It began the day that Christopher Columbus first set foot in the New World, on October 12, 1492. In his diary he wrote, "Indians could easily be made Christians because it seems to me that they have no religion of their own."

We can look back on that comment years later and say, "Well, that was a very quaint ethnocentric remark." But, in fact, if you look at Spain at that time it was a country full of religious intolerance. It was a newly formed Christian nation, it instigated the Spanish Inquisition, and it expelled the Jewish and Muslim populations. Columbus brought that religious intolerance with him to the New World. He imported it.

From that point in history right down to the present, the proselytizing religions of the Old World have claimed religious superiority over the indigenous religions of the New World. The attitude was "my religion is better than yours," and this attitude led to the belief that native religions do not warrant human rights protection. Ironically, the pilgrims who came to America searching for their religious freedom, in 1620, did not believe that what they saw was even religion. In their European eyes and minds, the ceremonies were strange and the reverence for animals was not religious. Instead, they decided all this was barbaric primitive superstition that needed to be stamped out.

We still see those kinds of superior attitudes in the world today, and they become dangerous as a human rights matter when the machinery of government is invoked and used to carry out those attitudes.

SMITH: Can you mention one direction or manner in which the government has been moving desultorily, procrastinating, where they might, instead, be moving toward granting native people the same sort of religious freedom everyone else has in America?

ECHO-HAWK: Historically, the policy of the government has been basically to ignore the First Amendment protections of many people. Both the establishment policy and the free-exercise-clause protections ultimately led to a complete ban of tribal religions, including the use of military force to stamp out the Ghost Dance religion and to outlaw the Sun Dance religion. For the United States, a leading democracy in the world, to completely ban the practice of tribal religion for generations is an unparalleled act. We have had very little legal protection for native religions in the United States.

LEGISLATIVE SUCCESS AND ETERNAL VIGILANCE

SMITH: Are you having any successes, and can you predict what the future might bring? Or do you believe in the need for eternal vigilance so that it's not one step forward and two steps back? It seems to me that no religious freedom can be taken for granted anywhere in the world.

ECHO-HAWK: Yes. I think we have had some successes. As you well know, in 1990 the U.S. Supreme Court ruled that the American Constitution does not protect the sacramental use of peyote as a form of native worship. That case—the *Smith* case—created a massive loophole in American law for worship, not only for native worship but for *all* worship. It created a human rights crisis. It led to unrest, to fear of prosecution, for native people across the land. But this time we didn't take the decision lying down. The case prompted a native civil rights movement that began on the reservations and in Indian country and ultimately found its way all the way back to Washington D.C. Since the judiciary deserted us we did an end run around it and took our case directly to Congress. In 1992 President Bill Clinton signed the Religious Freedom Restoration Act into law.

SMITH: Yes. That was a happy ending. Are there any other successes?

ECHO-HAWK: There have been other legislative successes. I think the repatriation laws of the 1990s are an example. These laws now require protection of native graves, dead bodies, mandating federally funded museums and other institutions to return millions of dead Indians who in the course of our history had been dug up and carried away to these museums.[2]

The repatriation issue was a religious issue because people have many religious beliefs and sensibilities relating to the treatment of their dead relatives. Unfortunately, this is an issue most Americans thoroughly take for granted for themselves, even for their pets. In the case of Indians, these religious rights have been massively ignored by American history, policy, and law. So here too we went to Congress and got it to pass a law requiring the repatriation of the dead. These successes illustrate the willingness of our lawmakers in the United States to address human rights problems.

The underlying problem is that the courts have pretty much abandoned their role as protectors of religion in the United States and relegated it to the political process, which makes it very difficult for Native American people. As minority groups, we are disadvantaged in the political process. If you are unpopular, it is hard to succeed in the cauldron of Washington's power politics. It's a very scary situation.

THE TWO-EDGED SWORD

SMITH: That's a wonderful caption to the picture of the religious conditions for native people. Now tell me about your feelings regarding the New Age movement and nonindigenous peoples who have a growing interest in Native American insights. How do you view the curiosity of outsiders? I suspect you think it's got its good and its bad points.

ECHO-HAWK: Yes, outside interest in native ways is a two-edged sword. It is good that non-native people are appreciating native religious traditions and finally learning a little bit about them. But there is a great danger in the New Age community of their exploiting and expropriating our traditions as their own. The native religions are not proselytizing religions. But there is now heavy regulation that we have to worship under because non-native peoples sometimes come into our communities to worship with us. So there tends to be abuse and exploitation, commercialization, which has led to different legal attacks on the body of law that protects native worshippers. It's a very, very complicated question and situation.

THE NATIVE AMERICAN GRAVES PROTECTION AND REPATRIATION ACT

The Native American Graves Protection and Repatriation Act (NAGPRA) is a federal law that was passed in 1990. NAGPRA provides a process for museums and federal agencies to return certain Native American cultural items—human remains, funerary objects, sacred objects, and objects of cultural patrimony—to lineal descendants, culturally affiliated Indian tribes, and native Hawaiian organizations.*

*NAGPRA affects government-funded organizations only.

SMITH: Now, this is a utilitarian question, and I am not very good in this regard, but is there anything the ordinary person can do to improve the relationship between the general population and native people?

> **Often in the stillness of night, when all nature seems asleep about me, there comes a gentle rapping at the door of my heart. I open it and a voice inquires, "Pokagon, what of your people? What will their future be?" My answer is: "Mortal man has not the power to draw aside the veil of unborn time to tell the future of his race. That gift belongs to the Divine alone. But it is given to him to closely judge the future by the present, and the past." Hence, in order to approximate the future of our race, we must consider our natural capabilities and our environments, as connected with the dominant race, which outnumbers us—three hundred to one—in this land of our fathers. . . . Before the days of Pokagon, I had my origin in the blood that ran through Pocahontas. I stand today as a living witness that the Indian is worth something to the world.**
>
> SIMON POKAGON (POTAWATOMIE), 1830–1899,
> FROM *THE FUTURE OF THE RED MAN*, 1897

ECHO-HAWK: It seems to me that there is one thing that could be done, not only in the United States but also in other countries. I think that people who immigrate to other lands should try to become native, which means to adapt to the land as the native people have done. I think that colonialism resulted in a number of settlers who failed to adapt to the places where they lived. Instead they imported their cultures, their languages, and their religions and marginalized the natives and their culture and religion in the places where they lived. A lot of newcomers remained aliens or strangers to the places where they lived. I think that is a challenge for all the people who immigrated to America. I'm not asking them to leave by any means. That's certainly not realistic. But I think to adapt as the native people have done to the place where they live is to make peace with the people and the land.

As the Iroquois writer Douglas George-Kanentiio has said, to respect the native people and come to a reconciliation with them means that new-comers or immigrants won't be *strangers* here.

SPIRITUAL CRISES

SMITH: I am concerned about the survival of many primal religions and cultures and the need to winnow the wisdom from them while we can. What about the future? Do you want to assume the role of a prophet? Is there any hope?

ECHO-HAWK: I think that the survival of native people, and of their religions, is at stake in the United States. The only way that native worship is made possible is through a patchwork maze of administrative rules and regulations and some litigation, which has resulted in the government being involved in comprehensive regulation of native religious practices. For example, the government has limited our access to our own sacred sites and to our eagle feathers, has narrowed our ability to worship in prisons, and has regulated peyote, which is used in the Native American Church. Our important native religious practices are comprehensive and are often intrusively regulated in the United States. And this is the only way in which the United States has found to allow the worship of its own native people.

So we have very significant challenges that face us in protecting worship at these places, in our prisons, where Indians are incarcerated in highly disproportionate numbers, threats from science when we try to repatriate.

SMITH: You have unfolded for us the picture of five hundred nations within one and given us a glimpse of what it means to be a nation within another nation all over the world. Of course the situation in the United States isn't the only case. We have His Holiness the Dalai Lama, the exiled leader of Tibet, who is holding out for exactly that kind of a concept in the nation of China. Also, it is an extraordinary fact that there are groups of people who have kept their identity for hundreds of years within the nation of India. How do you define the concept of a nation within a larger nation?

ECHO-HAWK: That's a global question, because the world has been subject to colonialism. It has formally repudiated colonialism, but its legacy is in Africa, in most of North and South America, Australia, and most of Asia, and all the present nations of the world that contain indigenous populations.

SMITH: It's a devastating chapter in history. I have heard it said that during its rule of India, in the nineteenth and early twentieth centuries, England plundered around $250 million a year from that subcontinent to line its coffers. So, yes, colonialism has ravaged the world, but as you say, native people are still here.

ECHO-HAWK: I think it is in fact a miracle that the Native American tribal religions have survived. I think that it is a testament to the human spirit that they have survived. But the paramount human rights issue confronting the United States today is survival. It is an issue not only for the United States but for all nations in the world that contain indigenous populations as a legacy of colonialism. There are at least seventy-two nations, which have 350 million people representing 6 percent of our whole humanity and are nations within nations, that confront the same question: Will the unique religions of these traditional indigenous peoples survive into and through this new millennium?

We aren't alone in the world. Tribal people everywhere are trying to survive with their distinct cultures and ways of worship. They need to be protected. I think the challenge of the religious community and the political community is to see that they are.

SMITH: But what of the hurdles you face in gaining equal political and religious rights for your people?

ECHO-HAWK: I think that our situation is a symptom of the larger issue that you, Huston, have referred to earlier as the spiritual crisis in the world today. Are we heading toward a more homogenous world spirituality within our human family? Or can we tolerate diversity? The United States proclaims itself a champion of religious freedom, but it falls short of living up to that claim. The way the United States looks at and addresses the religions of its native people will tell the world far more about its character than all the avowed statements about personal freedom it gives in international situations.

The challenge for native people as we go into this next millennium is to survive with our spirituality intact. It is our task to change the hearts and minds of this next generation of Americans and the American government to allow us to survive and flourish with our cultures intact. I think we owe it to humanity to do this. We may have to start inside the darkest corners of America—the prisons—to try and ensure that the traditional religious beliefs of all the prisoners are protected. If our country does not have the will to protect the right of the most helpless, powerless individuals in society to practice their faith—no matter how different it is—then it won't have the will to protect the religion of the free people in that country.

There is another challenge, which is to protect the sacred sites. The U.S. government simply has to acknowledge that its land is teeming with holy places, sacred sites that are far more diverse even than those in the Middle East, sites that predate the writing of the Bible and the Koran. Yet American law and social policy fail to recognize that fact. America should be more like the nations of the Middle East that protect these indigenous holy places for worship. In fact, America needs to return some of these places, such as the Black Hills, to the people they belong to. America should learn from its indigenous people—through their spirituality—to respect an environmental ethic that takes care of these ancient and holy places and the land in general.

Then the third and final challenge that arises is simply to respect and to place the indigenous religions of native people on a par with the rest of the world's religions, where they belong.

SMITH: Very well said. In conclusion, how do you feel about this pilgrimage to South Africa? Has it given you a different perspective on your own struggles back in America?

ECHO-HAWK: Coming here to South Africa has made a really profound impression on me that we native people aren't alone. Today the tribal peoples across the world are trying to survive with their distinct cultures and ways of worship. The tribal people here in South Africa were aware of Native Americans, and they recognized us and were very quick to share their experiences with us, which we found were very common to our experiences in the United States. It makes me feel that we as native people in the United States are finally finding *a seat at the table,* as far as respect for all the world religions is concerned. It's been a long time coming, and it gives me hope that *our way of prayer* is going to be protected into the future.

My vision for native people here in the United States, aside from the passage in the United Nations of the indigenous rights declaration, is that every Indian tribe, whether they be rich or poor, large or small, create its own cultural center and museum. Each tribe is struggling to continue its culture and its contributions to America's heritage. I think all tribes should have a place where they can archive their documents, their history, their music, their sacred objects, as well as their beautiful patrimony, for now and into the future.

SMITH: People often ask me if I ever lose faith; I tell them I sometimes come down with a case of the "spiritual flu." Otherwise, how can I not be optimistic?

DRAFT DECLARATION ON THE RIGHTS OF INDIGENOUS PEOPLES

Commission on Human Rights Chairperson: Ms Erica-Irene A. Daes, Sub-Commission on Prevention of Discrimination and Protection of Minorities, Forty-fifth session on Discrimination against indigenous peoples

"Affirming that indigenous peoples are equal in dignity and rights to all other peoples, while recognizing the rights of all peoples to be different, to consider themselves different, and to be respected as such."

ANNEX I DRAFT DECLARATION AS AGREED UPON
BY THE MEMBERS OF THE WORKING GROUP AT ITS ELEVENTH SESSION.

ECHO-HAWK: As a native advocate, I have to be optimistic that our religions are going to survive into the future. Native people will never give up. This is something we have to do. I think that as long as native people are here in this part of the world we are going to fight to protect our religions. There's increasing interest in indigenous peoples around the world right now.

A significant legal document is pending in the United Nations, the Draft Declaration on the Rights of Indigenous Peoples. It is a document that's been circulating and worked on for many years by indigenous leaders across the world. It contains most of the aspirations of native peoples, and prominent among them are the broad protections of our tribal religions, our cultures, our intellectual property rights, our land, our way of looking at the planet, repatriation of human remains. If enacted it will bring protection for the first time to indigenous peoples across the world. We also have pending right now in the United States some great interest on the part of Congress to introduce another bill to protect our sacred places in the United States.

All this gives me hope and inspiration.

3

ECOLOGY AND SPIRITUALITY

FOLLOWING THE PATH
OF NATURAL LAW

Winona LaDuke, 1996. Used by
permission of Winona LaDuke.

Winona LaDuke, internationally acclaimed activist, lives on the White Earth Reservation in Minnesota and is an enrolled member of the Mississippi Band of the Anishinaabeg. LaDuke is founding director of the White Earth Land Recovery Project and the Indigenous Women's Network and program director for the Honor the Earth Fund. In 1994 *Time* named her one of America's fifty most promising leaders under the age of forty. In the 1996 and 2000 presidential campaigns, she served as Ralph Nader's running mate for the Green Party. In 1988 she received the Reebok Human Rights Award. An accomplished writer, she is the author of *Last Standing Woman* and *All Our Relations*. In a 1996 interview LaDuke said, "Spirituality is the foundation of all my political work. In many of the progressive movements in this country, religion carries a lot of baggage. But I think that's changing. You can't dismiss the significance of Eastern religions, earth-based religions, and Western religions on political work today. What we all need to do is find the well-spring that keeps us going, that gives us the strength and patience to keep up this struggle for a long time."[1]

In their session at the Parliament of World Religions in Cape Town, Professor Smith and Ms. LaDuke delved into the eco-spiritual aspects of her life and work. The themes that emerged in their conversation include the inherent native belief in the great web of life, the interconnectedness of spirituality and the environment, and the role of cultural memory in spiritual heritage. What fires her life and work is the desire to participate in what she calls the "immense struggle for change" for indigenous people that she sees in many parts of the world. "You and I know that change happens," she said. "It's just a question of who controls the change. I've seen change at the hands of the native communities, which inspires me."

For Huston Smith, the dialogue illuminates his admiration for what he feels is the defining characteristic of the world's primal religions, their sense of "mutual relatedness," which leads to the community-strengthening practice of "mutual responsibility" he thinks is sorely lacking in mainstream Western culture. For him, the conversation was an opportunity to participate in the kind of exchange exemplified by the natural philosophy of many native elders he has come to deeply respect, such as Chief Luther Standing Bear (Brule Sioux, 1868–1939).

Of this natural philosophy of interconnectedness, Standing Bear said, "The man who sat on the ground in his tipi meditating on life and its meaning accepting the kinship of all creatures and acknowledging unity with the universe of things, was infusing in this being the true essence of civilization." But Smith's concern here delves deeper yet. His is a committed inquiry into Standing Bear's powerful indictment, in *Land of the Spotted Eagle,* about why the white man cannot comprehend the Indian's spiritual relationship to the earth. "The white man does not understand the Indian," Standing Bear wrote, "for the reason that he does not understand America. He is too far removed from its formative processes. The roots of the tree of his life have not yet grasped the rock and soil. The white man is still troubled with primitive fears; he still has in his consciousness the perils of this frontier continent, some of its fastnesses not yet having yielded to his questing footsteps and inquiring eyes. The man from Europe is still a foreigner and an alien. . . . But to the Indian the spirit of the land is still vested; it will be until other men are able to divine and meet its rhythms."[2]

For Smith, it is essential that modern religious life be in synch with those sacred rhythms.

Treat the earth well: it was not given to you by your parents, it was loaned to you by your children. We do not inherit the earth from our ancestors, we borrow it from our children. We are more than the sum of our knowledge, we are the products of our imagination.

INDIAN PROVERB

HUSTON SMITH: Winona, you have so much to tell us, so much that is important for us to learn. I certainly want the bulk of this time to go to you, but I'm going to take a few minutes to put our topic in perspective in my mind. The moment goes back to the height of the American protests against the war in Vietnam. I was in world religion at MIT during those turbulent years, and I wrote an article with a rather cute title, but I went for it anyway because I thought it made the point. I called this article "Tao Now," a two-word poem.

The deeper point was that the focus of the protests of the MIT students was on Dow Chemical's producing the napalm used in Vietnam.

The point of my article was that the opposites have met in this one word, "Dow," which is echoed in the way the word is pronounced. The "Dow" in Dow Chemical and the "Tao" in Taoism are pronounced exactly the same way. They are absolute opposites, and we have to choose which way we want to go, philosophically speaking. In the course of that article I made the statement that of the eight great religions I have steeped my life in, I felt Taoism was the most logical worldview the human mind had ever conceived. To illustrate my point, I'll just quote five lines from the *Tao Te Ching,* by Lao-tzu:

> Those who would take over the earth and shape it
> to their will never I notice succeed.
> The earth is like a vessel so sacred
> That at the very approach of the profane it is marred
> They reach out their fingers and it is gone.[3]

The essence of my article was that I thought the Tao was the most ecological religion, meaning that all the parts of its philosophy were interrelated. Now, the more I have come to learn about your religion, the more I think that I have to revise that statement. Now I think that the indigenous peoples' outlook on the world is ultimately more ecological even than the Taoist one.

With this brief preface in mind, I know that you live in northern Minnesota. Those of us who live in rather milder climates think of that as kind of harsh territory. Would you begin by telling us something about how you see the ecological character of the world?

WINONA LADUKE: I would start by greeting you, *"Aaniin Nindawaymuganitoog,"* "Hello, my relatives." The greeting itself is how we place ourselves in the world. I'm Bear Clan, Mississippi Band from Gaawaabaabanikaag, the White Earth Reservation in northern Minnesota. I'm very honored to be here with all these beautiful folks, in this time, in this beautiful country, and to meet the people who have so much courage in their hearts and have had so much resilience. I think it is a great lesson for all of us about their ability to survive.

In thinking about what you were saying, Huston, I would not presume to say that Taoism is less ecologically minded than the views of my own community, because I don't know that much about Taoism. I think that there is a lot of beauty in the other ways that people talk to the Creator.

What I would say is that our worldview is based on our spirit, our heart, and our physical being. All those aspects, which are our way of life, are reflected in our spiritual practice. In my community, the White

Earth Reservation, *Gaawaabaabanikaag,* we have religious practices that are perhaps considered more like institutions. We have the Midewiwin Lodge, which is the medicine society, and we have the Big Drum Society. These are teachings within a set of larger set of cultural instructions in our community. Those teachings are a way of life we call *Mino Bimaatisiiwin,* which means "to live a good life." As Anishinaabeg people and as indigenous people, that is what we are instructed to try and do: *live a good life in the best way we can.* That way of life is in recognition of all those relations, which are around us and are part of that web.

SMITH: To my mind, this mutual relatedness is the single greatest contribution of the primal peoples of the world. Can you give us an example of how the sense of relatedness connects you to the rest of the world in the great web of life?

LADUKE: Do you mean can I be real linear about it? What I would say is that we are taught in our stories that we are younger brothers and younger sisters of older relatives who came before us and gave us most of the gifts we have today. Our relatives are not only the two-legged. Our other relatives are four-legged; other relatives have wings; our relatives have fins. We are alive today and able to live our lives because of them. We are able to have the quality of life that we have today because of them.

For instance, our community is considered a forest culture, or a woodlands culture, by anthropologists or by people who categorize people in the way that makes some sense to them. What I find in the case of being a woodlands culture is that you have to have a woodlands! The Creator did not place us in the prairie. He didn't place us in a clear-cut. The Creator placed us in a forest that was full of life. In that forest we found our old stories that taught us how to be. We found our scrolls. There is a lot of talk about how our history is not recorded, but we have thousands of years of history written on birch bark, which are the scrolls of our practices. They exist. They are used as a way to remember our oral history in case we forget things, especially the most important details of our history. It's good to have memory devices.

SMITH: Scrolls are things that can be rolled up, right?

LADUKE: Yes. Birch bark rolls up. That is why they call it a scroll. Our teachings come from the forest. Historically, our medicines come from the forest. My reservation calls them the medicine of the Ojibway.[4] The medicine is used by our people, from the prairie to the pinelands. Many of the things that we need in our medicine come from the forest. The for-

Grand Medicine Lodge scroll, April 4, 1888. Minnesota Historical Society. Used
by permission of Winona LaDuke and DreamCatchers Productions.

est gives us life; that's one of our teachings. You can't afford to mess the
forest up, because that forest is what cares for you.

Sometimes, I use a little of our language when I talk because our language (Ojibway/Anishinabe) contains a lot of references to the relationship between those relatives and the Creator. One of the best examples
is something called *Manoomin,* which is our word for wild rice. The word
for the Creator is *Gichee Manitou.* It's the same word as a gift from the
Creator, a teaching given to us to respect that wild rice the Creator gave
us, which grows on the lakes. It is a reminder to us that it is one of our
greatest foods. It's a part of our world history, and it's a part of who we
are as indigenous people.

SMITH: Do I have this right? Your word for wild rice—one of your most
important staples—is the same as the word for the Great Spirit?

LADUKE: Yes, *Gichee Manitou* means "a gift from the Creator." In the
morphology of the word is the relationship we have to the Creator. Language is related to cultural practice. That rice was given to us. We say
that food not only feeds your belly, but it feeds your soul. You eat those
foods for ceremonies, and you are supposed to eat those foods to sus-

tain you, because the Creator did not give you Safeway. The Creator gave you this food out there on that land and instructions on how to take care of it. This is one of the reasons today that our community struggles with issues of biodiversity. The vast majority—three-quarters—of the rice produced in the world today comes from California. We don't have any word from Uncle Ben that he got that rice from the Creator the same way we did.

SMITH: That reminds me of a little whimsical thing that happened while I was teaching at MIT. Our house backed down on a pond, and there were mallard ducks all over it. We sent out for wild rice so that we could persuade the ducks to come over to our lawn. But on the opposite side of the pond lived a dentist. Every year he put in $400 worth of rice so that the ducks would come over to his side of the pond. I still feel resentment.

LADUKE: Yes, that's understandable, because there is actually a very long history of the relationship between ducks and rice. If you want ducks, have rice around. It's one of our teachings. One of the struggles we have today is that companies can take out a patent on rice. They patent something that the Creator gave *us* and make it their own. Then they call it *their* product, which is the issue of globalization and how it affects us. Those are some other examples in our community.

One of our most sacred relatives is the sturgeon, which in our language is *Name*. Commercial fishing in dams took out the sturgeon on our reservation. Our community is like other communities in that we have a clan. We have a sturgeon clan. So one of the questions that an indigenous community grapples with is, What happens when you lose your clan relative in your community? You have songs for that. You can have things to take care of that relationship and honor that. In my community now we have started to restore the sturgeon. We brought them from another watershed so we could bring our relatives home. All these things exemplify our relations to them and how they are revered, not as resources, not as something that is just for us, but as things that teach us how to be human. In the case of the sturgeon and in the case of the forest, we believe they teach us how to be human.

In the north woods of Minnesota, in the Great Lakes region where I live, we have a diverse forest that the Creator gave us to sustain ourselves. The first harvest of the year comes out of our maple sugar bushes, the *Ninitog*. The forest comes alive when we begin our harvesting cycle. This is how our people begin their year. We pray before we come out; we start with tobacco and we sing an honoring song, a praising song (that's what we call it), to thank the Creator for the harvest. This is a medicine for our people. It's used for a lot of our ceremonies, our fasting, because the maple sugar feeds our body as well as our soul. Our community has done this for a thousand years or so.

THE INVISIBLE LINE

SMITH: So your clan bridges the human and the animal world, in this case, the fish? Your clan does not draw a line but includes both the fish and the human beings. Am I right in that?

LADUKE: All I know is that as human beings you and I only know a little bit. What I would say is that it is one of the original teachings. I'm kind of a humble person and small within our spiritual practice. I try to pray most days. But I can't explain all the complexities. What I'm told is that our ancestors gave us the original teachings, and they are our relatives. For instance, we were taught by those animals, such as the bear, what all those medicines are in our community. You know a sturgeon can go almost seven hundred miles in a river system. They live 150 years. They are amazing fish who teach you about your humbleness in the big picture of things. They can go so far, live so long, and have so many descendants. They teach us through their existence. Over time our whole clan system, our government system, is related to them. That way of life— *Nimuwatozium*—is related to our whole ecosystem and to our land. Other communities are similar. I'm most familiar with my own.

SMITH: Is this what is meant by the invocation to live according to the ways of nature?

LADUKE: Yes. We all walk down the same path. In the end our simple teaching is that there is only one law. That is the Creator's law, the Breathmaker's law, or natural law. You and I live in societies that have made constructs of law that justify our own worst behavior and enable us to trade pollution credits or make various protocols that allow phaseouts of CFCs, or be in collective denial about nuclear testing. Those are the constructs of nation-states.

SMITH: Earlier you said that not all your ancestors were two-legged, that some of them were four-legged. I'm getting the impression that the line drawn so sharply by the modern world between the human and the animal realms is sort of perforated for native people. It is not a sharp dichotomy.

LADUKE: Yes. I would say our relatives are all those. I would also say that it is important how you reflect on the language itself because, as you know, a lot of industrial language considers things as humans and sub-humans, which implies that the animals are less than us, that they are subhuman. I doubt that any indigenous people would say that any of those relatives of ours who are so great—our elder brothers and our el-der sisters or our uncles, as we would call them in our ceremonies or in our practices—would say they are less. They would say we are lucky to be here, and we are lucky that they taught us how to be right. That's what I would say.

SMITH: I get the impression that not only do you not consider them to be less but that in some ways you consider them to be more. Now, I can't tell how much my imagination is getting ahead of me, but the reason they are seen to be more is that they are closer to the very source of be-ing. Maybe I'm moving into conceptual science today. In the evolution-ary conception the two-leggeds came before the four-leggeds, and that places them closest to the source. Of course, in science the source has no major qualities, but your source is the Great Spirit. So are the four-leggeds and the sturgeon not only not less than us, but even exemplary for us, by virtue of their being closer to the source? That would mean that we humans are more derivative, further away from the Great Spirit.

LADUKE: What I would say, and I think that most humans have the same experience, is that we are only human, and as such we botch things up. Every ten generations or so we make some big mistakes. All our com-munities have these teachings that say, "Okay, we made mistakes." Then they are corrected. Then we are supposed to stay on our path or get back on our path. That is one of our teachings. It is a really important con-cept, because I would say that there is this kind of industrial mythology that indigenous peoples want to "go back." It is not about going back—*it's about being on your path*—staying on the path that the Creator gave you instead of going over here or over there. It is not a going-back path. It is the path of following your instructions. So what I would say is that because we are human, we often stray. We hope that we can correct our-selves through prayer or through our community. But sometimes it takes divine intervention to correct us.

SMITH: I want to stay with your notion of not going back, because it resonates very deeply with me. I have spent my life trying to understand the world's greatest religious traditions, and I get charged right down the line regularly that I am concerned with the past. My retort, which I firmly believe in is, no, I'm not interested in past, present, and future. I'm interested in what is *timeless,* what is so true that it was true then and it is true now, and it will be true in the future.

Winona, you give me great reinforcement and encouragement for that view of things when you talk about your concentration on the present moment.

LADUKE: That is the best we can do. My community is the one I'm most familiar with, and I think it is a microcosm of indigenous communities on a worldwide scale where you have a spiritual practice that is integral to your cultural practice. It's not separate. Some other fine native people have also said this. In order to have that, the Creator said, *"There is a place where your medicines are."* It's the place you go to recharge your spiritual practices, because that is where you have your ceremony every year. There are relatives in there, whether they are the *Name,* the sturgeon, or the *muskategge,* the buffalo; those animals are part of your teachings. They are doorkeepers, they are part of your spiritual practice. You invoke them as you talk to the Creator, as you talk to your relatives. You always remember that relationship between the Creator and your animal relatives in your practice.

But what you find now is that indigenous communities everywhere are facing the crisis of living in an area where their sacred site is a place someone wants to mine, or someone wants to log; or they want to put in a ski resort or a telescope. Soon you find that the animals that are part of your prayers, like our sturgeon, aren't even in your ecosystem anymore. They are over in a zoo someplace. Or you find that the foods that you eat are poisoned. The Creator didn't say, "Have macaroni soup for all your ceremonies." There are sacred foods you are supposed to use to feed the spirits.

On a worldwide scale, you find that sacred sites, or parts of them, are threatened, and whether it's the animals or the plant relatives, they are not present. In the case of the Cree up in northern Quebec, or the Inuit up in Labrador, their whole ecosystems are under water because of some big dam project.

But the United States consumes a third of the world's resources. You can't do that and live in accordance with natural law. That is simple logic. You cannot consume more than you should. Most of our teachings say that. And you cannot consume a third of the world's resources without violating other nations' human rights. You have to take from someone else to do that. So we need to cut our consumption. In that process of transforming our economies we need to protect those things, just say that some things cannot be taken. A lot of us have children and know that sometimes you have to put limits on them. You have to say to them, "You cannot eat every piece of candy even if you have a quarter and can buy it. You will get sick." That is the case with us. You cannot mine every site that exists. You cannot dam every river. You cannot cut every tree. You cannot put a telescope every place you can put a telescope. You have to just not do it. Some of those places that need the most protection are sacred sites. Those are the places where the Creator listens the best. Maybe that's where the direct line is. Those places have to be protected.

THE LARGER SPIRITUAL CRISIS

SMITH: There are no two places in the whole world exactly alike; no two places like this one or have what is *present* in this place. That belief has worked into the verse of the popular song "There's No Place Like Home." That has a double meaning, but the abstract meaning is that there really is no place like home. I would like to take a moment to concretize that abstract statement. When I was talking about this point about land and spirituality with Oren Lyons on the Onondaga Reservation, he helped me to see this distinction. What he told me has remained with me as a powerful anecdote. Oren told me he was the first one from that reservation to go off to college. When he came home for Thanksgiving vacation his uncle took him out on a canoe on a lake, and after he got him midlake, he said, "Oren, you've been to college and you must be pretty smart. Now tell me, who are you?"

Of course Oren was taken aback and said, "What do you mean? I'm Oren Lyons."

His uncle said, "No, *who are you?*"

After he tried a few more times, and the uncle wouldn't have it, he gave up and said, "Okay, who am I?"

His uncle said, "Do you see that huge pine over on that shore?"

Oren said, "Of course."

His uncle said, "You are that pine, and the bluff on that side, Oren, you are that bluff, and this water that is supporting this canoe, Oren, you are that water."

Nowhere in my gallivanting around the world had I come upon this notion of the very identity of the person as inseparable from the environment that played a part in bringing him into being. That may be an extreme example; nevertheless, the general point I'm hearing from you is that religion just pervades the indigenous outlook. Is that correct?

LADUKE: I think that is very correct. In our case *Anishinaabeg Akiing* means "the land of the people." But it also means the land to which the people belong. That is the same general concept. In all our stories, in our oral history, we say this is where the giant went to sleep, or this is where the great river was made. All those stories are contained in the land itself, and they are not contained elsewhere. That is why our people may live all over the country, but when they say, *"Gi-way,"* "I go home," it means they are going back to their land, which is their real home.

In the time we are in now, cultures and industrialization are causing people to uproot, to be constantly moving. What is happening is a result of colonialism. You have this idea that there is a constant frontier. There is always a new place to go, a new place that is going to be better. This is a belief that pushes totally against who we are as indigenous people. Our teachings say that *this* is the place where we are, and that we are okay here.

What happens through this process of constantly moving ahead is what you see today—an ecological crisis—which you and I know is what's happening in the world right now. We are in a fix. We are down here in South Africa, and I'm worried about how thin the ozone layer is. You learn that Dow Chemical creates these things that go into the atmosphere, like we heard about today, and they show up in the breast milk of indigenous women up in the Arctic. All around the world you have this crisis as a consequence of a larger spiritual crisis in society, of not having a place to call home, to be responsible for. That is one of the challenges facing us in the new millennium.

SMITH: I think this is one thing that is becoming very clear to everybody. I don't think that any informed person—a scientist or someone simply informed—can argue that we are on a sustainable course. It would be ignorant, simply ignorant, to deny that we are in a very serious ecological crisis. The "haves" consume far more than they really need. They rob nature of irreplaceable endowments and turn them into waste and pollution. No, it's clear that we are on an unsustainable course. Whether we have passed the point of no return is less clear. We can hope that we haven't and that we will do what we can to reverse the course we are now on.

LADUKE: I don't believe that any scientist or expert on those hallowed grounds of academia could make the argument today that industrial society is self-sustaining. This level of consumption of the world's resources by a linear society that takes raw materials and produces so much waste and so much pollution has no semblance of sustainability. You can't cause more extinction in the last ten years than has occurred since the Ice Age and say that is a sustainable pattern of living.

SMITH: I couldn't agree more. Show us an industrial society that is sustainable and not contributing to our environmental problem. Now, I may be asking you to extend yourself a little, for at the start of this interview you were modest and said that you only knew about your own community. I'm going to ask you to hazard a comparison, because this is such a crucial issue you are raising. I personally think that indigenous people might provide a model that the rest of the world should be working toward— the model of sustainable communities. Do you agree? If so, do you think that the world has passed the point of no return, and we are beginning to try to mend our ways?

LADUKE: I do agree with the model part. As for whether the world has gotten the point or whether more people are aware, that's hard to say. I think that people are becoming increasingly aware of the environmental crisis. I hate to say it, but some people say we won't figure out what the problem is until white men realize the industrial productions in the world are causing their testicles to shrink. Then there might be some realization!

SMITH: Maybe that might do it.

LADUKE: The challenge is to get people to wake up out of denial and to decide to do something about it. Do indigenous people have something to offer? Yes. I know mostly about my community, but I've also had the privilege in my lifetime to listen to many remarkable leaders from other native communities. They teach that natural law is the highest law, higher than the laws made by nation-states or municipalities. We would do well to live in accordance with natural law. We live in a society that trades pollution credits and resorts to disposal as a method of pollution abatement, thinking that if you pour pollutants into a river that takes care of the problem.

SMITH: That's a case of industry shuffling the pack, isn't it? It's absurd. It reminds me of a line from a Tom Lehrer folk song, "The sewage they pour in San Francisco Bay, they drink for tea in San Jose."

LADUKE: Two or three hundred years ago, our old people were pointing out that if you put it in the air, you're going to breathe it. If you put

it in the water, you're going to drink it. That is not only common sense—
that is natural law, and you and I are accountable to it and must conform to it. We can live out any fantasy we want, but in the end it will
catch up with us. We're only human. That is our teaching and our spiritual practice. One should strive to live in accordance with those teachings and live as simply as you possibly can. Not to do so is to assume
that you are greater than natural law. That is not an assumption that I
would make.

SMITH: There is so much wisdom in what you put so simply and powerfully. Your words make me realize once again that wisdom is more important than knowledge. Wisdom is knowledge that makes a difference
in how we live.

THE UNIQUE CONTRIBUTION

LADUKE: Huston, in your travels around the world, have you found
that what I'm saying to you is unique? I don't think it is. These are things
that other people who are much older and wiser have said in other practices. It seems to me that these struggles—whether they are in your ecosystem sustaining the wellspring of the gift of the Creator, or in what it
is about us that is human—must be struggles that a lot of these other religions are dealing with.

SMITH: Now, in my mind the unique contribution of the indigenous
peoples is to focus on this point of *mutual relatedness*. Therefore, mutual responsibility with such single-mindedness is what I don't find in the
other traditions. I've heard similar statements about the Earth being our
Mother and about the limited resources of the world. I have often heard
that what could make people happy is living simply. But I wonder how
we can connect the land with religion.

It is true. There are echoes of what you have said in all the great religions. This is a near-perfect instance of what religion is about, for it is
common knowledge that *religion* derives from the Latin word *religio*.
Our word *ligament* comes from *ligio*, and when we put all this together,
we see that religion is about *rebinding* or *binding together*, knitting the
frayed fabric of life (your phrase is the "web of life") back together again.

LADUKE: It's good to hear that we are all praying. Our teaching is that
there is a Creator that gives us all this and that all these things are sacred as well. A lot of times when we pray we pray to all these spirits. But

we have a belief in the Great Spirit. I think that it is the same thing as "God," if you want to say it that way, but we use the term the Great Spirit.

SMITH: As you indicate, truth is one, and so the truth does surface in these other traditions. I don't think there is a simple fix to this problem. It's deep in our nature that the tangible things are the most evident. So we reach out for more and more of those things that will satisfy what we really want, which is something for each of us to deal with. Can you describe to us what you mean by the "good path" in life?

LADUKE: The teachings in my community—the one I know best—is that we should try to seek this way of life, this powerful life. It's a way of life called the "good path." The Creator instructed us to go down that way, because if you go you'll find that's the way to live in harmony with all the rest of your relatives. The way to live is in accordance and respect to the *Akin,* the Earth that cares for us, which is our Mother. That's what we are taught in our community.

Each of us has those teachings, but in a different way. In our community what that means is that you reaffirm those spiritual teachings from your ancestors in how you live your life, in how you make your prayers, in how you make your songs, and how you treat your relatives, who, we are taught, are of all kinds. It is within that context that a lot of us find ourselves. It is a difficult situation, because just to carry on that simple life you are given is a struggle in the face of industrialism. It is a struggle as we look on a worldwide scale or in North America. It is a struggle when you consider that 50 million indigenous people live in the world's rain forests and that those forests are being hacked down at an alarming rate, when you consider the fact that millions of indigenous peoples worldwide are being relocated for dam projects. When your ecosystem is under water, it transforms what your teachings are supposed to be about. Many of our people, when they try to live a simple life, are faced daily with immense violence and the fact that the vast majority of wars being fought in the world today involve indigenous people.

In our North American context we find we are in a very similar situation. We are kind of a microcosm of that war. We have two-thirds of the uranium resources in the United States on Indian lands. Native communities in northern Saskatchewan are the largest uranium producers in the world. We have most of the low-sulfur coal on our land, the biggest hydroelectric projects in North America. They have flooded our territories; in northern Manitoba, they turn rivers into sewers, full of contamination. A dam project is not an ecologically sound project when you consider that you are putting a whole ecosystem under water.

But we are still the people who still have trees and biodiversity. Yet my reservation was clear-cut at the turn of the century by those who wished to amass great fortunes, like warehousing, like the Pillsbury family. There is a relationship between poverty and wealth, and we understand that. Our trees are now recovering. Now we look, and they have come back to take the trees again. Our communities have this wellspring belief that "they left us that," which means the "leftovers." The word in our language for our reservation is the same word for "leftovers." We have this beautiful land, and we simply ask to keep it. That is the issue of survival that we struggle with in our communities. Just to simply survive will be a way of life in this millennium.

In the end, I would say that you and I know that this is not just an indigenous issue. This is about the survival of all of us. You cannot mine uranium without producing radioactive waste. You cannot burn coal without producing acid rain and the greenhouse effect. You cannot dam every river without destroying the salmon and the land.

PRAYER, PRACTICE, AND PROPHECY

SMITH: I'm completely with you. Say more. Did your ancestors see this coming? Do you have prophecies about this dangerous crossroads in history? What do your teachings tell you about the coming years?

LADUKE: We have this teaching that the Anishinaabeg are the people of the Seventh Fire. These teachings are from the prophecies of a long time ago that said hard times would come to our people, the time of the Sixth Fire, when other people would come to our lands and many things would be lost and taken away. But the teachings said that a time would come when our people would turn around and find things that had been taken and put in museums, and we would bring them home. I assume these to mean the repatriation movement, and the return from our boarding schools, and the return of language and songs.

So this is the time of the Seventh Fire, the time when we bring back our people's remains that were taken, the time when we find things that our ancestors were forced to hide because they were afraid that they would lose them. This is the time when we bring those sacred things back out of hiding and recover those who are on that path. The prophets said that our people would remember who they were and would look ahead for the path they would take.

The teachings say that our people would have two choices, that there are two paths ahead for all of us. One path is well worn but scorched. The other path is green. The choice is between individual will and the collective will of societies, but it is still a choice. I believe that that is really where we are; each of us must consider what tangible things can be done. Each person has his or her own niche, and I would not presume what someone else's niche is.

I come from North America, and here I sit, in South Africa, and listen to these people from these land commissions, these people who were in prison for so long, talk about their hearts and how they reconcile. I am so amazed at how they engage in this process of reconciliation. I ask those who are from here to put their whole heart into that and to realize that reconciliation is a spiritual process, but that it also must deal with economics and justice. If only 13 percent of the population still controls 83 percent of the wealth, then you do not have justice.[5] And I ask the people from the United States to bring that home too, because we need that reconciliation process. Some whites say that because it happened eighty years ago, we should forget about it. But we don't forget. Forgetting doesn't make it go away. We must still all practice our respective spiritualities in the effort to reconcile. We have to have the courage to engage in that dialogue. That dialogue doesn't occur in abstract ways only in other countries. So, speaking as I am in the place of all these prayers, and all this beauty, I ask our listeners to reflect on what we have said in this conversation.

SMITH: Political change is never easy. Look at the situation with His Holiness the Dalai Lama in Tibet. What does it take for a culture to change or to develop a reconciliation process?

LADUKE: In the immense struggle for change there were many things that were quite hard here in South Africa. There are still a number of people who are very poor. But the people had a political will for change, which is not necessarily what we have in the United States. But they have overcome immense odds in order to make that change. And so as I look at my own community, I see that these odds are sometimes daunting for our community, but in comparison, we have come a long way, and we don't have that far to go in regaining more control of our destiny in our own community on the White Earth Reservation.

Over the past year, I undertook a political campaign myself [on the 2000 Green Party ticket] in the interests of leading the transformation to a political will like we see here in South Africa, where there is such disparity in views. I was thinking, Why could we not begin that process in the United States? A lot of my thinking now has to do with the idea of reconciliation and reparations. Both ideas are inherent in the political transformation in South Africa and I think are absolutely essential here—reconciling our relationship with the Earth and with each other—because through a healing process, that is how we move forward as communities of people who live together here on Turtle Island.

In my life, I've seen a lot of things change, and I am very thankful for that opportunity. I mean, all of us have. I think of my grandparents, the massive amount of change that occurred. But I think that one of the things that you and I know is that change always happens; it's just a question of who controls the change.

I've seen change at the hands of the native communities, which inspires me. In my own community, I've seen that some of our land has been returned. About thirteen thousand acres have come back to our community over the past ten years, which is a good start. I've seen people return to the sugar bush in great numbers. I've seen in my own community the return of a traditional corn variety that had not been grown for forty years, which helps us meet the food needs of our people.

This society is so dominant and pervasive in its message, which is why there are more shopping malls than there are high schools in the United States. There's far more money spent on prisons than on Head Start programs, and more on weapons than pretty much on anything else. Those lessons are not about renewing life. They're not about the Creation and your faith. Your spiritual practice is what helps you remember those eminent things.

The gift that the Creator gives us all is the ability to live each day. I'm very thankful to be one of the people here today and also to be one of those who gets to watch all these other people who pray in their own way. We each have our own way of talking to the Creator, and that's a good thing.

SMITH: You've said that your religion is about staying on your path. How do you do that when there are so many forces pulling you away from it?

LADUKE: I dance at powwows, and I've seen an increase in the numbers of dancers, the number of young people who know a lot more of their traditions. I see more young people who know our language now, compared to when I was a kid. I couldn't speak Indian when I was a kid, but now I think we have more young people who are speaking their native language. Those are signs that people are waking up.

What I should say is that I survive because of the Creator and the many gifts that are around. I think that in the broader context spiritual practice is essential for renewing your relationship to the Earth. It is essential to renew your relationship to the world around you, to remember that you are only a small part in it all, to remember your humility in a broader spectrum of things, and to renew your vows to your values and your teachings. A spiritual practice is essential so that you remain on your path.

SMITH: I couldn't agree more. I hope our conversation has been of some help in inspiring others to engage in the much-needed process of reconciliation.

4

THE HOMELANDS OF RELIGION

THE CLASH OF WORLDVIEWS OVER PRAYER, PLACE, AND CEREMONY

Charlotte Black Elk, 1999. Photograph by Don Doll, S.J.
Used by permission of Don Doll, S.J.

Charlotte Black Elk is a cultural leader of the Oglala Lakota tribe. She holds numerous degrees, including one in molecular, cellular, and developmental biology, and she is also an investment banker and an attorney. Ms. Black Elk is a primary advocate for the protection of the Black Hills and is noted for the Black Owl Ruling, a rule of evidentiary procedure that uses science to verify Lakota oral tradition. She is the great-granddaughter of the Lakota medicine man Nicholas Black Elk, who gained renown through John Neihardt's classic *Black Elk Speaks,* and lives with her family on the Pine Ridge Indian Reservation in South Dakota.

In the third forum at the Parliament, Ms. Black Elk and Huston Smith explored the problems of enduring threats to Native American sacred sites. Although many Native American sites such as the Arctic Refuge, Yucca Mountain, the Petroglyph National Monument, and Medicine Lake are in peril, Ms. Black Elk concentrates here on two particularly egregious cases. What the Lakota call Mato Tipi (and whites call Devil's Tower) is now an international site for rock climbers, six thousand of them every weekend. The problem is, as she told *High Country Times* in 1997, "Americans haven't been taught to deal with other cultures and religions. We know how to behave in a court, but I think there's a notion that Indians practicing their religions are less than religious. People come to Devil's Tower and think, 'We're on vacation, we're going to go see Indians and take videos of them doing their ceremonies while we drink beer and wear short shorts.'"[1]

In response to Smith's question about her vision for the future, she issues a "Call to the Seven Generations" to fight for the right to "freely exercise their religion within their culture." For those New Age practitioners or spiritual tourists who approach her for a spiritual quick fix, as if seeking weight-loss pills, she recommends that they "go prepare for seven years."

While people of faith can pray anywhere, Ms. Black Elk admits, it is important to the vitality of the community's religious life that native people be allowed access to their own sacred places and the right to perform their ceremonies. Rather than be discouraged, she vows to "never back down" every time she witnesses a desecration of Indian sacred lands.

For Smith, the rare scholar who has traveled to and lived in the lands where the main eight religions of the world that he has written about are practiced, the native perspective on land and religion is of particular interest. He holds the steadfast belief that holy sites are places where something numinous occurred and thus are worthy of respect and reverence, and moreover, that native peoples should be granted the freedom to participate in ceremonies on their own land. Ms. Black Elk concludes that it is important to the vitality of the community's religious life that native people be allowed access to their own sacred places. Rather than be discouraged, she vows to "never back down" every time she witnesses a desecration of Indian sacred lands.

And that is because the Power of the World always works in circles, and everything tries to be round. . . . The life of a human being is a circle from childhood to childhood, and so it is in everything where power moves.

**NICHOLAS BLACK ELK (HEHAKA SAPA),
OGLALA SIOUX MEDICINE MAN, 1931**

HUSTON SMITH: Charlotte, your credentials are awesome. We have just heard that you are a lawyer and investment banker, and that you developed a new procedure for verifying oral tradition. I am awestruck. Our topic is sacred sites. To open up that subject, let me ask you how you perceive the broad outline of sacred lands before we get into specifics and examples.

CHARLOTTE BLACK ELK: Let's look at the Black Hills. Our name for the Black Hills is *Wamaka Ognaka I-cante,* "the heart of everything that is." It is a word in Lakota for all things physical and all things spiritual. In our origin legend when the Earth was created, the Earth was given a heart. We were told that all the universe was given a song and that each piece of the universe holds a piece of that song, but the Black Hills hold the entire song. We say that the Black Hills are the heart of our home and the home of our heart. It's shaped like a heart. When you see it from outer space it looks like a heart, and each season it beats as it goes through cyclic changes.

It's also important to look at the word *sacred,* what that word means to us. As Lakota people we possess three languages. These are dialectical languages. We have Lakota, Dakota, and Nakota. They have regionalism. I'm Oglala, and we say that we are the children of warriors, so we speak much faster, much harsher, when we speak English. The Eastern people, the Dakota, are village people who were more agricultural; they had summer and winter villages, and they speak much slower. We also possess a formal language called *Tob Tob.* It's a language of one-syllable words. Then we have a sacred language, which is *Hanbloglagia.* This is a language of tongues and frequencies through which comes our sacred teachings. It is spoken only by women and is taught only to women.

SMITH: Did I hear you correctly that this sacred language is spoken only by women?

BLACK ELK: Yes. Only by women. We have a word, *Wakan,* that is our word for God. In our household language *Wakan* would mean sacred or mystery, and *Takan* would be magnificent, great. So you could get the expression *Wakan Tanka,* "Great Spirit," in the household language. But in the formal language, *Wakakagano, Wa-ka* means "that which is that it is." The word *"Ka"* means "to possess power beyond comprehension." The word *"Ta"* means "that which makes it what it is." And *Ga* means "that with no beginning and no ending." So it is a philosophical concept that contains our word for God, but within that is the word for sacred—"that which is that it is."

From Wakan-Tanka, the Great Mystery, comes all power. It is from Wakan-Tanka that the holy man has wisdom and the power to heal and to make holy charms. Man knows that all healing plants are given by Wakan-Tanka; therefore they are holy.

MAZA BLASKA, "FLAT IRON," OGLALA
SIOUX CHIEF, LATE NINETEENTH CENTURY

SMITH: I'm reminded that in the Torah Yahweh says, "I am that I am," which is an echo of that concept, and in Hindu mythology one of the most profound tenets is *Tat tvam asi,* "Thou art that."

BLACK ELK: Except that there is a very strong difference between Judeo-Christian notions and native beliefs. In the origin legend of Genesis you have a transgression, a banishment to the Earth. So the Earth could be seen as an enemy. In the Lakota origin legend, the Earth is our Mother, and Earth took of herself and created her first child, the growing and moving. Then she took of herself a second time and created a second child, the winged. The she took of herself and created a third child, the four-legged. And then she took of herself and created the fourth child, which was two-legged, and said, "This child will be my special child." She named the child *Mato*, "I am esteemed." This child she gives wisdom. This child is the bear.

Much later, she decides that she will have a child who makes choices. She took of herself and created bone and covered it with flesh, and gave this being hands to carry out choices. This is woman, *Winyan*, the "Maker of Choices Who Is Complete." Then she takes of herself, creates bone, covers it with flesh, makes this being in a shape compatible with the maker of choices and names this being *Wica*, "A step from completion." This is man.

Part of this legend takes place in the Black Hills, where we go back and perform each of our ceremonies to bring forward the song of the universe. When we perform all seven of our sacred ceremonies, the whole song is realized in Creation.

SMITH: Can you pick up on one point in this story of Creation where woman is complete and man is one step short of completion?

BLACK ELK: Yes. That's as it should be.

SMITH: Okay, I'm not going to argue. There was one other question I wanted to ask. When the heart of this *whole song* is in the Black Hills, would this belief be parallel to that of other tribes in other parts of the country?

BLACK ELK: Many tribes recognize the Black Hills as a sacred place. I have a preference not to read translations if I don't speak all the languages of all the tribes in the area whose origin legends I have been studying.

SMITH: Now, this lays a very solid foundation for our topic of sacred places. This is a sacred place for the reasons that you have made very plain, and I'm getting the impression that worship in your tradition of prayer is really *inseparable* from place.

BLACK ELK: Absolutely.

SMITH: In Christianity you can pray any place you want to. Am I right in thinking that here, in South Africa, you are free to pray, but your prayers lack the fullness and completeness and perfected substance of your prayers back home? That for the Lakota, spirituality is indivisible from the Black Hills, just as it is indivisible from the economic and the political?

BLACK ELK: That's correct. The Black Hills in our language is *Paha Sapa*. In our origin legend *Sa* is an established place, and *Pa* is out of the Earth. Those mountains were the first established place on Earth. And the color of what was established is black. We say that the Black Hills contain the center of the universe, and when they were created, all the land of the Earth was in one piece, and there were great mountains that ran from the West to the East. In the middle of this great land were the Black Hills. As the Earth separated into two, then four, then seven pieces, the center stayed as the original piece of land, as the rest of it moved away. That is why the Black Hills are geologically the oldest place on the Earth.[2]

SMITH: Of course, the scientific view of our planet's origin is very different. But in it there's no place for the sacred. Is this where your science is coming in? And if so, how do you reconcile the two?

BLACK ELK: Our sacred ceremonies teach us science. They teach us philosophy; they also give us the foundation of our laws. A sacred cer-

---

BLACK ELK'S VISION

Then I was standing on the highest mountain of them all, and round about beneath me was the whole hoop of the world. And while I stood there I say more than I can tell and I understood more than I saw: for I was seeing in a sacred manner the shapes of all things in the spirit, and the shape of all shapes as they must live together like one being. . . . And I saw the sacred hoop of my people was one of the many hoops that made one circle, wide as daylight and as starlight; and in the center grew one mighty flowering tree to shelter all the children of one mother and one father. And I saw that it was holy. . . . But anywhere is the center of the world.

NICHOLAS BLACK ELK (OGLALA SIOUX), 1863–1950

---

emony is also a scientific teaching. For example, what's called a vision quest is actually a calling to hear the voice of the sacred. When we perform those ceremonies we also call the thunder beings and the thunder to return, and we say that the thunder charges forth from the Earth and then comes back down. When you study lightning you find that it is necessary for life to exist. Actually, lightning springs from the Earth, and when it hits the bottom of a cloud, then you see it coming back to Earth. That process enriches the air. It puts nitrogen in the air and in the water.

Our sacred ceremonies teach us to stand in a defined sacred place to pray, that the laws we set for ourselves as humans are only as good as the way we observe them. It gives us our societal rules, the legal structure for our society. Every one of those places in the Black Hills has a specific relationship to us and to our origin legend going back to the beginning. It is important for us to be there.

The unfortunate thing for us in the Black Hills is that they are also one of the richest resource areas of the Earth. The world's largest producing gold mine is there. If you have ever traveled the plains of the United States you have alkaloid water all around until you get to the Black Hills. The one river that never dries, even in times of severe drought, and we have had cycles of twenty-eight-year droughts on the plains, comes out of the Black Hills, the Cheyenne River, that beautiful river.

So it is necessary to go back to those places that come from your origin legend and that take you back thousands and thousands of years. While you can pray anywhere else as though you were in the Black Hills, it is important to actually be there, to make that pilgrimage.

SMITH: Yes, I agree. Pilgrimage is always to a site that for the pilgrim is the center of the world. But let me now quiz you a bit on whether your views of the age of the Black Hills squares with textbook science. You said that your great legends tell you the hills there are the oldest place on Earth. I'm wondering if carbon dating establishes this.

BLACK ELK: Oh, yes. In fact, when geologists determined the age of the Black Hills they had to redo the textbooks to set back the age of the Earth. They had been saying that the Earth was four billion years old, and then they found that the age of the rocks in the Black Hills were *four and a half* billion years old.

SMITH: That's pretty impressive.

BLACK ELK: In our teachings we set out to look at our presence in the

Black Hills. How long have we been here? What we found was that our teaching says our sacred pipe is very new. We have only had it for three thousand years. So we are just now learning about it. We set out to verify that the sacred pipe was brought to us in the Black Hills more than three thousand years ago, and we could do that scientifically. We have pictographic writings and petroglyphs that tell the story, but most anthropologists would look at our stories and call them "random peckings," as if some juvenile came by and just vandalized one of the canyons.[3]

SMITH: What came to mind when you were describing the holiness of these hills—what flashed through my mind—is the image of "Devil's Tower." Slapping that phrase onto a holy place seems like a white desecration, another violation of something sacred to native people.

BLACK ELK: That incident was interesting. The story is that there was a gentleman traveling in the Black Hills who said that there was a tower so ugly he was certain devils lived there. That is quite a different view from our attitude of the holy place.

To us, the Black Hills boom, they beat. The very heartbeat of the world pounds there. The sound travels, and sometimes when you are standing there you can hear it. An early white visitor wrote, "It's no wonder the Indians take off their shoes and walk in prayer when they come into the Black Hills. The very gates of hell are here, and the demons are screaming to be released." Again, we have a very different viewpoint.

One of the issues that we have had to deal with in modern times is the notion that if you violate a law you must be punished—unless it's an Indian law. Then it's quite all right. If you do something wrong against Indians, that's fine. So now most of the Black Hills are under private and federal ownership, and when we go back to these places we have to get permission from the government, or we have to sneak in as tourists to pray.

My name is Charlotte Black Elk, and I have requested permission

---

A NATURAL FIT

The American Indian is of the soil, whether it be the region of the forests, plains, pueblos, or mesas. He fits into the landscape, for the land that fashioned the continent also fashioned the man for his surroundings. He once grew as naturally as the wild sunflowers; he belongs just as the buffalo belongs.

LUTHER STANDING BEAR, OGLALA SIOUX CHIEF, 1868?–1939

---

to pray in the Black Elk Wilderness, a place that's named after my grandfather. I paid $40 for a special-use permit, but I was still denied and was not allowed to use one. There were sixty-six special-use permits requested at that time. Three were by American Indians for religious purposes, and those three were all denied. The other sixty-three were allowed. Sixty-one of those were by mainline Christian groups, the sixty-second was by the Hell's Angels for a millennium gathering. The sixty-third was by the Rainbow Coalition. Those were all approved. But those of us who wanted to pray in the Black Hills were denied that liberty, even though we had paid to be able to pray on our ancestral land.

In fact, we have tried over the last fifteen years or so to get many of our sacred sites—such as Harney Peak and Devil's Tower, which we call *Mato Tipi,* or the Bear's Lodge—purchased by the federal government as public trusts. That would afford us a degree of protection and ensure that the sites would be accessible to everyone. Another great example is the Hot Springs, which is a special place to us. Now it has a roof over it, and you have to pay to go swim there. So we keep trying to make places like these public holdings. We don't specifically put out maps that say "Indian sacred sites," but some of them are well-known. Pipestone is one of them. It's now a national park.

SMITH: Is that regulation still enforced? I'm trying to imagine what would happen if a Christian pilgrim were required to pay a permit fee to pray at one of her holy places, such as Notre Dame Cathedral, but it's almost unimaginable.

BLACK ELK: Oh, yes, because there is a notion in Western society that if you own something you have property rights, and those rights are greater than the right of native people to exercise their religious and cultural uses of that place.

SMITH: Among your people, even the notion of selling land is an absurd idea, isn't it? I recall reading somewhere, Chief Joseph wrote it, I believe, that you should "never sell the bones of your mother or father."

BLACK ELK: It is. All things that live on the Earth are children of the Earth, and they are our relatives. I don't have a greater right to live than a tree does. An elk doesn't have a greater right to life than a fish does. We all have equal rights. Our ceremonies teach us that *everything* desires to live, and because we were created to make choices we can perform ceremonies that will enable all life to live together and to live well.

SACRIFICE AND SACRILEGE

SMITH: Mount Rushmore is in this territory we are talking about. Would you say something about this monumental sculpture? I think it is a sacrilege.

BLACK ELK: I love Mount Rushmore, because every time I look at that monstrosity I know that I will never back down on being Lakota. Every one of those gentlemen up there represents institutionalized genocide against the American Indian people. George Washington, the father of the United States, institutionalized scalping and killing Indians, the wholesale genocide of Indian tribes. Thomas Jefferson articulated the Manifest Destiny principle, which says, "Roll over, you Indians." Abraham Lincoln, on the day he gave the Emancipation Proclamation speech, signed a document that was called "Nits Make Lice." This policy of genocide said, "Kill Indian women because if you don't they will have children, and kill Indian children so they won't grow up to be warriors and keep fighting." Then Teddy Roosevelt said that if America is going to realize its Manifest Destiny, the tribal masses must be crushed.

So as long as that thing, Mount Rushmore, sits in our sacred lands, I have a responsibility to live my culture.

SMITH: That's a very powerful statement. I have heard that there is a move to try to balance the record by creating another colossal sculpture, namely, Crazy Horse, in South Dakota. I think I know what your response is going to be, but please, give it anyway.

One does not sell the land people walk on.

CRAZY HORSE (TASUNKE WITKO)
(OGLALA SIOUX), 1840–1877
SEPTEMBER 23, 1875

BLACK ELK: I belong to the people of Crazy Horse. Crazy Horse was a man who was never photographed, who attempted to live as strongly Lakota as he could. Our most sacred lands are being desecrated, supposedly in honor of the man who was never photographed, and they are misstating his remark that "my land is where my people are buried." Our tradition is to take our ashes back to the Black Hills after cremation.

We have a responsibility to tell the story of the theft of those lands, the desecration of those lands. We have a responsibility to make sure that when we pass through this Earth that the Earth has not been desecrated during our time here by something like an open-pit gold mine, or a Mount Rushmore, and the like. We have a responsibility not to change the Earth in ways that we can't repair. Such changes are violations against God.

SMITH: I honor you for shouldering that responsibility.

THE PRIMACY OF CEREMONY

SMITH: Responsibility to one's ancestral lands is echoed among primal peoples everywhere as a responsibility to future generations. How do indigenous peoples move, then, from belief to better action in the world?

BLACK ELK: I am a Sun Dancer. I participate in the ceremony.

SMITH: I didn't know women participated in the Sun Dance.

BLACK ELK: We participate, but in a different way than men. When we move to music we are seeking to take on the pain of the universe and to make the universe complete again. We believe that as humans we only own two things. While we live we own our name, and we own our power to choose. We can choose to love, to hate, to give pain, or to take pain away. In this ceremony we dance to take on the pain of Creation so that other things don't have to suffer. On the first day you dance, you know you are doing something good so you are very strong and you dance from sunrise to sunset. On the second day, hunger sets in. Most of us in modern times have not known famine, but we have known hunger. Maybe we've missed a meal, we didn't like the food that was there. So hunger is familiar.

SMITH: But what about water?

BLACK ELK: On the third day when you thirst for water, that's when you realize that you are not above all Creation. When I dance, I always remember every stupid person that left ice water on the table. I know that if they were in front of me right then, I would slap them. Then I get beyond myself, and I look around and see the trees. I realize that that tree is probably thirsty, but unlike the human who can make the choice

Sun Dancers. Painting by Black Hawk (Lakota), 1881. Used by permission of George Braziller, Inc.

to leave a religious ceremony and go drink water, or the next time they sit in a restaurant, to drink up that water, the tree cannot exercise its choice to have water. In every little thing you do when you casually leave water or throw it out, that's water that those trees will never have, water my great-grandchildren will never have. The Sun Dance ceremony really makes you look at all the thoughtless choices we make each day, and how the related ceremonies remind you of the sacred.

SMITH: I hear an echo of what you are saying in a story about Dogen Zenji, a thirteenth-century poet and Zen master. There is a bridge in Kyoto, Japan, called the "Half-Dipper Bridge." It gets its name from Dogen's practice. When he crossed the bridge he would take a dipper of the river water, but before drinking from it he would pour half of it back into the river. When we take we must also give. I hear an echo of this in your point that we live by the grace and the bounty of this Earth. In the Sun Dance you give back to the Earth, which only seems right and respectful.

BLACK ELK: That's right; that's correct.

SMITH: I want to come back to the notion that I find very moving about the relationship between prayer and place, which are synonyms for devotional rights. I can't think of anywhere else where the slice is quite as tight. Let me try a couple of fanciful images. First, I think of the way a Christian might feel if rock climbers seeing the steeple of Notre Dame were to say, "Say, this is a challenge. Let's put on our pitons and our ropes and climb to the top and become celebrities. That certainly would be a great accomplishment." I can see how that would be regarded as a desecration. Listening to you, I get the sense that you get the same kind of the feeling with regard to what's happening in the commercialization of your sacred land.

BLACK ELK: Yes, that's correct. There is an attitude in the world that man has a God-given right to be *entertained*. When that comes in conflict with places that are sacred and special to native people, then native peoples are dismissed as being behind the times. It's inferred that we should get modern and be a part of this entertainment culture. Or worse, that our religious ceremonies should be part of that entertainment.

SMITH: Regarding the depth of this desecration of your sacred lands, perhaps another way to think of the violation might be to consider Mount Tabor, in Palestine, known as the Mount of Transfiguration, where Jesus and two disciples were transfigured into glory. What you are talking about is the same as if people were to say, "Let's set up a concession stand there and sell soft drinks and snacks to the pilgrims." Or, "Let's open a water-skiing concession on Lake Galilee." What I'm hearing from you is that that sense of desecration should be expanded to all the commercial intrusion on the Black Hills.

Human history becomes more and more a race between education and catastrophe.

H. G. WELLS, *THE OUTLINE OF HISTORY,* 1920

BLACK ELK: That's correct. I think people should go to the Black Hills and pray there. But not just to the Black Hills. I think that there are many sacred places all over the Earth, and they all need to be respected. I think that when we look at what it means to have a place to pray, that notion is very much in conflict with the notion of secular governments. As government becomes more removed from the culture of the people, there is a tendency not to respect prayer. People pilgrimage to pray in sacred places; prayer takes you back, in every culture, to sacred places. For us, the Black Hills are that place.

LAW AND EDUCATION

SMITH: Not everybody here at this conference would recognize that prayer takes you back to a sacred place, but I find it a very important and suggestive idea. Now, let's turn to another of your competencies, the legal arena. Are you getting anywhere in pressing for those rights that the dominant culture just takes for granted?

BLACK ELK: Yes and no. A lot of it has to do with *educating* people. For all the bad press that television gets, I credit it for allowing that dialogue to go forward. I have a history here. My grandfather, Ben Black Elk, was on the first commercially broadcast satellite image on TelStar. So I have this affinity for satellite technology. We are fighting on every front with legislation, some of it in court battles, but the greatest battle we have to wage is in the war of ideas. When you teach somebody something new, you are teaching something that allows them to be better than what they have been. Teaching other people to respect our ways is our greatest struggle.

As we struggle to have our lands returned to us, I think we are engaged in what I call the battle for spiritual title to our culture and religious tradition. We need to know why our places are sacred, and to perform our ceremonies, and to have the young children take part in them. My children are Lakota in a way that nobody has been since we were put on the reservations in the 1800s. I see that as a tremendous victory.

SMITH: This reminds me to ask you about your emphasis on education as an avenue of enlightenment. Just last month in the newspaper there was a report of a Gallup poll that asked, "Which religion other than your own would you most like to learn more about?" The first two responses were 54 and 53 percent for what happened to be the dominant religions. I think Catholicism topped it by two points, but then came other ones. The third one was Native American, with something like 34 percent of the people or something like that, and then there was a large drop to Judaism and Islam. That gives some encouragement that public interest is turning in your direction.

BLACK ELK: That is a hopeful sign.

SMITH: Yes, I agree.

BLACK ELK: I hope it will lead to the day when my grandchildren and great-grandchildren can freely exercise their religion within their culture.

SMITH: Let us fervently hope.

THE BRINGER OF LAW

SMITH: You have spoken about education, and thinking back over this conversation I think I'd like to hear more about the "instructions" you have received from your ancestors.

BLACK ELK: For Lakota people to be who we are, we must follow the instructions given to us by the Bringer of the Law; we have a responsibility to have the lands of the Black Hills returned to us. It is our teaching that when the universe was created, each piece of it was given a song. When we go there and do our ceremonies we bring that whole song into play. When the song of the universe is being sung, then all Creation can rejoice.

We were told that we were given certain ceremonies, not just for ourselves. As humans we were made to be makers of choices. But the Earth had other children. There are other forms of life, and all Creation desires to live. When the makers of choices choose to do their ceremonies, it allows all Creation to walk the soft Earth in a dancing manner together, and I think that is the responsibility we have. Every culture was given a way of prayer. Every culture was given responsibilities that come with that prayer. To simply sit and pray without doing all those things that God tells you to do is not to pray at all. It is what we call "howling in the wind."

When you follow the responsibilities that come with prayer, then you can bring out the song of the universe. I think that is a responsibility we all share. But all people who agree that we have to live under laws going back to the divine teachings have to really look at those laws and make sure that they are actually realized. In the United States that means returning stolen lands to the native people. It means that when nations say that one of the primary constitutional principles is respect for religion, they must mean respect for the religion of every tradition.

SMITH: There has been so much talk about the globalization of the world and its effect on indigenous people. Where do you stand on these issues of diversity?

BLACK ELK: I think the world loses when globalization of religions mimics the globalization of the economy. I think we need to have diversity in the world. This world was created diverse; it needs to remain diverse. You respect Creation when you have diversity.

As someone who has struggled for religious freedom for many years, I find it ironic to be back in South Africa. I have been here before, as an observer during the first democratic elections. In that case, the United States had argued that the majority had to be respected and must not be marginalized here in South Africa, and also that minority views had to be respected here. The United States used its economic might to create embargo in South Africa. But in its own backyard it oppresses its own native people. This is blatant hypocrisy.

I'm Lakota. We are a warrior nation, so we are going to fight against that hypocrisy.

THE CALL OF SEVEN GENERATIONS

SMITH: What can the average person do to educate herself, even to help?

BLACK ELK: I advocate that people vote and become active within their own governments. The greatest thing is when foreign diplomats come to the United States and know more about Indians than the American government. It forces the government to become much more knowledgeable. It forces them to study, when they know they are going to be asked questions like, Why aren't the Native American people allowed to freely practice their religion? All of a sudden we start to see changes in attitudes and behaviors. We Lakota live our culture, so we are not as fascinated with my grandfather, Black Elk, as people who don't practice their culture are.

AN OGLALA SIOUX PEACE PRAYER

I hope the Great Heavenly Father, who will look down upon us, Will give all the tribes his blessing, that we may go forth in peace, and live in peace all our days, and that He will look down upon our children and finally lift us far above this earth, and that our Heavenly Father will look upon our children as His children, that all the tribes may be His children, and as we shake hands to-day upon this broad plain, we may forever live in peace.

RED CLOUD, LATE-NINETEENTH-CENTURY OGLALA SIOUX CHIEF

There has to be a calling by people of faith for every government to do what it is supposed to do. There has to be a calling so that seven generations from now the great-grandchildren of my great-grandchildren can be Lakota and the great-grandchildren of your great-grandchildren can be who they were meant to be.

5

NATIVE LANGUAGE, NATIVE SPIRITUALITY

FROM CRISIS TO CHALLENGE

Douglas George-Kanentiio, 2000. Photograph by Joanne Shenandoah. Used by permission of Joanne Shenandoah.

D ouglas George-Kanentiio, Mohawk-Iroquois, was born and raised as one of seventeen brothers and sisters in the Akwesasne Mohawk Territory and is a member of the Bear Clan. He is vigorously involved in many issues surrounding the survival of the Six Nations, including sovereignty, the environment, social problems, land claims, and the revival of tribal languages. He is co-founder of radio CKON, the only native-licensed broadcasting station in North America, co-founder of the Native American Journalists Association, and a member of the board of trustees of the National Museum of the American Indian. George is co-author, with his wife, Joanne Shenandoah, of *Skywoman: Legends of the Iroquois* and author of *Iroquois Culture and Commentary*. They now live in Oneida Territory, in New York.

In the fifth dialogue at the Parliament, Douglas George and his former professor Huston Smith discussed the often bittersweet topic of native languages. As *Whole Earth* magazine reported in spring 2000, "Languages are going extinct twice as fast as mammals; four times as fast as birds."[1] At the current rate, somewhere in the world a language dies every two weeks. In an issue devoted to vanishing languages *Civilization* magazine reported, "In the 19th century, there were more than 1,000 Indian languages in Brazil, many spoken in small, isolated villages in the rain forest; today there are a mere 200, most of which have never been written down or recorded."[2] In 1996 Red Thunder Cloud, the last living fluent speaker of Catawba, a Siouan language, died. There remains only one living speaker of Quileute, eighty-seven-year-old Lillian Pullen, of La Push, Washington. "Of the 6,000 languages still on earth, 90 percent could be gone by 2100," wrote Rosemarie Ostler in *The Futurist*.[3]

While some observers regard language loss as inevitable, even desirable, if it lessens ethnic tensions and promotes global communication, most indigenous people view it as a crisis that must be transformed. There must be a collective will to preserve and revitalize the traditional languages. To community activists like Douglas George, language is a symbol of the tribe's group identity, and the threat to its vitality is a diversity and a human rights issue, as well as a spiritual one. He believes language to be a spiritual gift, which means its loss can trigger a spiritual crisis in the community. He makes the case that the great web of life is not only biological but also verbal and cultural. To George, rescuing the endangered languages of the world's indigenous peoples is akin to saving their spirit. As George carefully relates, the preservation of the "mother tongues, the languages of the earth," is essential not only for educational purposes but for the very survival of indigenous people.

For Professor Smith, the crisis in languages is directly related to the crisis in religious and political freedom. What all three situations share is the need for minority groups to speak freely. The preservation of one's inherited language, he observes here, is especially key in oral traditions because it is the very safeguard of the community and "increases the capacity to experience the sacred through nonverbal means." Without language, the ability to express or experience one's spiritual life is diminished, so language is a profound religious issue.

We wait in the darkness!
Come, all ye who listen,
Help in our night journey:
Now no sun is shining;
Now no star is glowing;
Come show us the pathway:
The night is not friendly;
She closes her eyelids;
The moon has forgot us,
We wait in the darkness!

**FROM "DARKNESS SONG,"
AN IROQUOIS INITIATION SONG**

HUSTON SMITH: I cannot be more overjoyed at the prospect of this conversation, because you play a unique role in my life. Before we turn to our topic of native languages, I want to tell the audience what that role is. In my five decades of teaching at Syracuse, you were the only Native American student I have ever had. Never could I have anticipated at that first class meeting what would happen of enduring importance in the course of that semester.

The story, as you may remember, is that during that semester my older brother, Walter, died. One morning at 6:00 A.M., I received a phone call from my remaining brother informing me that the previous evening Walter had keeled over from a blood clot in his brain. Our class was to meet at 10:00, and I debated about whether to have the departmental secretary go to the classroom and tell the students that the class was canceled. Finally, I decided to hold the class but be up-front about what had happened and ask the students to understand if at times my attention wandered. I wanted them to understand and excuse me if I was a little less coherent than usual.

For the next hour I taught as well as possible and made it through. As I was gathering up my notes I noticed that you were lingering. Without saying a word, you fell in step with me, and we walked together with downcast eyes for about ten minutes. When we arrived at my office you came in. I closed the door. Then you said, "Professor Smith, when something like this happens among our people, we sit together. I'm sorry it happened." With those simple words, you proceeded to sit for twenty minutes with me in my office without saying a word. Then you rose and left the office, closing the door quietly behind you.

I don't have to tell you the impact of your action. It was an experience I shall never forget, and I thank you again for that. So it sent a thrill through me when I discovered we were going to have another hour of learning together.

Turning now to the topic of this hour, native languages, let's begin by your giving us an overview of what the language situation is among the Iroquois.

DOUGLAS GEORGE: I was born in 1955 in a time of great transition within Iroquois society. I was actually raised on the Canadian side of what is the only reservation in North America that actually straddles the border. [The Blackfeet Reservation, in Montana, also shares an American and Canadian border.] In our history we have experienced times when the very foundations of our lives have been shaken. The 1950s were one of those times.

Specifically, I was born in those times and was raised among the Mohawk people. Mohawk is one of the Six Nations that also include the Onondagas, the Tuscaroras, the Oneidas, the Senecas, and the Cayugas. Our homeland is what is now central New York State. At time of contact, in the year 1492, we estimate there were a quarter million Iroquois living on those native lands. Currently there are around 80,000 Iroquois people, the majority of whom live on the Canadian side of the border. That is because after the American Revolution, many of our people felt they owed a deep allegiance to the British Crown. They were somewhat apprehensive about the reaction of the Americans to the victory and elected to fulfill their treaty obligations and live close to the British.

When I was born, there was virtually complete knowledge and fluency of the Mohawk language among the adult population. After the Second World War there was a move by the Iroquois to become wage earners. They were displaced from their aboriginal territories, especially the Mohawks. With the construction of the St. Lawrence Seaway and various other capital works projects by the state of New York and the U.S. federal government, our people were displaced from the land. When that happened the adult population realized that their children had to be prepared to earn a wage, whereas formerly we could exist by extracting natural resources from the land and the river. That was no longer the case. Their children had to be prepared to compete in a job market, in a capitalistic system. A conscious decision was made by the adult population that their children would be educated, instructed, and taught to think in the English language. The Mohawk language was by and large abandoned, and we experienced a great break among the generations, a break we are still feeling the effects of. You could almost say to a given year when that break happened. For us it has created a tremendous amount of internal trauma.

SMITH: So within one generation you have endured a slippage from virtually 100 percent knowledge of your language to 25 percent. My, oh, my, what a tragic loss for any period of time, but to think that it happened in one generation—

GEORGE: Yes, the estimate among the Mohawks is that fluent Mohawk speakers make up approximately one-quarter of our population. Among the Iroquois, we have the most Iroquois speakers existing in the Mohawk nation. In other Iroquois nations the situation is even graver than that in our communities.

I think what needs to be emphasized is that at the time of contact with the Europeans there were upward of roughly six hundred languages spoken in North America by 30 million people. A hundred years ago the native population of North America had dwindled to about 170,000. As for the current situation, I believe we have about 157 languages that are still spoken. However, the majority of those languages are spoken by people entering their elder years. There have been moves by native communities to restore language. There has been legislation passed on a national level in the United States to make funds and resources available to help us recover from former government mistakes when they outlawed languages, to make means available to those native groups who still want to retain their language. That is a most admirable thing.[4]

There is one Mohawk teacher who has had an international impact because she designed a curriculum under which some Mohawk students are currently learning about the world through Mohawk eyes. Her name is Dorothy Lazar, a former nun in a Catholic tradition, who put aside her orders and now devotes all her time to teaching ways to retain Mohawk language. She is a remarkable person. A very humble, very nice, wonderful person. That curriculum is being replicated among the Maori in New Zealand and among the native Hawaiians in Hawaii. There are tangible, creative responses to the situation we are in. But I cannot emphasize enough that the teaching of our elders, passed on to each one of us and delivered here now, is that if native people lose their connection with the natural world, then the world itself is lost. That is the situation we are faced with now.

SMITH: You indicated the cause of the tragic loss of language among your people. Now, what do you see as the cost of losing that particular world?

GEORGE: My own experience is the best way to tell it. When I was a fairly young boy I was taken away from the reservation. The Canadian government decided that I was going to be their ward. Like literally thousands of other native children I was put into an institution, a very sterile institution where the very last vestiges of native language were eradicated from the minds of the children. That was probably the most odious and reprehensible act that the government engaged in, the actual displacement of our children.[5]

These children were taken away from the nurturing and loving atmosphere of their own communities and put in these institutions, where they were overseen by people who were, if nothing else, rigid and brutal. You will see that among native people, time and time again. They will give you heartrending testimony of what happened to them when they were taken away from their families, even when those families might have been in a state of crisis, and put into these institutions.

If there was one act initiated by the United States and Canada that was meant to finally eradicate native people by destroying their spirit, that was it. This singular act of removing children by design, by federal policy, from their homes to institutions that were nothing short of penal colonies, laid them wide open to substance abuse.

That is one of the things I went through. If there is anything that stamped out the last vestiges of pride in our ancestry, it was the way our children were put into these schools. This is not an exaggeration. It's a highly emotional issue for Indians who have gone through this. The removal of our children was the primary cause of the destruction of our native language.

SMITH: You have written that the learning of your mother tongue was actually discouraged by the elders for a time because they thought that it might interfere with their assimilation. That's a heartbreaking story. How do people recover from such a cultural calamity as convincing parents that it is in their children's interest to be raised in a whole other tradition?

GEORGE: One of the most amazing, most beautiful, and most heartening things about the Iroquois people is how much we have retained when it comes to our ancestral values, when it comes to our ancient ceremonial activities. We still practice an elaborate set of rituals that follow the lunar phases of the moon. We are pleased to say that among all native peoples in North America, despite the enormous loss of language, our people are still holding on to those things that make us indigenous people.

SMITH: And in those rituals is the language native?

GEORGE: Yes. It has to be. We are taught that native language, the Iroquois language, was developed and born in the land in which we find ourselves. We are taught that it is the language of the Earth. It is the language in which we communicate with the natural world. When our spiritual leaders, our political leaders—they are one and the same—when they gather together, regardless of whether it is a social event, a national meeting, or a ceremony, they have to speak very specific words of thanksgiving. It's called the opening address, or "Thanksgiving Prayer." During the course of this prayer they acknowledge the different elements of Creation, beginning with Mother Earth and going on to the waters, the insects, the plants, the trees, the winds, our grandmother moon, the human

---

THE SACRED WORD

A word has power in and of itself. It comes from nothing into sound and meaning; it gives origin to all things. By means of words can a man deal with the world on equal terms. And the word is sacred.

N. SCOTT MOMADAY, *THE WAY TO RAINY MOUNTAIN*, 1969

A THANKSGIVING PRAYER FROM THE IROQUOIS (SENECA) PEOPLE

Gwa! Gwa!
Now the time has come!
Hear us, Lord of the Sky!
We are here to speak the truth,
For you do not hear lies.
We are your children, Lord of the Sky.

Now begins the Gayant gogwus.
This sacred fire and sacred tobacco
And through this smoke
We offer our prayers.
We are your children, Lord of the Sky.

Now in the beginning of all things
You provided that we inherit your creation.
You said: I shall make the earth
On which the people shall live.
And they shall look to the earth as their mother.
And they shall say, "It is she who supports us."
You said that we should always be thankful
For our earth and for each other.
So it is that we are gathered here.
We are your children, Lord of the Sky.

Now again the smoke rises
And again we offer prayers
You said that food should be placed beside us
And it should be ours in exchange for our labor.
You thought that ours should be a world
Where green grass of many kinds should grow
You said that some should be medicines
And that one should be Ona'o
The sacred food, our sister corn
You gave to her two clinging sisters
Beautiful Oa'geta, our sister beans
And bountiful Nyo'sowane, our sister squash
The three sacred sisters, they who sustain us.

This is what you thought, Lord of the Sky.
Thus did you think to provide for us
And you ordered that when the warm season comes
That we should see the return of life
And remember you, and be thankful,
And gather here by the sacred fire.
So now again the smoke arises
We the people offer our prayers
We speak to you the rising smoke
We are thankful, Lord of the Sky.

TRANSLATED BY CHUCK LARSEN (SENECA), FOR THE CENTER
FOR WORLD INDIGENOUS STUDIES AND THE FOURTH WORLD DOCUMENTATION PROJECT, 2002

leaders, our elders. They go through this in order to put our minds into a kind of collective spiritual state, and they have to do this in a native language, because we are told that is the means by which we can effectively communicate with the natural world. If we don't have that language, then we can no longer talk to the elements. We no longer can address the winds. We no longer can address the natural world, the animal species. If we fail to do that, if there is some time in our history when we lose that ability, then the balance is upset between humans and nature, and there will be an attendant and possibly a violent reaction.

SMITH: I'll put on my historian of religions cap for a moment. I'm thinking of a parallel in Islam. You mentioned that in your rituals the native language has to be used. So too in the *Sala,* the prayers, even though most Muslims do not know Arabic, those prayers must be said in Arabic, so everybody knows those. That's the similarity. But the difference is that Muslims relate to the language as the language of the divine, of Allah, so the language brings them closer to God. Whereas for you your language is related to the elements of the Earth, and you cannot be effectively bonded, or thoroughly bonded, without that.

GEORGE: We are taught that language is essential in the spiritual world as well as the physical world. The Iroquois believe this is one of an infinite number of spiritual dimensions, and we are meant to extract certain lessons from our time on this Earth. When our time is completed, we are sent on a journey back to the Creator, and the shell of who we are returns to Mother Earth because it was a gift from Mother Earth. But the spirit—*the spark of our being*—goes on a journey back to the Creator escorted by our relatives.

Now, one of the reasons that the Iroquois are greatly apprehensive about the loss of our language is that when we make that transition, when we die on this level, our spirit goes to the next level of existence. We have to be greeted by our relatives, our ancestors, and if they can't speak to us, if we don't know their language, then we are going to be trapped between two worlds, and if that happens it is going to be a great despair for our people.

BEYOND THE CRISIS

SMITH: What can be done, what is being done, about the crisis in native languages? Have you passed the point of no return, or are there ways to turn the situation around?

GEORGE: What I like about being a member of the Six Nations Confederacy, especially the Mohawks, is that whenever there is a crisis we respond by organizing. We will meet the challenge. Many things have weakened us as a people, but we still hold on to those things that define us before the eyes of the Creator and the natural world. This threat of losing our language was one such challenge.

We who belong to the generation born after the Second World War were confronted by this break when we no longer could hear the words as they had been passed down over thousands of years. That's when we decided we would take firm and decisive steps to try to counter the loss of language.

It is, of course, very difficult. In my home community there are nine thousand residents. Of that population, which is expanding very quickly, I would say that at least half is of the age to obtain formal education. Our people decided to respond to this acculturation to educational systems that are not of our own design by designing and creating our own school system. We decided to design our own curriculums in four of our communities, and those curriculums would be taught in a Mohawk language. We would go even further than that. We would offer complete immersion in the Mohawk language from kindergarten to grade six.

SMITH: It is thrilling to hear of your attempts to revive your language for reasons that supersede the requirements of state education. In my understanding the oral tradition safeguards the community. Tribally speaking, the maintenance of one's inherited language increases the capacity to experience the sacred through nonverbal means. To do that, though, you need to maintain control of your very means of communication, which is your language.

GEORGE: One characteristic of Iroquois leaders, from when our confederacy was formed to the present, is our love of communication. We are instructed to carry our experiences as individuals and as representatives of our respective nations throughout the world, and we have done that aggressively. We are not comfortable being passive victims of any situation; we like to take charge. A generation ago the Mohawk people realized the overwhelming power of the media, the printed media and the visual and audio media, in creating impressions that people had of who we were. Those impressions were easily and readily converted into political action, so we decided we would start our own newspaper. Rather than relying on outside media, we would take over that thing in accordance with our traditional beliefs, and we would become journalists.

Our radio station does not have an American or Canadian license the way all broadcast stations are supposed to. It was meant to tell people, "This is who we are as Mohawks, we are communicating with you," and also to provide the listeners with various forms of native entertainment.

So the media is a mixed blessing for us. We do try to tailor it to fit our specific needs. Just this past October in Canada, several of our nations banded together and formed the Aboriginal Peoples Television Network. We just decided, okay, the media is here. We have to deal with it, so let's do it in a creative way, a way that enhances who we are as a people, and at the same time communicates the best of who we are to our neighbors. That is the guiding philosophy of the Iroquois. We try to find tangible ways by which we may live in peace and harmony with all that is around us. So we went into the media deliberately; we did so because we realized that is the basis on which people make decisions regarding our future, either internally or externally.

SMITH: Isn't that happening among the Onondaga? Aren't you trying to encourage the learning of the spiritual dimension of language?

GEORGE: Yes, the Onondaga are beginning to do that. One of the problems we have experienced in implementing these creative responses to this crisis is that there has been an endless series of political problems with the Iroquois as we try to aggressively defend our rights as independent peoples. We are not Americans, and we are not Canadians. So as we try to expand our internal economies we meet resistance either from the federal governments or the state agencies, or in some cases our own

---

THE CONSTITUTION OF THE FIVE NATIONS

In all your deliberations in the Council, in your efforts at lawmaking, in all your official acts, self-interest shall be cast into oblivion. Cast not away the warnings of any others, if they should chide you for any error or wrong you may do, but return to the way of the Great Law, which is just and right. Look and listen for the welfare of the whole people and have always in view not only the present but also the coming generations, even those whose faces are yet beneath the surface of the earth—the unborn of the future Nation.

FROM THE CONSTITUTION OF THE FIVE NATIONS,
OR THE IROQUOIS BOOK OF THE GREAT LAW, 1916

people, who have recently developed different opinions about the direction of the Iroquois society. Whenever we stray into this crisis mode we have to put out the fires directly in front of us. Every year that we are involved in these political struggles is another year when another elder has passed on.

That's another reason that our children have not had access to their language when they have needed it to live in harmony with themselves, needed it to maintain and perpetuate the best of who they are. But we are trying. We do offer these schools that are designed with a curriculum to state Iroquois philosophy. We have something called an opening prayer in which we address Mother Earth. We designed a curriculum, again totally in Mohawk, to follow that circular type of spiritual value. The children learn science in the context of the opening prayer. They learn mathematics; they learn contemporary issues. They learn grammar in Mohawk. The hope is that at the conclusion of their term they will think in Mohawk, and they will be able to address, once again, their elders and the natural world in the language they should have been born into.

THE RELIGIOUS DIMENSION OF LANGUAGE

SMITH: A distinctive and very important feature of the oral tradition and of song is that the feeling among native peoples that sacred teachings are really too precious to be committed to impersonal, frozen, static writing. Religious education should come from the older generation telling the myths and the stories. Is that the case with the Iroquois? I'm thinking about your fundamental philosophy about the relationship between religion and language. But I'm still a little perplexed about how the loss of language, no matter how tragic, is a *religious* dilemma.

GEORGE: Certainly. One of the things that the first visitors from the East would remark on is the manner in which our children were taught. We didn't have a formal education system, meaning that our children were not pooled together in a rigid classroom structure. They learned by emulating their elders, by being with their elders. When it comes to things that were essential to our *collective* well-being, like music, education was associated with being with the person who knew that song, and then learning that song simply by memory. We were always told that our oral traditions are collective memories that are passed down by certain people who have the gift of retention. These are people who can memorize things to a most amazing degree. This is an absolute truth in Iroquois society, because these people cannot misinterpret, they cannot lie, they cannot willfully tell us something that simply isn't true.

This is why there is a complete reliance by the Iroquois on the stories, the experiences of our elders as passed on over generations. I'll give you one example. Around eight hundred years ago, a governing set of rules was given to the Iroquois by a prophet we call "Skennenrarwwarring," which means "the Peacemaker" or "He is making peace." He established a confederacy as the world's first truly democratic institution that recognized the inherent rights of people to govern themselves. He also acknowledged the biological right of women to take an active role in the determination of public affairs.

The Creator made it to be this way. An old woman shall be as a child again and her grandchildren shall care for her. For only because she is, they are.

HANDSOME LAKE (SENECA), CA. 1735–1815

SMITH: Now, is he different from Handsome Lake?

GEORGE: Yes, he is the predecessor to Handsome Lake, the Seneca chief who received what we call the "Great Law of Peace" from the Peacemaker. That tradition, the intricacy of this great law, was given to people who had the intellectual capacity to memorize that very elaborate structure, and they passed it on over the generations for eight hundred years in an unbroken line to the present.

TRADITIONAL INDIAN LAW

Among the Indians there have been no written laws. Customs handed down from generation to generation have been the only laws to guide them. Every one might act different from what was considered right did he choose to do so, but such acts would bring upon him the censure of the Nation. . . . This fear of the Nation's censure acted as a mighty band, binding all in one social, honorable compact.

GEORGE COPWAY (KAH-GE-GA-BOWH), OJIBWAY CHIEF, 1818–1863

That original law, the Great Law of Peace, was meant for all humankind. It was supplemented, in 1799, by "Skananiateriio," which translates to "Good Water," "Nice Lake," or "Handsome Lake." He came to us and gave us a set of moral codes in a time of great stress, similar to what we are experiencing now.

Those moral codes were to guide us through the treacherous period when we would have to live next to and sometimes be overwhelmed by our European guests. That tradition is passed on. Both these sets of rules that define Iroquois society are given every year at certain times when people gather together and are able to hear these things from our speakers.

SMITH: This entire conversation is about the relationship between language and meaning. You came very close to making that link when you said that language determines how you think. The question for linguists is whether you can think the same thoughts if you are using different languages. I happened to be a colleague at MIT of Noam Chomsky. I asked him about this, and he said he did not think that there is any thought in one language that cannot be translated into another, though it may take longer to say it in the other language. I am not sure I believe him because of this intimate relationship between language and thought. I happen to have grown up in China, so I had a problem similar to yours. I will share it because it's really a way to pave the way for you to give an example of a thought that you really can't put into English. My example was when the American, President Nance, of Soochow University (now Suzho) was away on business, and the Chinese dean of the university had to chair a faculty meeting.

Well, while the cat is away the mice will play. The absence of President Nance gave the faculty an opportunity to air their complaints about the president, and this put the dean in the luckless position of having to defend him against their complaints. My father (who was teaching English at the university while he was learning Chinese) told me that there came a point in the meeting when the dean said that the president was not "devious," which is *"dyao be"* in Chinese. But *dyao be* has a subtlety that I don't find in English. As a gesture to the faculty, he conceded that he was a little. . . . He paused as he searched for the Chinese word for the quality he was trying to describe, finally gave up, and asked my father for the Chinese equivalent of *bullheaded*. My father thought for a moment or two and then said, "There isn't any."

Speaking for myself now, there just isn't a word in Chinese for that degree of confrontational stubbornness that is impounded in the word *bull-headed*. You can search the length and the breadth of Chinese, and you will not get a word that has that sense of challenge and defiance. This is my prelude, Doug, to asking you if you can think of an equivalent in your language in which meaning is tied this tightly to native language.

GEORGE: During our times of recent crisis in a couple of our Mohawk communities, there was a group of people that decided they were going to apply the best of our spiritual disciplines to try to secure peace. They formed a group and called themselves a "Mohawk *Kanekenriio*," which roughly in English means "a good mind." But it means more than that. I don't think there is an English translation for the word. To the Mohawks, it means a person who is dedicated to using the best of who they are to reach that state of peace that would allow them to secure and restore tranquility to a community. To them that meant the best of who the Iroquois people were, not passive people, but people who actively use the powers of persuasion, patience, tolerance, and love to restore harmony to the community.

SMITH: That's a beautiful example.

THE GENIUS OF THE ORAL TRADITIONS

SMITH: Let's get back to this whole idea of a tradition that is transmitted exclusively through oral means. Our culture considers that a limitation, a handicap.

GEORGE: Yes, it is difficult for you to grasp our thoughts on this matter. We are told repeatedly by our elders that perhaps more should have been done to retain our language. I think they realize, in retrospect, that had we done so, we might have less of a break between the generations, and that we have to act quickly in order to recover from this.

The Iroquois starts by respecting and abiding by what our ancestors did and what your ancestors did, meaning upholding the treaties. That is the essence of respect. Abide by your constitution. Abide by the words of your ancestors. If we can do that, then I think reconciliation is possible. But without the acknowledgment that you have that agreement, that in fact it is a supreme law of your country, everything else is secondary and almost without power. For the Iroquois it starts with respecting and honoring your treaty commitments with the native peoples.

There was a time when words were like magic.
The human mind had mysterious powers.
A word spoken by chance
Might have strange consequences . . .
Nobody could explain this:
That's the way it was.

INUIT SAYING

Within our longhouse, we dissuade people from using the written language. We feel that if people are writing it down, then they are retaining it in their heads, not in their hearts. So within the traditional teachings, the way we pass on traditional values is by memory. We are very reluctant to put things in writing because then it is subject to misinterpretation, and it doesn't have the same spirit, the same enthusiasm, the same emotion and passion as it does when you are learning directly from someone who has committed it to memory. There is a lot written about the Iroquois, probably more so than about any other native group in North America. But to get the true essence of who we are, you would have to spend a considerable amount of time listening to the rhythms of speech, to our teachers.

THE GREAT CULTURAL DIVIDE

SMITH: I think of Hebrew and how much the Jews identify their religion with their language. Hebrew, with its canonical prayers, is to them a sacred language. Christianity has no canonical language, although it used to have the liturgical language of Latin. That's gone, and now you can pray in any language you want. But that's not so for the Arabs, or the Jews, for whom the canonical prayers must be said in Hebrew. Now you have a similar situation to yours in the State of Israel, where it's more under their autonomy and they have revived Hebrew as a living language. That is your objective but under more difficult circumstances.

GEORGE: I understand exactly what you are saying. Here is the *fundamental division* between the Iroquois and the Christians. It is that we believe the Creator speaks through all the natural elements. We don't worship the different forms of Creation. We realize that the Creator speaks through those elements of Creation. We realize that life is fundamentally good, that we are given all the blessings to enjoy this Creation, and that we have to act as custodians. We believe in an infinite number of Creators, not just a singular God, that when we return to our spiritual world, it is not a time of trauma for us but one of great release. Our primary role on this Earth as human beings is to act as custodians and to extract whatever beauty from this world will enable us to return to the Creator in peace and harmony. That is our fundamental philosophy. But along with that is the question of whether or not we can actually call ourselves spiritual without access to language.

When I said that the Iroquois language is the language of the Earth I meant that it is essential to the physical well-being of our people. We rely on a whole series of plants and herbs to effect good health for our people. We are told that when you approach that plant to release its healing powers you have to do it in a native language, in an Iroquois language. The plant responds to that language and releases its healing power. Can you actually maintain these elaborate ceremonies without Iroquois language? My personal belief is that you can't. You have to be able to speak to the spiritual beings when you ask them to join us, and when they do join us during these collective rituals, you have to be able to speak the language. And if you have our spiritual beings entering into our ceremonial building and trying to dance with us, trying to speak to us through dreams, and trying to eat with us, but we can't communicate with them, then the power of that ritual is negated. That is a situation we are confronted with right now.

SMITH: We are having this conversation during the Parliament of World Religions, and part of our responsibility is to face some mistakes, some sins of the past. Has the Christian community, I'm thinking of missionaries, made your problem more difficult?

GEORGE: Oddly enough, within our community, there has been a real distinction between the Protestant and Catholic sects of Christianity. By and large the Protestants were the most in favor of integration, the people who put their language and their culture first.

SMITH: You can say that out loud. I'm a Protestant, and I have witnessed that very much. But first let me just complete this thought. Years ago, I went to Alaska and came to know the tribes up there, the Eskimo or Inuit, who were converted by the Russian Orthodox missionaries. But when the Protestant missionaries came, their treatment was in marked contrast to that of the Russian Orthodox—who adapted and enfolded the native traditions and *included* the native religions within their

Christianity—whereas the Methodists put them in business suits and ties and things like that.

GEORGE: That's true. You can actually see the physical distinction between the Catholic Mohawks and the Protestant Mohawks. The Protestant Mohawks were more capitalist oriented and more attuned to the styles of the day, and the Catholics were just a little more frayed around the edges. I was actually raised a Roman Catholic, and in the church that I went to—I lived within the shadow of the Roman Catholic Church—was a Jesuit mission. Until recently, it was one of the only Jesuit missions left in North America, and they still—even after three hundred years—have not given up the idea that they are going to convert the Mohawks. Our people seem to have a particular fascination with the Jesuits. Our experience initially in the early 1600s was less than pleasant, and we wound up executing a few of them, and they never quite forgave us for that. So when I went to church, what the Catholics did is rather than

---

THE NATIVE AMERICAN PROPHECY

Being asked to sing at the opening of the Parliament of World Religions was indeed an honor. I was there representing other native people across America, but also to bring the beautiful message of our "prophecy." That song says we are to awake and stand up and be counted, for we are being recognized in the spiritual world. Certainly all religions have that in common.

Looking back at the Parliament and my experiences in South Africa, I think about the beauty of the land, the beauty in the souls that we met, and the beauty of the messages, which were so simple but profound. Especially when it came to comparing cultures and religions, ah, there were so many similarities.

One of my favorite memories was being on the hillside listening to the Dalai Lama talk about how we are responsible for ourselves and for our families and for our nations. It made me think that's what that song was all about. To hear that in such a simple and beautiful way just verified for me that we were on the right path, we were thinking along the same lines. And not necessarily just for me, but all the native peoples of America.

It's a beautiful message that no matter where we come from, no matter what age or race or religion, we all have a right and responsibility on this Earth. To do that through music is a very beautiful thing for me. It's like the birds have their responsibility to sing, and the stars and the moon and the sun, they shine; the wind blows, everyone has been given a special gift. Singing is mine.

JOANNE SHENANDOAH, GRAMMY AWARD–NOMINATED
SINGER, WIFE OF DOUGLAS GEORGE-KANENTIIO, 2001

---

overwhelming the Mohawk culture by preaching, or using their enormous powers of persuasion that we know the Jesuits have to convert us to speaking French, they learned Mohawk.

They adapted to a considerable degree to the norms of society. When I was a child, there were only two languages spoken in our Catholic Church. I was an altar boy. We would speak Latin during the mass, and the priest, who was a Mohawk and a Jesuit, a very fine orator, would speak in Mohawk and would be very adamant in his condemnation of the traditional practices, the longhouse rituals. But nonetheless he kept up that language within the church. It was the church that kept this really amazing set of records in the Mohawk language that our people now turn to when they want to follow the trail of their ancestors or find the names that were used when our children were brought into the world.

So in an odd way the church can help us recover some of our ancestral beliefs. To me that is an amazing thing. But certainly the Catholic Church has been a kind of mixed blessing for us.

THE SPIRITUAL TEACHING OF CHILDREN

SMITH: I would like to speak about the religious life of children. I might begin by describing something that happened when we took our trip to Robben Island, outside Cape Town, and were shown the prison cell where Nelson Mandela was incarcerated for seventeen years, out of his total of twenty-seven years in prison. Our guide, Mr. Kathrada, who was imprisoned with him for about sixteen of those years, told us that what he missed most was *children*. He said that they never saw them because children were not even permitted to come in. The spouses were allowed to visit, maybe twice a year, but children never. Now, when we speak of children, of course language is so integral to their growth. Have you any thoughts about the relation of the language issue to the raising of children?

GEORGE: Yes, of course. The primary means of transferring cultural information, history, and communal norms, within Iroquois society, does not happen necessarily between the child and the child's biological parents. It happens because we are a collective. When a child is born into a clan, he or she is born into an extended family. That child learns primarily from the elders, and it's the elders who are entrusted with actually giving the children instructions. They are the ones to pass on the information that is vital to the well-being of our people.

When that connection is broken, as it has been over the last forty years, then we experience a great deal of internal trauma. That child is left to its own devices, at the mercy of the Western media, which in our communities is overwhelmingly powerful in teaching them how to dress, how to act, and how to be. That's one of the great traumas that the Iroquois people are facing today. We need to find and reestablish that connection between the elders and the children when our children are brought into this world. We consider every child a gift from the Creator. When they are given a name before the people, the name is taken from the clan, and that name might very well be two or three thousand years old.

SMITH: I have known you now for some three decades, but I must confess I do not know your Iroquois name. Can you tell us?

GEORGE: My Iroquois name is "Gunadeo." The name comes from the Mohawk Bear Clan. The Mohawks have three clans: the bears, the wolves, and the turtles. Whenever a person has a name that is associated with water, he's a turtle. Whenever they have a name associated with the sky world, the stars, or the sun, that's the Wolf Clan. And because the nature of the bear in the natural world is that of a creator that moves about in plants and digs in trees, anything to do with plants and trees are Bear Clan names.

When our children are brought before the people within the longhouse, they are carried to the center of the floor. There is a song that goes with them as the chief and the clan mother bring that child before the people. They go in a circle, counterclockwise—the way the Earth moves—and they present that child to the spiritual world, and to all the people who are assembled, and they give that child their clan name. That child will carry that name from that time until they leave the world, at which time that name reverts back to the clan.

SMITH: I respect your philosophy of moving, through sheer willpower, from crisis to challenge.

GEORGE: With the Iroquois we are trying to do things like have retreats that would allow the children to be removed from the demands and pressures of reservation life. Reservation life is not something that is idealistic by any means. It can be a very bitter experience for a lot of children, but to have places where people can actually physically remove to can effect some kind of healing. We have initiated some very creative approaches to childhood trauma as a result of language displacement. We have psychological training programs, we have people who are certified counselors in our Iroquois tradition, to respond to the needs of the children, but it can't be just the children. The children are just an extension of the experiences of their community.

So the community needs healing, and one of the serious problems we have had is that the outside world won't leave us alone long enough for us to heal. The Iroquois are always being challenged by external forces that want to tear us apart. These forces don't want an identifiable, secure, strong native community in their midst. This battle is going on now in the state of New York. We have the federal government and various other public groups that are demanding an end to this thing called the Iroquois. It is very dangerous, and it could become an actual physical threat to our survival. That is the situation we are in now. What we need most is something that I have never known in my life, and that is, a few years when we don't have to deal with crisis, when we can just devote ourselves to responding to the needs of our children and healing those wounds.

SMITH: Douglas, what has been the greatest benefit, for Native Americans, that has emerged out of the Parliament?

GEORGE: One of the most important things to come out of the Parliament is the Truth and Reconciliation Commission organized by Bishop Tutu and President Mandela. It shows us how we can apply that profound act of forgiveness in our own Iroquois territory, because we have experienced things that are similar to the trauma South Africa went through. We have had a difficult time reconciling the different elements within our society.

In our Iroquois Confederacy we are trying to find appropriate ways to reach forgiveness. One of the most important aspects of our spirituality is the collective act of forgiveness.

I personally have a great deal of hope for the Iroquois, because we are a very creative people. Although we might be diminished in terms of our language and other aspects of our culture, I've seen the dawn of a new century in which people are pooling their resources. There are so many lights of hope; there's still a tenaciousness, almost beyond reason. That's why I have every reason to believe that our Iroquois people will survive and prevail as distinct political and cultural entities.

SMITH: As you know, I have been working on a book about why religion matters in the modern world. I believe it matters because only religion provides us with a sense of meaning and purpose and allows us access to transcendence, the loss of which is a terrible blow to the modern world. So let me ask you, Douglas, why does it still matter to you, to the Iroquois?

GEORGE: Religion matters because it's religion that connects us to the divine. As Iroquois people we are taught that we live in a world that is but one part of an infinite number of dimensions. It is our spiritual disciplines, our collective rituals, our thanksgiving rituals that allow us to live in a state of peace and harmony on this dimension and that prepare us for that journey along the stars when we leave the Earth and return to the Creator. It's our sense of spirituality that I think is essential to our survival, because it establishes a certain and very important relationship between the human species and the other forms of life on this planet. It's through our spiritual values that we are sympathetic and have some degree of understanding of our place in the world. Religion gives us a sense of direction, a sense of being. It gives us morals and values. In an ideal sense it establishes the principles on which we govern ourselves, and so it is one of the miracles of Iroquois society.

Finally, I think that when everything else begins to retreat in a state of chaos, as has been foretold by our elders, it will be religion and our spiritual values that will provide us with the stability that we will need to survive.

SMITH: Of course, I don't know you well enough to say this with any confidence, but as you were describing the characteristics of the Bear Clan I could see you, Douglas, as having fit into that mode. We wish you the best.

6

THE TRIUMPH
OF THE NATIVE
AMERICAN CHURCH

CELEBRATING THE FREE EXERCISE
OF RELIGION

Frank Dayish Jr. delivering the opening prayer at the Parliament
of World Religions, Cape Town, South Africa, 1999. Photograph
by Phil Cousineau. Used by permission of Phil Cousineau.

Frank Dayish Jr., Navajo, is a lifelong member of the Native American Church of North America and has served two terms as its president. Dayish is currently the vice president of the Navajo Nation and serves as co-chairman of the Sovereignty Protection Initiative. He is active on issues of Native American religious freedom and is currently serving as the president of the Native American Church of New Mexico. He now lives with his family in New Mexico, where he breeds, raises, and shows Appaloosa horses.

In this dialogue Dayish and Huston Smith explore the "triumph of the Native American Church," the story of the stunningly victorious struggle to obtain legal protections for the ancient practice of peyote, a deeply religious way of life that affects a quarter of a million Native Americans who regularly attend its prayer meetings.

For around ten thousand years the indigenous people of North America have been making pilgrimages to gather the peyote cactus plant they believe to be a sacrament, holy medicine, placed on Earth by God to heal them and give them spiritual guidance. Tribal people have used the medicine solely for sacramental purposes. Ceremonial use of peyote is believed to teach righteousness, humbleness, and sacred knowledge. Its uses include curing wounds, providing protection in times of war, relieving hunger and thirst while on pilgrimage, prophecy, and divination. The practice is organized into what is known the Native American Church, the largest indigenous religion in this country.

In the words of the late Winnebago Road Man, or leader of the dusk-to-dawn peyote ceremony, Reuben Snake, the church is "a way of life . . . a way for God's truth to come to us through to us . . . a way we can try to live in peace and harmony with creation." This reference to "the way" reflects the elegant simplicity of many indigenous forms of spiritual practice, for peyote religion is considered by its worshippers a spiritual road, a way to directly experience God. As the Comanche chief and Road Man Quanah Parker warned, peyote may not taste good but "it would keep you on the right path." This journey down the "peyote road" is believed to be an encounter with divine forces that can heal body, mind, and spirit.

"White people go into their church houses and talk *about* Jesus," Quanah said, "we go into our church and talk *to* Jesus."[1]

For Professor Smith, one of the world's leading scholars of "entheogens" (natural plants used to aid the direct experience of God or the gods), the Native American Church has proven to be a test case in the "free exercise of religion." His dialogue with Dayish reveals his belief that peyote is the "oldest and most misunderstood religion in America." As described by Smith in the book he co-authored with Reuben Snake, *One Nation Under God*, peyote is the "spiritual bulwark of a quarter million native people whose roots extend into the twilight zone of prehistory, before the rise of Christianity or any historical religion."[2] When the rights of the church were suspended in 1990 by the U.S. Supreme Court, Smith joined a coalition to help overturn the decision. Of his work on *One Nation Under God,* he says, "This is the only book I have written on a single religion. I gave two years to the project, and it has enriched me no end."

This chapter reveals the Native American Church's remarkable political victory in the early 1990s when President Clinton signed into law the American Indian Religious Freedom Act Amendments of 1994. In so doing, as Smith says, "he brought to a close the latest chapter of the epic struggle to protect an American religious practice that predates by millennia the whites' invasion of America." For Smith, the coalition of faiths was a "landmark triumph over centuries of adversity." However, over the last decade there have been repeated challenges to the sacramental use of peyote, even arrests for possession of the sacrament as a "second-degree felony." Today, various courts continue to rule that Indian people cannot be prosecuted for religious use of peyote, but Dayish and Smith argue here that eternal vigilance must be maintained to protect the dignity and the legality of this ancient spiritual practice.

The Creator, our Great Spirit, the Creator who takes pity on us, You have blessed us with your presence on this occasion, here on this great land in your blessing way, You, the Creator of our spirit, the Creator who takes pity on us, You created earth for the five-fingered beings of all nationalities and You have brought us together.

**FROM FRANK DAYISH JR.'S OPENING PRAYER
AT THE PARLIAMENT**

HUSTON SMITH: Frank, this is a unique experience for me. Over the years I have known many members of the Native American Church and have valued them tremendously. Yet I think this is the first time that I have been able to speak with what we might call a "prelate of the church." I feel like I'm sort of talking, if not with the pope, then at least with the archbishop. That's supposed to be humorous and lighthearted. But it's really an oxymoron, because your church is built very much from the ground up and not given to hierarchies and dictatorial requirements from on high. Still, it adds a piquant note to this conversation.

To begin with, I would like to ask you to acquaint us with the history and the practices of your church. I know that the roots of peyote practice go back about ten thousand years. But since our country has categories for churches—inside and outside—that had to change and take on some form. So would you give us a brief background?

FRANK DAYISH: Yes, but first I would like to say that I am delighted to be here with you. The feeling of honor is mutual. We are on even ground. I would like to begin by saying that I was born into the Native American Church, I didn't come across it through sickness or ailments. I wasn't drinking; I wasn't going through some terrible hardship. I was born into it. My parents were worshipping this way, and their parents before them, and their parents before them. When I came to understand what was going on around me with this beautiful way of life I realized I wanted to be a part of it.

Now, when you talk about history, you go back quite a few years, as you say, Huston. The roots are so old, and there was no one around to record these events, but I've heard stories from the elders and I've read our beautiful folklore, which is our people's way of passing on our stories from generation to generation.

I have learned that the history of the Native American Church is less than a hundred years old, but the way of life with the peyote is ten thousand or more years old. It came from South America up through Mexico and into North America. During those times it was the indigenous people who were worshipping that way. The central part of the church is the peyote, which we refer to as the medicine.[3]

SMITH: I cannot resist adding that peyote is a harmless cactus, which is impossible to become addicted to, and to which not even a single misdemeanor, let alone a crime, has ever been traced. To members of the Native American Church it is a sacramental substance. When you compare that with the misuse of the sacramental substance of the dominant religion of our country—alcohol—the infamy of this difference brings the issue to very vivid light.

DAYISH: The tribes have many different ways to talk about how the sacrament has been used. There are many stories that date all the way back to how it was found, how the altar was set in place, and how the prayers and the special tobacco smoke go along with it. Those details were passed on without documents from tribe to tribe and from generation to generation. The actual organization of the church didn't start until 1918. Unfortunately, that effort to be recognized officially by state and local governments was initiated because of political situations that were similar to what happened to us in the *Smith* case. Outside forces have periodically made it necessary to approach Congress to ask that it recognize the Native American Church. Back then there was a movement pushing for the assimilation of native people, which was based on discrimination and those sorts of issues. The reason, both then and again more recently, was to get legal recognition for the church and to preserve its legal status in the states where the religion was being practiced. So in 1918 the Native American Church was first incorporated in the state of Oklahoma. From that point on the church grew, and various organizations came out of it.

Today there are several organizations of the Native American Church within the United States. There are five hundred or so tribes in the United States, and a majority of those tribes have members who belong to various chapters of the Native American Church. To name just a few of the key organizations, there are the Native American Church of North America, the Native American Church of Oklahoma, and the Native American Church of Navajo Land, and so on.

These five hundred or so different tribal groups in the United States all have their own traditional religions. Then you have the Native American Church chapters, which conduct their ceremonies within many of those tribal environments, and really without too many major differences

---

THE POWER OF PEYOTE SONGS

In the prayer songs that bring our hearts together, we offer our single, united heart to the Great Spirit. That is what Peyote is all about because it is interfused with God's love. It does good things for us.

REUBEN SNAKE, WINNEBAGO ROAD MAN, 1993

---

between them. For instance, the Native American Church of Navajo Land is located on the Navajo Reservation, and they have their own beliefs and thoughts and what they think they can do based on the environment they live in. Oklahoma has the same situation. They have their own environment. They have their own issues that they need to deal with where they reside. Our practices and procedures are actually very similar.

SMITH: When you say they *belong,* that means that there are branches of the church in the tribe. That doesn't mean that the entire tribe is a member.

DAYISH: Absolutely right. More recently, we wanted to address various issues confronting our church. Out of that need, a coalition was formed, sort of a National Council of American Churches. What that did was bring all these organizations together so that we could take a unified position on the serious issues facing our faith and our church.

THE CRISIS IN THE NATIVE AMERICAN CHURCH

SMITH: Let me move in a very pointed way to the recent crisis that has been dramatic both in its inception and in its outcome. Namely, that on April 17, 1990, the Supreme Court handed down a decision, in *Employment Division of Oregon v. Smith,* that the "free exercise of religion" clause in the First Amendment to the United States Constitution does not extend to the Native American Church because of its sacramental use of peyote. The decision stripped the church of its constitutional religious rights to practice its religion because its sacrament was peyote.

Now, I would like you to speak directly to that decisive event. Against that background was the infamous *Smith* decision. I'm eager to say that we are not referring to the Huston Smith decision. No, it was the Al Smith decision.

If I recall correctly, Al Smith was laid off from his position as a counselor in a rehabilitation center, in Portland, Oregon, because he was a member of what his boss called an organization that takes "that drug." But Al Smith insisted that he never took what they called, with disdain, "that drug." Instead, he admitted, "I did take the *sacrament* of peyote." He refused to back down, and for eight years he took the case up through the courts until the Supreme Court of his own state, Oregon, sided with him. They said he was in the right on this issue, and that he had the legal right to practice his religion. But then the U.S. Supreme Court moved in and overturned the decision of the state of Oregon. Their decision violated the reason the founding fathers instituted the separation of church and state, which was specifically to keep that kind of thing from happening.

I believe I am right in giving these facts.

With this background in mind, can you tell us the story of your church's response to the *Smith* decision and how that devastating decision came about?

DAYISH: Yes. That's absolutely correct. The *Smith* case was a real tragedy. As I said earlier, a lot of the members of the church like Al Smith were confronted by discrimination from various organizations. In this case it was the state of Oregon. Smith was released from his employment as a drug and alcohol counselor because of his participation in the Native American Church. He was told that if he continued to practice his religion while working as a counselor he would be terminated. Eventually, he was released from his employment. That is precisely what happened. For eight years or so, the case went back and forth, and finally reached the Supreme Court.

At the time I was working for NASA in Maryland, which is close to the capital. We got together with a lot of the practitioners in the Native American Church, and we talked about the issues confronting the church. We discussed the most troubling aspects of the problem, such as discrimination, the fear generated by the dominant culture's war on drugs, a misunderstanding of the nature of our sacrament peyote, the way we Native American Church practitioners use it. We also talked about the

---

THE FUNDAMENTAL RIGHT TO EXERCISE RELIGIOUS BELIEFS

The right to freely exercise our religion is a right that millions have sacrificed their lives for. It is a right that is so fundamental to our way of life, no matter whether we are Christian, Jew, or Buddhist or Muslim. Should any of our religious practices be threatened, we join together in defense of our right to exercise our religious beliefs. Except perhaps, when it comes to the religious practices of the Native People of this country. These are the religious practices that are little understood and which in recent years, the rulings of the courts have systematically undermined. We should all feel threatened, when the religious rights of Native People are challenged. For today it may be their rights, someone else's religious rights that are discouraged, but tomorrow it may well be ours.

SENATOR DANIEL INOUYE, D-HAWAII, CHAIRMAN OF THE
SELECT COMMITTEE ON INDIAN AFFAIRS, PORTLAND, OREGON, 1992

deep undercurrent of religious superiority and intolerance of people who practice other faiths.

We realized that discrimination had been going on for decades. Our previous church leaders had confronted government representatives in an effort to educate them and secure our religious rights. But suddenly there we were again, facing the same old challenges to our right to practice our religion. That's really why we initiated a strategic movement to bring the sacrament of peyote back to the attention of government legislators to try and educate them all over again.

Then came the *Smith* decision.

Huston, I want to tell you that I just don't have the words to say how devastating it was to have the federal courts come to us and say, "You don't have your freedom of religion anymore." There are no words to adequately express the concerns and the thoughts that everyone—I'm talking about Native American Church members—had at the time. The thought that we would not have the right to practice our religion was incomprehensible. During this period when our religion was banned our thoughts turned to what we needed to do next.

SMITH: Frank, I must tell you that it is immensely moving to me to have seen how members of so many different faiths across the country rallied to your side when you were trying to regain your rights of religious freedom. The Christian clergy rallied in support, as did the Quakers, the Amish, and the Buddhists.

DAYISH: First, we were bombarded with discrimination for our religious belief and practices, and then on top of that we were told, "You can't even practice your religion."

So in this mess of confusion and misunderstanding, there were a lot of bad feelings. I can say that because I felt that way, too, because I went back and forth across Indian country and met with the other practitioners or members of the Native American Church and discovered that they felt as bad as I did.

On top of all that, we did not understand how the federal government, the courts, came to the decision they came to. We did not understand what the courts were calling the "compelling interest" portion of the law, so we never understood why Al Smith was put into the position he was put into. Our people didn't understand the issues, they didn't understand what had to happen so that they could continue to practice their religion legally.

Fortunately, there were various organizations at the time that tried to help. One of them was the Native American Religious Freedom Project

(NARFP), whose members, led by Reuben Snake, organized a coalition. Those of us in the Native American Church of North America [the largest organization of Native American Church members, who have a yearly national convention] looked to other organizations such as the Native American Rights Fund and the Association on American Indian Affairs to provide us with assistance and guidance.

SMITH: I recall Al Smith saying so humbly but so perceptively in an interview for the film *The Peyote Road,* which was shot during the Senate Select Committee on Indian Affairs hearings in Portland, Oregon, "It's always been a misunderstanding between cultures."

DAYISH: We are just practitioners and trying to worship in our own way, in our own church. In doing so we inadvertently broke the laws of the United States. So we were forced to consult experts in different fields to help us and to move our movement forward. A broad coalition, which I described before, was formed, and it included chapters of the church from tribes clear across North America. What this did, again inadvertently, was to bring all the members of the Native American Church together.

SMITH: The name of Reuben Snake, the Winnebago chief and peyote Road Man, should not be omitted from this discussion. If one had to pick one individual who had the vision to produce the coalition and for the first time bring virtually every tribe into a concerted movement, it was Reuben. He was the prime mover in securing the passage by Congress of the American Indian Religious Freedom Act Amendments of

---

WHATEVER AMERICA DESIRES FOR THE WORLD

In 1952 the president of these United States, Dwight D. Eisenhower, said these words: "Whatever America desires for the world, must first come to pass in the heart of America." Today our national leaders, our president, and members of his administration, the secretary of state, travel to the four corners of the globe professing the support of human rights in all the different nations of the world. They say, "Live up to your teachings and protect the human rights of people." But while they are doing that, right here within this country, the indigenous people of this land continue to suffer from gross injustices and deprivations of our religious freedom. So in closing, I want to say, Senator [Daniel Inouye], quoting Edmund Burke, "The only thing necessary for evil to triumph is for good men to do nothing."

REUBEN SNAKE, COORDINATOR, NATIVE AMERICAN
RELIGIOUS FREEDOM PROJECT, PORTLAND, OREGON, 1992

1994, which President Clinton signed as Public Law 103–344 on October 6, 1994.

DAYISH: Absolutely. That's why I mentioned NARFP. Reuben was the person who put together the coalition and started the movement after the *Smith* decision came down. From that point many organizations started to come together to educate us on how to address Congress, how to address congressional members, and how to address congressional aides, so they could understand the issue we were confronting. A lot of organizations came together, such as DreamCatchers and Kifaru Productions, who produced several documentary films to educate not only legislators and the American public but also members of our church and the religious freedom coalition.

As I said earlier, the intent was never to convert anybody. The church doesn't even have a lot of money. It doesn't have a lot of resources. It doesn't have a lot of talented people to go to and say, "This is what we would like to say, or this is how we would like to articulate our position." We met with experts such as non-Indian professors of law and of religion, including you, Dr. Smith. We had assistance from the National Council of Churches, the National Conference of American rabbis, and many other religious and human rights organizations. I think we were very fortunate and blessed that people appreciated what we were confronting.

Another thing to remember about the Native American Church of North America is that we don't have a website, we don't advertise, and we don't invite other people to our ceremonies. All we want to do is to preserve and protect the religion we have.

SMITH: I suspect that the leaders from other faiths, including Quakers, Jews, and Catholics, all those who stepped in to help your cause, believed they could be next on the list of those prosecuted for practicing their religion. You didn't have a lot of money, but you still fought for your rights. Was it because of what Indian rights lawyer James Botsford has called the "fear of a knock at the door"?

DAYISH: Our religion was in jeopardy. Regardless of what was to happen, I think there was no way for the courts to suppress us from continuing to worship. Regardless of the *Smith* decision, Native American Church members continued to worship.

The other day we were touring the prison on Robben Island with a South African gentleman by the name of Mr. Ahmad Kathrada, who had been incarcerated there with Nelson Mandela for seventeen years. Mr.

Kathrada mentioned the years that they, as political prisoners, had spent on that island. They were jailed at that time because of a belief that they had about their right to religious and political freedom. I likened their fight to the outcome of the *Smith* decision and our response to our struggle to continue our way of worship. We continued to pray that the courts would understand our situation and continue to do things to preserve our religion.

SMITH: Last evening we were having dinner together in Cape Town, and you made a very eloquent gesture when you were talking about this problem. You said, "We continued even though it was illegal, we continued even to worship and to pray because for us without our religion." Then you made a dramatic gesture as if you were cutting your own throat. In other words, the sustainment of your life was coming from this ancient form of worship, and it would be like *death* to live without your religion.

DAYISH: That's absolutely right, Huston. Our way of life was threatened.

AN INTERFAITH ALLIANCE

SMITH: But now I want to move into another aspect of this profoundly important fight for religious freedom, which is the way in which this case was directed against your church. It became explosive for many other denominations, such as the Quakers, the Amish, even Christians and Jews, when the government began coming down on their religions. It's terribly ironic, because people came to this country to escape centuries of governmental persecution of their religion. When these other religions saw you targeted they saw the writing on the wall. If they are first, we could be next. But freedom of religion has always needed to be guarded.

DAYISH: That's absolutely right, Huston. As I stated earlier it wasn't just a few tribes that banded together. That's where the initial coalition started. We started to have the annual events with interfaith impact, like the one we staged at the United Methodist Church, which is headquartered in Washington, D.C., to lobby congressional members. If Native Americans could be stripped of their religion, they must have said to themselves, Who's next?

SMITH: Exactly. Their worst fears were realized. They thought they might be next—and they *were* next. There were several cases involving the prosecution of Catholic priests and Jewish rabbis, using the *Smith* case as precedent.

In my understanding, the largest coalition of religious groups in America ever to have come together asked the Court to reconsider its decision. The Court refused, and, therefore, the judiciary having deserted them, they did an end run around the courts and took the issue directly to Congress and in 1993 did succeed in passing the Religious Freedom Restoration Act. This was necessary because in the *Smith* decision the courts had lowered the bar at which governments could interfere with religion. They had to show a compelling state interest before they had a right to intervene. But with that decision they *lowered* the legal threshold to an irrational basis.

For those of us who are not lawyers, maybe that difference doesn't sound very great. But for constitutional scholars the decision was, as they described it, "a huge lowering of the bar." That's what sent a shock wave throughout the religious body and caused them to get together and help pass the Religious Freedom Restoration Act.

Now, there is an ironical moment. I'm really saying this to make sure I have it right. The Native American Church tried to join that coalition. But it was turned down on the grounds that the coalition was put together in such a fragile manner that if you brought in a religion whose sacrament is a "drug," in the eyes of the Court, they could shut you out of the coalition. When you realized what could happen you had to do your own end run around the Court.[4]

A year later you were successful in passing the 1994 Amendments to the American Indian Religious Freedom Act. In 1998 a test case came up to the Supreme Court that said the law that had been passed by this huge coalition at their instigation was invalid, and so that law was knocked down, but your law still stands. Is that correct?

THE RESTORATION OF RELIGIOUS FREEDOM

DAYISH: I'm happy you brought that up. It's called the Religious Freedom Restoration Act of 1993. We approached the group, and they felt that our organization was a threat because of precisely what you said. Our cause was very controversial because of the unfortunate confusion with hard drugs. They thought an association with us might affect and even delay the amendments that they were hoping to achieve. So we were denied in adding our law, our protection of our sacrament and our ceremonies, to their coalition.

But when we were denied we didn't walk away upset. We kept fighting. We assisted them in passing the 1993 amendment. As we went through that process, we decided that the fight had to be carried on, and so the

Native American Church and other organizations continued to pursue the protection of freedom of religion for all. I can remember this because I participated in Native American Church services, where we prayed for guidance so that the right people would come in and assist us in achieving what we were hoping to achieve. It seems to me that it was right that they denied us, because down the road the Supreme Court decision was overturned. So it was a success on our part that we didn't join that coalition. It was a success from the standpoint that we were forced to work for the passage of our own legislation protecting the Native American Church, specifically.

SMITH: What an ironic moment in American history. The large coalition turned you down, but what happened was that their law got struck down, and since you were turned down, you went for your own law, which is still in place. Am I correct in saying that the Native American Church is the only religious body that is named in law as having religious freedom?[5]

DAYISH: That's exactly what happened. It was great.

Now, Professor Smith, I'd like to ask you a question. I have some thoughts that came to me after talking with my elders before we came down here to South Africa. Because of the sacredness of the church our intent is not to go out and recruit members. My question to you, Professor Smith, is, What qualifications do you have, what are your criteria, for bringing the Native American Church onto the world stage, and for talking about the things that we have addressed up until this point?

SMITH: I would say that we historians of religion make a distinction between the historical religions and the indigenous religions. If we look at human history, and through archeological artifacts, we can go back twenty thousand years, maybe fifty thousand years ago when all human religious philosophy was in the oral mode of indigenous people. In comparison to that are the historical religions, which are defined by the fact that they have written text, not just oral myth. They have cumulative history because of those written texts. The Christianity of the Middle Ages was not the Christianity of the apostolic period. The Christianity of the apostolic period was not the Christianity of the patristic church fathers. There are changes, but the historical religions are virtually the only other ones that are present at this conference. There are some debates about the Gaia movement, but the historical aspects of those are still under discussion.

So the way I see it, this whole conference in Cape Town is like the tip of the iceberg resting on this huge foundation of indigenous religions, which is the way humanity has lived out their religious impulses and longings and hopes for seventy thousand years or so. As Walter Echo-Hawk said, this World Parliament is a chance to give native people "a seat at the table."

DAYISH: That's very helpful. I agree. I think that it is important, from a religious freedom standpoint, to have national- or international-level events, like this Parliament, that bring together so many of the leaders of different faiths to try to understand the issues of the Native American Church. However, if the word does not get down to the level of local communities, there will probably still be religious discrimination.

SMITH: You've spoken eloquently about the devastating feeling you had when the *Smith* decision was handed down. What was your feeling when the law was passed that now grants you protection? What kind of celebrations did you have?

DAYISH: There were a lot of celebrations held throughout the United States. We had ours in Kansas. The Navajo Nation had theirs in their capital, Window Rock, and there was pure elation. There were ceremonies across Indian country with the understanding that there is still a lot of work to be done. We were successful, but we understood that there is still a long way to go.

SMITH: Without a nickel in your coffers, you and your stalwart friends challenged the highest court of the land, and reversed four centuries of prejudice against your sacrament. I see the case also as a warning that the practitioners of minority faiths must be ever vigilant, and willing to stand up for their faiths if and when the need arises. It is a story that deserves to be documented, remembered, and retold for generations, for it carries hope for freedom lovers throughout the world.

THIS WAY OF WORSHIP

SMITH: In closing, can you tell us about the sacred dimension of your religion, and why it matters so profoundly to you that you were willing to fight for your right to practice it?

DAYISH: Religion matters because it's the central point of our existence— for me and my family and my people—and I resort to it for my health and it's how I ask to be blessed. Religion matters to me because it reflects the physical life that I have on my land that was settled by my grandfather, who was a land board member for the Navajo Nation. We came upon this land through our prayers, and we continue life that way. This way of worship, requesting blessings, surrounds my life. I get up every morning thinking good thoughts of the Creator, as well as during the day, from dawn through the spreading of the sunlight right up to the evening when the sun sets. So those are my thoughts regarding the purpose of religion.

SMITH: With so much about the survival of indigenous peoples all around the world, it is remarkable that you have such faith in the future of yours.

DAYISH: My culture will survive because of the beliefs that were passed on to us and the beliefs that we have today. If I may share a story with you, you will see how we relate to the way everything around us has a spirit, even the Earth, the way it spins, the direction it takes.

I was told way back when I was a boy that Johano-ai, the sun god, travels from the East to the West. Every day he gets up and does his chore, to take the sun over the Earth. Johano-ai goes about his chores with his five horses. He's got a red shell horse; he's got a horse of turquoise; he's got a pearly shell horse; he's got a white shell horse; and he also has a horse of coal. And one very nice day when it's sunny and the skies are blue and everything is calm, the sun god gets on his turquoise horse (or

---

SONG OF THE HORSES

How joyous his neigh!
Lo, the Turquoise Horse of Johano-ai,
How joyous his neigh,
There on precious hides outspread, stands he;
How joyous his neigh,
There of mingled waters holy, drinketh he;
How joyous his neigh,
There in mist of sacred pollen hidden, all hidden he;
How joyous his neigh,
These his offspring may grow and thrive forevermore;
How joyous his neigh.

DINE (NAVAJO) SONG

---

his red shell horse or his pearly shell horse or his white horse or his horse of coal), and he takes the gold disk of the sun and takes it across the sky from East to West.

Now, because his horses help him achieve this goal on a daily basis, he gives his horses the best water that he can find, the ceremonial water. Then he takes his horses to graze on good, blooming flowers, which grow on the most beautiful property where there are rich hides and the best woven blankets. This is where the sun god corrals his horses. He provides the best things for them every day. And when these horses shake off the dust from their daily rides, they are shaking off all these valuable minerals from the most beautiful land. They say that when a horse is running, the dust he makes is not dust; it is corn pollen that medicine men have offered up to Johano-ai, the sun god.

And that's what we use in our traditional life. In all our ceremonies we use the best we can find.

The traditional ceremonies, stories, myths, and folklore that have been passed on to us are things we interact with daily. So we are continually reminded of the physical existence of the different spirit beings here on Earth by the culture, by the stories, that we have go along with them. I think that's the reason that our culture and our religion will exist for a long time to come. And I will continue to pass on what I shared with my children so that we continue to pass on the culture that was passed on to us.

7

THE FIGHT FOR NATIVE AMERICAN PRISONERS' RIGHTS

THE RED ROAD TO REHABILITATION

Lenny Foster, 1999. Photograph by Phil Cousineau.
Used by permission of Phil Cousineau.

L enny Foster, a Dine/Navajo from Port Defiance, Arizona, has been involved in the struggle for prisoners' rights for the last thirty years. He is the director of the Corrections Project of the Navajo Nation Department of Behavioral Health Services and spiritual advisor to approximately two thousand Native American inmates in ninety-six state prisons and federal penitentiaries across the United States. He has authored state legislation in New Mexico, Arizona, Colorado, and Utah permitting American Indian religious practices in correctional facilities, a development that has led to a significant reduction in prison returns. From 1969 to 1981 Foster also participated in many American Indian Movement (AIM) campaigns, including the Occupation of Alcatraz, the Trail of Broken Treaties Caravan, Wounded Knee, the Longest Walk, and Big Mountain. He has traveled extensively around the world as an Indian rights activist and received many awards and accolades for his work, notably the Martin Luther King Jr. Civil Rights Award. Mr. Foster is also a Sun Dancer and a member of the Native American Church.

The seventh session of the delegation explored what Vine Deloria describes as the grimmest and toughest of all religious freedom issues for Indian people: prisoners' rights. In this deeply moving conversation between the formidable spiritual counselor and Professor Smith, we learn of the startling gap between prisoners' rights among the general population and those among Indian inmates. For Foster, the struggle is against a general ban on native ceremonies, an injustice that has its roots, again, in the reluctance of the larger society even to recognize Indian practices as religious. The lack of equal access to ceremonies for native prisoners is due to the objections many prison officials have to native ceremonial practice. Not only is the ban wrong, argues Foster, but it makes it unconscionably difficult for Indian inmates to practice their religion.

His view of the paramount importance of ceremony is backed up by scholars such as anthropologist Victor Turner who writes: "Religion, like art, lives so far as it is performed, i.e., in so far as its rituals are 'going concerns.' If you wish to spay or geld religion, first remove its rituals, its generative and regenerative processes. For religion is not a cognitive system, a set of dogmas, alone, it is meaningful experience and experienced meaning. In ritual one lives *through* events."[1]

Likewise, Joseph Epes Brown, the chronicler of Nicholas Black Elk's life, said in an address at the American Museum of Natural History, in 1982, "All spiritually effective rites must accomplish three accumulative possibilities which may be termed: purification, expansion—wholeness or virtue—and identity." His prime example in the talk was the use of the sacred pipe. Smoking the pipe in a ceremonial setting, he said, or "in a sacred manner," as his mentor, Black Elk, said, the participant takes part in a communion, a purification, an offering (to the Great Mystery), a sacrifice. It is then and finally an understanding of the closing phrase, *"Mitakuye oyas'in!"* "We are all related."

For Lenny Foster, access to ceremony is a human rights issue. Twenty-five years of counseling have taught him the healing power of sacred rites such as the pipe ceremony and the sweat lodge, which are the basis of his spiritual instruction, the most effective way of dealing with native prisoners.

The discrimination reveals what Vine Deloria Jr. calls the "great inequality of the law" that reduces religion only to a belief system. "If you're in a cell you can believe what you want, but that doesn't help you deal with your situation. And you can see great inequality in the law, because if you restricted the Christian and Jewish religions to their essential ceremonies or essential rituals, all the Christians would ever be able to do would be to baptize, and all the Jews would ever be able to do is to circumcise."

For Foster, this struggle is a lifelong commitment to ensuring that native prisoners enjoy the same religious freedom as those of any other religious faith. For Huston Smith, the struggle for these prisoners' rights is the most egregious examples of inequality before the law that native peoples face today. As he makes clear here, it is a basic human right to be allowed equal access to spiritual healing ceremonies.

American Indians share a history rich in diversity, integrity, culture, and tradition. It is also rich in tragedy, deceit, and genocide. As the world learns of these atrocities and cries out for justice for all people everywhere, no human being should ever have to fear for his or her life because of their political or religious beliefs.

LEONARD PELTIER, 1975

HUSTON SMITH: Lenny, you have an impressive list of endeavors for the cause of your people. But before we turn to the specific focus of your work and this conversation, would you say a little bit to us about how you see yourself?

LENNY FOSTER: I greet you in the traditional manner, which we always use to introduce ourselves to the holy people first.

SMITH: Thank you. The morning after we arrived in Cape Town, we were taken out to Robben Island, and on our tour we were shown the prison cell in which Mr. Nelson Mandela spent seventeen years out of the twenty-six total years he was incarcerated. Being in that prison aroused powerful emotions in all of us, but I must believe that the emotions that were awakened in you were of a distinctive character because you have made the center of your life working with prisoners. Can you tell us what was going through your mind?

FOSTER: I felt that the visit to Robben Island was a pilgrimage for me. I had heard so much about Nelson Mandela and his being incarcerated for such a long time and what he represented to people in a struggle throughout the world. The authorities were unable to break his spirit or his will, and that was quite an inspiration to me. The prison itself reminded me of some of the penitentiaries in the United States, such as Leavenworth, Lewisburg, Santa Fe, and Lompoc and the Native Americans there who have been incarcerated as political prisoners. At this time, there is Leonard Peltier, a Lakota or Ojibway from North Dakota, whose struggle parallels that of Nelson Mandela. Leonard has been incarcerated for approximately twenty-four years. He was alleged to have been in the area where two FBI agents were killed, on June 25, 1976, and has been incarcerated at the U.S. penitentiary in Leavenworth, Kansas. He is one of the most famous political prisoners in the world. When we were at Robben Island I thought of the struggle that he has had to endure as part of his liberation, and, just like with Nelson Mandela, the authorities cannot break his spirit. So my visit there was very spiritual, very emotional for me.[2]

SMITH: Yes, yes. Now I would like to get into the specifics of the way you minister through your sacraments and rituals to your people who are incarcerated. But let me do so by asking if your people have the same rights in this matter of incarceration. I'm talking about in practice, not in principle. Is there an inequality in the way in which law officers put native people behind bars? Do you suffer a special handicap in that respect?

FOSTER: The concept of penitentiary prison is a foreign concept that was brought to North America. We never had that type of incarceration or detention for individuals who committed offenses against the community or individuals. Traditionally, there were efforts made to restore justice through the peacemaking process. This isolation and deprivation and punitive punishment are foreign and highly damaging concepts to Native Americans.

I don't have the exact numbers, but I think the latest survey information said that there were over seven thousand Native Americans incarcerated in our prisons. As far as the specific numbers on death row go, I couldn't tell you.[3] But I think what you need to understand is that in some of these state prison systems, such as South Dakota, Montana, and Oklahoma, 20 to 40 percent of the prison inmates incarcerated in their respective prisons are Native Americans. The percentage is severely disproportionate. When 40 percent of the prison population is Native American, something is wrong.

SMITH: I might just give a parallel in my experience. I grew up in China, and my mother was born in China also, and in her time if someone had committed an offense against the community, they too would not incarcerate them. That was a foreign concept to them. I have photographs from that period of someone who had committed an offense. Their punishment was a form of the medieval stocks, a technique that utilized two boards with holes for the prisoner's hands and neck. So the person would be at large, but they wouldn't be cut off from their family and other people. They were entirely dependent on other people because they couldn't feed themselves, but at least they weren't totally cut off from society. Perhaps it's a poor analogy, but let's remember that that is a form of punishment from a people who adjured the notion of putting people away and cutting them off physically from the community. Our system in the United States stands in dramatic contrast. We incarcerate and isolate more prisoners than just about any country. My question to you is this: Do you think law officers treat your people fairly, or are Indians more harshly treated when they are incarcerated?

FOSTER: There exists a double standard of justice in the United States, because Native Americans are incarcerated at a far higher rate than any other nationality. The indigenous culture of this country and its traditions and spiritual beliefs are discounted and undermined and not appreciated. There is a real effort, or struggle, at this time to obtain those equal rights. That is what we are engaged in. Perhaps prisoner rights is

the most serious crisis among our people. Many of our people are incarcerated because of alcohol- and drug-related offenses, perhaps 90 to
99 percent of offenses. That's a major problem, because alcohol has devastated our communities; it has broken up families; it's undermined our
spirituality. We are focusing on that because we feel that spirituality is
the answer to our abuse problems. That is why we are so adamant about
using the sweat lodge, which has been very successful in addressing these
problems. Inside the sweat lodge you have to be open, and you have to
be willing to put your mind into the prayers and the songs and be willing to admit that you are having some problems.

For these reasons, it is our obligation to work with our people to ad-
just and correct the drug and alcohol situation. We find that returning
to traditional spiritual beliefs is the best way to address those problems.
But ignorance and racism and the complete lack of awareness of our spiritual ways result in the complete denial of our efforts to work with our
own people; it results in lost opportunities.

THE OLD WAYS OF INDIAN MINISTRY

SMITH: Take us now, as it were, by hand with you inside a prison. All
prisons have chaplains, but the spiritual needs and resources of your
people are different from the kinds that the nominal official chaplain can
offer. So what do native prisoners need to carry them through this difficult
period, and how do you provide that?

FOSTER: For the last thirty years there has been a movement across the
United States, a recovery or healing movement. It's really a spiritual healing that is taking place among Indian people, a return to the culture, the
practices. This effort has resulted in the revival of a lot of pride and dignity in Indian country. It's no different in the prison setting. I think many
of our people are incarcerated because of a lack of awareness about their
culture or beliefs. So prison becomes a place where a great deal of spiritual and historical learning is taking place, where Indian men and women
are relearning the songs and the prayers and the ceremonies. A lot of education is taking place, but it has been a struggle because the wardens,
the chaplains, the federal bureau of prison systems have been very reluctant to approve of such traditional native practices. They use security
concerns as an excuse for why these practices cannot be held in prisons.

SMITH: You are going into prisons as if you were on a mission as a chaplain or a minister to help native prisoners face up to their spiritual needs.

But you face certain blocks. That is what I'm hearing. You keep coming up against certain prohibitions or prejudices, which do not allow you to do what you feel you need to do to help.

> **The American Indian has faced so many difficulties in life that it's time that we all go through an individual healing for the benefit of the generation that's coming behind us. I'd like to call it *"Ataka Wokushkushka,"* "something holy moving," because that's what I see that's happening across the United States and Canada today.**
>
> RICK THOMAS (SANTEE SIOUX), 1994

> **We have, at the very core of our being, more power than anything human kindness has ever made ever since the beginning of time. That's how powerful we are. The Creator gave us this gift. So no matter what has been done to us, any type of abuse or historical grief, whatever has been done to us, that we have all the power internally to be able to overcome anything. We can, in any given second, start that healing process and walk a healing road.**
>
> GENE THIN ELK (LAKOTA), 1994

FOSTER: Exactly. Certain requests are made from the inmates themselves through correspondence. Family members come into our offices requesting that we visit their loved ones who are incarcerated; they are in need of spiritual counseling, they are in need of specific ceremonies. We contact the chaplain's office and the warden's office to request that we be allowed to go into these facilities to conduct our ceremonies, such as the sweat lodge ceremony.

SMITH: Do they cooperate?

FOSTER: For the most part they approve. But there are times when the requests will *not* be approved. There are some facilities, in the state of

Texas and in Oklahoma, that are now approving us. But there are still some correctional facilities that are not approving any sweat lodge ceremonies, for example, because the officials claim it's a security concern to them. It's really fear and ignorance and lack of awareness of our ancient ceremonial practices.

SMITH: You mention the sweat lodge. Are there other rituals that you have trouble taking in or working with the inmates on?

FOSTER: The sweat lodge is an ancient ceremonial practice that cleanses the body, the mind, and the spirit. Prayers and songs are made that really help an individual while they are imprisoned. It makes a person feel real good. It's a beautiful, very spiritual ceremony. We also find the talking circle, where individuals are brought together in a circle and an eagle feather is passed, to be very therapeutic. Each individual is encouraged to express himself, and there is no interruption while that person is speaking. The sweat lodge is a very spiritual, moving experience.

THE FIGHT FOR SACRED CEREMONIES

FOSTER: For Native American prisoners, the pipe ceremony is also very important. The tobacco and the pipe and what they represent help take our prayers to the Creator. Of course, we have to teach and encourage the brothers and sisters to relearn the prayers and the songs. It is a real effort. It has to be consistent for those ceremonies to be complete and also to benefit the individuals participating. It is very successful, but it

---

PRAYING WITH THE SACRED PIPE

With this pipe you will walk upon the Earth: for the Earth is your Grandmother and Mother, and She is sacred. Every step that is taken upon Her should be as a prayer. The bowl of this pipe is of red stone; it is the Earth. Carved in the stone and facing the center of this buffalo calf who represents all the four-leggeds who live upon your Mother. The stem of the pipe is of wood, and this represents all that grows upon the Earth. And these twelve feathers which hang here where the stem fits into the bowl are from *Wanbli Galeshka*, the Spotted Eagle, and they represent the eagle and all the wingeds of the air. All these peoples, and all the things of the universe, are joined to you who smoke the pipe—all send their voices to *Wakan-Tanka*, the Great Spirit. When you pray with this pipe, you pray for and with everything.

NICHOLAS BLACK ELK TO JOSEPH EPES BROWN, 1931

---

has to be done consistently. This is what we are advocating, the right of every Native American who is incarcerated to request these traditional spiritual ceremonies and to have them approved. This is what the whole struggle is about—our *complete* religious freedom.

SMITH: How about eagle feathers—do they enter into this question of the right to express one's religious beliefs behind prison bars?

FOSTER: Yes, eagle feathers, sage, cedar, tobacco, and quartz are all sacred items that are used in our holy ceremonies. But they are also protected by federal law, and we advocate having these sacred items available so that the ceremonies can be complete. But again, there is a lot of misunderstanding on the part of the government and prison officials. We have had some of our eagle feathers confiscated, and sometimes destroyed. Some of the sacred pipes have been confiscated, broken, and taken from us. Our sweat lodges have been bulldozed. There are documented cases on that. It hurts when our sacred items—which we believe have a living spirit—are treated disrespectfully. It hurts. We ask that they be treated with the utmost respect. This is one of the most pressing issues in our struggle for religious freedom for prisoners.

SMITH: My impression is that you are making your legal and moral points, finally and after long effort, and that there are fewer objections to taking these sacred items into prison. Is there any more improvement?

FOSTER: Right now prison officials have visitors (even spiritual counselors) put your hand in a detection machine to see if you have been touching any chemicals. Based on that, they can deny you entrance into the facility. The situation now is that when we bring in any sacred items such as the pipe or a medicine bundle, they require us to open them and do a visual inspection. We fought their right to touch our sacred items, but accepted the compromise that they would do a visual inspection but not touch the bundles.

We would like to pursue new avenues of review on each of these cases. But recently the courts have not been open to our issues. The courts are not friendly to our religious freedom.

SMITH: It sounds like you still face considerable obstacles in your pursuit of, as you say, *complete* religious freedom.

FOSTER: We refrain from taking any cases into the courts now, because it established bad case law. We have also pursued introducing legislation at the state and federal levels. That has been very difficult.

We have to lobby and get witnesses together and impress upon the legislators, the Congress, and the Senate that this piece of legislation is very important for our people's cultural integrity and the ability to protect our religious practices.

More recently we have engaged in intertribal and interfaith dialogue, and we formed a coalition called the National Native American Rights Advocacy Coalition. It consists of various groups, national organizations, such as tribal groups, the National Congress of American Indians, Native American Rights Funds, different activists. We formed a coalition to address this at both the state and federal level and requested a meeting and engaged in a dialogue with state administrators. These are individuals who represent the state department of corrections throughout the United States, and there are fifty of them, and we have met with them on one occasion to explore the possibility of creating a uniform standard of Native American religious practices in their respective state prison systems.

SMITH: You have been working at this a long time; you've dedicated your life to this fight for prisoners' rights. What I'm reaching for is whether you are experiencing any *softening* of the resistance to your life's work. When you go to a prison to minister to an inmate, are you more welcome, or at least more understood regarding what you are there for than you were when you began this work?

FOSTER: I would say that after doing this for the past nineteen years, some of the wardens and some of the chaplains have come to know who we are and what we do. They approve our requests to visit these facilities and perform these ceremonies. We also encourage the chaplains once a year, at their annual convention, to participate in the sweat lodge ceremony so that they themselves will appreciate it and have some aware-

---

THE HEALING TRADITION

The traditions of our people are handed down from father to son. The chief is considered to be the most learned, and the leader of the tribe. The doctor, however, is thought to have more inspiration. He is supposed to be in communion with spirits. . . . He cures the sick by laying on of hands, and prayers and incantations and heavenly songs. He infuses new life into the patient, and performs most wonderful feats of skill in his practice.

SARAH WINNEMUCCA (PAIUTE), 1844–1891

---

ness of what it is all about. It seems to have lessened the resistance from them, and they have a better appreciation of and sensitivity toward our beautiful ceremony.

SMITH: I'm sure there is still a long way to go, but what I'm hearing now is that your nineteen years of spiritual counseling are bearing some fruit and that there is less resistance now than before.

FOSTER: We still feel that a very intense human rights crisis exists in this area of religious freedom in prisons. Our work is not done by a long shot, and it has to be done on a consistent basis, and we encourage Indian people to become involved by visiting the prisons. We feel that equal access to the sweat lodges and the pipes and the sacred items and equal access to spiritual leaders coming into the prisons is necessary to teach and to lead. There is also a ban on the cutting of long hair, which is another issue that seems to be causing problems. In California, for example, they placed a hair-cutting policy in effect for Native Americans who follow the traditional beliefs. Native prisoners who have long hair are being forced to cut it, which can result in a very severe and deep depression. It's a form of spiritual castration when they make our people do that.

THE CRY FOR DIGNITY

SMITH: I have heard a very moving story about your ministration to one of your people on death row. Could you tell us that story?

FOSTER: Yes. There are a number of American Indians on death row in the United States. One of the people on death row was served a warrant of execution, and afterward he contacted me. His name was Derrick Gerlaugh. He was a member of the Pima Indian Nation, and he was incarcerated in the Arizona state prison in Florence. I started visiting him and taking the sacred pipe into the prison. I requested through the chaplain and the warden at that facility, and they approved my visits. We prayed with the pipe and sang songs. It made him feel at peace, because he wanted to get ready for his execution on Wednesday, February 5, 1999.

I visited him for two and a half months, and finally it came close to the date of execution. Late in January of that year, I made a request to the chaplain to take my brother to a sweat lodge ceremony as part of Derrick's last rites. He didn't see any problem with that. But when I went to the warden, he said no because of security risks. He claimed that the prisoner was going to be moving out of his chains and out of his cell, and that we were going to be using a fire in our ceremony, which he couldn't approve of because he thought that the ceremony posed a security risk. I tried to impress on the warden that I had taken this individual to the sweat lodge on several occasions throughout the last fifteen years. But he said Derrick wasn't allowed to leave his cell and was going to be executed.

Eventually, I appealed to the director of the Arizona Department of Corrections. We had a discussion, and the director said he would give the idea of a spiritual ceremony some thought and would get back to me the next day.

Well, eventually the director approved our request. This was the first time in U.S. history that an imprisoned Native American was given approval to participate in a sweat lodge ceremony and allowed to use the sacred pipe as part of his last rites. Finally, when the Department of Corrections approved it, the department stated that I would have to go through a complete strip search and the type of process that a preacher would not submit to. Reluctantly, I went ahead and agreed to the stipulation. Once I did that we were approved for one sweat lodge ceremony and one pipe ceremony a few days before Derrick Gerlaugh's execution.

It was a very beautiful ceremony, despite the fact that there were eleven guards, three chaplains, one German shepherd police dog, and two cameras present. The prison authorities had their reasons for having that many security people around. They wanted to document our ceremony and make sure we didn't do anything like try to escape.

Altogether, we spent five to six hours outdoors. It was just me and my brother. We built a fire, and prayed, and covered up the sweat lodge, and once the rocks were ready we put them into the sweat lodge and we did four rounds. We prayed and we sang, and by the end of the ceremony Derrick was ready to meet his maker. I told him that he had to let go of his pain, his anger, that he might still have in him. I reminded him that to meet the Great Spirit he needed to have some love and some joy and some happiness in himself.

Finally, he was ready. After we smoked the sacred pipe, he made one last request. He wanted to braid his hair before he went to meet the Great Spirit. On Wednesday, February 5, he was allowed to braid his hair. Then he was executed. The lethal injection took two minutes. I was a witness to the execution, per the family's request that I be there for him as his spiritual advisor.

Again, I want to say that this was the first time anywhere in the country that a request to use the sweat lodge and to use the pipe as part of the last rites was approved for an incarcerated Native American. This decision opened the doors to and set a precedent for future requests of that kind, which is important to us because the reality of the situation is that there are Native Americans on death row in California, Arizona, and other places who will at last have the right to use the sweat lodge.

I think that when my friend Derrick took his journey into the spirit world, he went with some dignity and some pride and was able to feel good about himself that he had finally made amends and was repentant of what he did to be in that situation.

The sweat lodge was a beautiful ceremony that prepared him. That is what the whole thing is about, allowing our people to have some dignity and pride in who they are, which is the heart of the recovery movement and the spiritual healing taking place among our Indian people. It's happening right here and now. So we have to continue to advocate and push for that, whether it is through negotiation or legislation.

SMITH: It is an immensely inspiring story, while at the same time just stark in indicating the discrimination, as you say, toward you as a recognized spiritual counselor. In contrast, the notion of a Catholic priest being forced to a strip search as you were would be regarded as a profanation, and yet in the case of your people it is a routine practice with no thought of the tremendous indecency involved.

FOSTER: Yes, we have been subjected to many degradations and been made to feel ashamed of who we are, but we still stand up, and we resort to our spirituality as a foundation, as a base, so we can have some pride and some dignity about who we are. There is a real recovery effort throughout the Indian communities where the sweat lodges and the pipes are used to return to our traditional beliefs. We have endured, and we have prevailed. Through our prayers and through our ceremonies, those blessings will come. That's how we believe in the Creator.

What is occurring with our native brothers and sisters who are incarcerated is a discussion about how one day they will be coming home. We tell them that we want to be able to welcome them home knowing that they have made a change in their attitude, in their behavior, in their lifestyle, in their sobriety, in their sense of responsibility about themselves. We are allowed to go into the prison and teach so they can learn.

SMITH: There is one more formal disparity that I can think of. As I understand it, under U.S. law a Native American officer cannot arrest a white person, even if the white is on a reservation and doing an antisocial thing. Is that true?

FOSTER: The federal and state governments have not recognized our courts, our way of life, as having any validity, even though we are talking about sovereignty. And, of course, sovereignty is given to Indian people from the Creator. It's the natural law and the spiritual law. Then you have the white man's law, which they say supersedes everything, and in that context the tribal courts are not recognized as being on an equal basis with either the state or federal government. It's a real effort to have that recognized, but of course it's an intense struggle whether it is through legislation or through court proceedings. Probably one of the most pressing issues in Indian country today is to have the non-Indians recognize the Native American Indians. We are still here. They couldn't kill us off. We are also here in South Africa being recognized, along with the other sacred colors of the universe. We are being allowed to express ourselves in this arena, and I think that's a blessing that has come through our perseverance.

SMITH: I would like to revert once more to what I understand as being a federal law. Behind that I sense a feeling that it would be undignified for a Native American to place a white person under arrest. But you turn that around, and you see an unleveled playing field.

FOSTER: I think when you have anyone come into a community, they have to abide by and respect the laws of that community. You don't expect to come in and beat someone or rob someone or break into their home. You have to observe the laws of that community and respect their families and their home. That's common sense. Yet it's not so in many places, and so that issue is being tested in the courts. It's a tough situation.

THE RED ROAD TO REHABILITATION

SMITH: As you look ahead, I cannot imagine you *not* continuing your efforts on this matter of justice. I can only think of you looking toward it, struggling toward it, with a focus on the prison situation as the one you have prioritized in your efforts. Is that the way you see it as long as you live out your days? Can you tell us about any efforts on the part of Indian people to try their own traditional form of rehabilitation?

FOSTER: One of the proposals pending in Indian country, by the Dine, or Navajo Nation, is for a two-thousand-bed facility. The contracts were being proposed between the state and the federal prisons to send medium- and minimum-security inmates to this facility, and certain rights would be given to be allowed to practice one's culture and spirituality as part of the rehabilitation.

Right now you don't have any real rehabilitation taking place in the prisons. The current concept is to detain, to isolate, which is just punitive. There is no real official effort to rehabilitate a person. It only happens if people from the outside go into the facility to teach and instruct. But I think we could put an Indian flavor on that type of private-prison concept, where we would work with our own people, teach them a trade, and teach them the language and the culture and have them relearn. On my own visits to these facilities, I see that many native people don't understand their language or their culture. The prison is the one place they are given that opportunity to relearn. When it's offered I think the majority are trying that.

SMITH: Recently, I heard from my friends in Indian law, such as Indian rights lawyer James Botsford, that there are attempts at reviving traditional forms of peacemaking because the current system is just not working for native people.

FOSTER: Yes, there is an initiative by the Dine/Navajo Nation to return to what's called a peacemaking process. There you bring together the two parties in conflict to create some resolution. Let's say you bring two families and their problems together; then we use a prayer, we use the Creation stories to highlight what went wrong. We might try some restitution, some work, some solution that does not involve an adversarial process but where an understanding is created. It works. It has worked for thousands of years, and we are finally using that practice again. Anyone wishing to use that practice today, as opposed to going to court, is able to, and I think that each particular Indian nation in the United States could have some form of a traditional peacemaking process.

This is an idea that needs to be further developed, but I see the trend going that way. Of course, we need to have this movement recognized by the state and federal agencies of the government.

I'm just one of many who are involved in this struggle. I think it's a beautiful cause, it has been a beautiful spiritual journey for me. I'm always learning. I look to the elders, to the medicine people, to their knowledge and their wisdom and knowing that we are trying to make things better for our people. Maybe we will never see it in our lifetime, but the journey that we are undertaking is very fulfilling and satisfying to me. I have an obligation to help those who are less fortunate and are incarcerated. This is my calling and my passion, and I'll continue to fight for their religious rights and their practices and the ceremonies.

SMITH: In summary, can you explain to us what your struggle is *for*? You have mentioned the need to have access to ceremony, but what does that mean to someone who is incarcerated?

FOSTER: I have felt very honored to have been here among my colleagues, my brothers and sisters, to express some of the most profound issues confronting Indian country today. On behalf of our relatives who are incarcerated I would like to say that the most profound issue affecting the families, the loved ones, of those who are incarcerated for long periods of time, is the request for a *spiritual healing* to take place through our ancient ceremonial practices. This is a request for the cleansing and the purification of the mind, the body, and the spirit, and through it a healing of our nation is taking place. However, there has been an intense struggle to prevent and to suppress this healing, and it has been mounted by the forces of the U.S. government. Those are strong words, but that is the reality of the situation for the original people of Turtle Island.

I have been involved in this struggle for thirty years. It is a very intense struggle for the liberation of the mind, the body, and the spirit and can only happen if our incarcerated relatives are allowed to participate in these ceremonies and to ask blessings from the Creator. We feel that the cleansing and the purification will allow this healing of the prisoners to take place so he or she can go on to be a productive person once again and to assume responsibilities and to have respect and to be sober. These teachings come about only through the visits made by our spiritual leaders.

A spiritual healing is taking place in a movement throughout the country, but the authorities continue to suppress the practices, the beliefs, and the ceremonies, which is tantamount to cultural genocide. Again, those are very strong words, but one must look at the evidence. So we continue to seek the support, the prayers, the sympathy, the solidarity of concerned people around the world.

If the United States truly wants to reconcile with its original people, then they could do some good by releasing our brother Leonard Peltier. They could also allow our Indian people in prisons consistent ceremonies once a week so they can have that healing of the mind, the body, and the spirit.

I feel very honored and humbled to have been part of the Parliament.

SMITH: Well, blessings on you as you continue this noble work.

STEALING OUR SPIRIT

THE THREAT OF THE HUMAN
GENOME DIVERSITY PROJECT

Tonya Gonnella Frichner at the Parliament of World Religions,
Cape Town, South Africa, 1999. Photograph by Phil Cousineau.
Used by permission of Phil Cousineau.

Tonya Gonnella Frichner, Onondaga, is a lawyer and adjunct professor of Native American law, an activist devoted to the pursuit of human rights for indigenous peoples, and president and founder of the American Indian Law Alliance. In 1987 she served as legal counsel to the Haudenosaunee tribe at the United Nations Sub-Commission on Human Rights/Working Group on Indigenous Populations, in Geneva, Switzerland. She has been an active participant in international forums affecting indigenous peoples, including the establishment of the Permanent Forum on Indigenous Issues, the negotiation processes concerning the draft U.N. Declaration on the Rights of Indigenous Peoples, and the proposed Organization of American States Declaration on the Rights of Indigenous Peoples. She was awarded the Harriet Tubman Humanitarian Achievement Award and was named the American Indian of the Year by the American Indian Thunderbird Dancers in New York City.

This dialogue between Ms. Frichner and Professor Smith centers on a subset of the publicly financed Human Genome Project, which has been heralded for its decoding of the human genome. Alternately deemed the "life script," the "stuff of life," the "secret of life," even the "genius within," the human genome represents the entire amount of DNA present in the cells of a species. The medical significance of the decoding can scarcely be overestimated; some scientists are speculating that within the next half-century gene-based therapy for many diseases will be commonplace.

"Genomics is now providing biology's periodic table," says Eric Lander of MIT's Whitehead Institute. "The new study of genomics promises novel ways of ending disease. A gene, then, is an instruction, like the directions in a bead-making kit but written in molecule-ese. Humans have perhaps [35,000] genes, and we are 99.99 percent identical. . . . We are learning that each letter in the text can spell the difference. . . . That one-tenth of one percent is what makes us unique and different."[1]

But it is the investigations into that one-tenth of 1 percent that has the indigenous peoples of the world worried, especially the specter of patents on genes and the ethical implications of genetic profiling. The decoding of the so-called book of life poses daunting moral dilemmas and profound ethical issues, which have arisen with the controversial methods of an offshoot of the HGP called the Human Genome Diversity Project. Their methodology has galvanized widespread condemnation among indigenous leaders around the world, who are concerned about the spiritual and moral implications of collecting hair, skin, and blood samples from indigenous peoples throughout the world without their knowledge or consent. The project's recent change of methodology has not diminished the concerns of those people whose genetic samples or those of their relatives were taken without informed consent and are still under the control of the project.

For these reasons, there is a dire need, in Tonya Frichner's view, to closely guard the very essence of native spirituality—biology and dignity. To her, allowing unfettered science runs the risk of viewing indigenous people as the next resource to be exploited, the next grand experiment, rather than attempting to help the indigenous tribes they believe are in danger of becoming extinct. In turn, for Smith, the issue is how the Human Genome Diversity Project reveals the modern struggle over the very image of God and is a test case for how sacred we regard our deepest essence. To this effect, he has said recently, "We're saying we're gods, but deep down we know we are not. This project *shows* we're not even close." To Smith, the scientific quest for the genetic causes of diversity is another example of *scientism* or an illustration of what Gregory Bateson described as "mistaking the menu for the meal."

In the fall of 2004, a similar experiment was revealed at Arizona State University, where researchers persuaded members of the Havasupai Nation to give blood under the pretext that their sole concern was the tribe's diabetes epidemic. Instead, researchers used the blood samples, and sold samples to other nonassociated researchers, to study tribal schizophrenia, inbreeding, and migration patterns, without getting the proper permission to do so.

In 2000 *El Pais* of Madrid published an editorial saying that "the new possibilities are of such importance that their deployment will require great prudence while at the same time inspiring curiosity, which is probably one of the definitive traits of the human genetic sequence. . . . Penetrating the code of life of humankind is a thrilling adventure."[2]

For Frichner and Smith, that adventure is as spiritual as it is scientific, and it must be conducted with honor and humility.

The struggle of being Indian. I think a lot of stories turn on that. The struggle of how and why it is important to be Indian in order to retain one's heritage and identity. . . . This process of colonization, that is, usurping the indigenous power of the people, taking their land and resources and language and heritage away—that has to be struggled against. We cannot ignore that.

SIMON ORTIZ, QUOTED IN *WINGED WORDS*, 1990

HUSTON SMITH: Tonya, I believe that the Human Genome Diversity Project has given rise to one of the most hateful issues of our time. For over four hundred years, through the methods of science, we have been probing the depths of the universe, discovering that it is some 15 billion light years old. Now we are scientifically probing ourselves, but on a relatively superficial level. But we are entering the foundational area of chromosomes and genes, the most fundamental building blocks of human life, the human genome. I think we should recognize that it looks like the scientific and cultural mood seems to signal that it's full speed ahead—with the one exception of cloning, where the outrage was so great that the research was prohibited. With that in mind, we should realize that there are many, many people other than Native Americans who are concerned about this old conflict between science and religion.

The biologist Lewis Thomas was one of the most beloved popularizers of science and a major thinker. He saw a great danger in technology that allows us to get our fingers in and monkey around with the chain of genes that makes up our being. He gave a warning about tampering with genes in his classic, *Lives of a Cell.* Thomas wrote that he'd rather enter the cockpit of a Boeing 707 with no knowledge of flying, turn off the automatic pilot, and presume that he could bring the plane down safely than experiment with human genes.

So we are aware of the problem with genetic research in a general way, but your focus as a Native American is on the biodiversity subset of the well-known Human Genome Project, namely, the Human Genome *Diversity* Project. So please tell us of your concerns, and how they relate to the overall issue of the struggle for Native American religious freedom.

TONYA FRICHNER: I'm very glad to address your opening remarks, Huston. You mention cloning, and I think people's reaction to it has been basically one of repulsion. We think that it has been stopped, but it has not. Cloning is only illegal in three states in the United States. There has been a ban on it, but only at facilities that are publicly funded. So people need to have more information about this project. My duty here today is to further and deepen the talk about the struggle for Native American religious freedom. In this case it's the Human Genome Diversity Project. What it amounts to is the *secret* gathering of the blood, hair, and tissue samples of indigenous people worldwide. Basically, this is the gathering of their genetic material without their consent; this is scientific studies being done without their permission.

This highly secretive project began in 1991, but we only heard about it in 1993. What is this all about? Well, I believe it is based on scientific interest in human diversity. The human population has about five thousand communities of peoples throughout the world identified as distinct. Within those five thousand groups there are 720 groups that are distinct, but also indigenous peoples and nations. That is where our concern comes in, not only as individuals, but as citizens of a nation.

Let me just share this reality with you in black and white. In 1993 I was at a conference in Geneva, Switzerland, being briefed by the Maori people of New Zealand. While there I had the chance to look at a document that they were presenting to all the indigenous delegates. When I thumbed through it, I found listed—to my absolute amazement—the name of my own tribe, the Onondaga. I also found the Cayaga, another people who are part of the Confederacy of the Six Nations. It's a pretty comprehensive list.

SMITH: Now, why do the project scientists want to take this route? Why do they want to seek out these people and get the genetic information on them?

FRICHNER: That's the big question that we have not been able to get answered. What is clear to us is that for a long time many groups of indigenous people, in many regions of the world, have been so isolated that there hasn't been much intermarriage. By reading the Human Genome Diversity Project documents we found that our genes and our bloodlines may have something unique in them. In other words, indigenous people may be more "pure" than other communities or other peoples.

SMITH: You said you didn't know the rationale that would lead them to secretly gather this genetic information, but it seems to me that your hypothesis hits the nail on the head. I assume that the project wants to know what is in the chain of genes, which is very long and complicated, that is identical for all human beings. But they also want to know what segments, what genetic sequences, are negotiable, in the sense that you can still have human beings, but with variations. To find that answer, I need to reach for my pocketbook when I realize how much public money is going to go into determining this factor. The way they are targeting communities that have been isolated is reminiscent of those birds, the finches, on the Galapagos Island whose beaks differ from those of the others because they'd been isolated. So, Tonya, I think you said it. The reason the researchers are performing these studies is because they *can*.

FRICHNER: With the Human Genome Project, the idea has been to map the entire genetic code of human beings. It is so complicated and so lengthy that it is going to take quite a few more years to get to the point where the human genome will be completely mapped and available and on paper for scientists to use. The research hasn't been completed, but scientists are already jumping to the next step, which is the diversity involved within the human genome. The problem is that they are missing the beginning, or the first building block. It doesn't quite make sense that they would jump to the next piece of research when they don't have foundational information to begin with.

THE VAMPIRE PROJECT

SMITH: I am completely with you on this but need to hear from you what the *spiritual* concern is here, what the implications for the primal religions of the world might be. I have my own suspicions but would like to hear it in your words.

FRICHNER: The Maori people have a name for the gene, and it's called *Iratangara,* which means "the life spirit of mortals." The Maori say that the life spirit connects you to all the people around you and to your ancestors, that it is handed down to you, that you inherit it. They say that when you receive the life spirit it is enriched; therefore your spirit belongs to the nation, the people, and to the community. They say it does not belong to you alone.

The Human Genome Diversity Project, or what indigenous people refer to as "the Vampire Project," has been gathering the blood, the hair, and the tissue samples of over seven hundred indigenous peoples. All this genetic material has been earmarked for this project. The project has identified many of us as "isolates of historic interest," or "endangered." Essentially, this means that these scientists think we are on the way to extinction. Four speakers in our delegation here in Cape Town are defined this way, as "isolates of historic interest." This includes me, Frank Dayish, Walter Echo-Hawk, and Lenny Foster. Also, the Onondaga Nation,

the Navajo Nation, and the Pawnee Nation have all been identified by
the project as endangered or going extinct, which I find deeply offensive.

SMITH: I have a hypothesis. It's uninformed, but it just jumped to mind.
These isolated peoples may disappear before we get the "big picture."

FRICHNER: Yes—that's the language the project uses. They say that
these peoples are in danger of becoming "extinct," which is language that
I find rather pejorative. That is the basis and the foundation of the project.
The project couldn't go forward unless they were using peoples who were
identified as being in danger of becoming extinct. That is another nega-
tive piece of the project. But if you go one step further, why not go to
the communities and offer something that would help that community
not become extinct? To help it survive? That is how I see it.

When you talk about probing, it isn't superficial probing. It's a dig-
ging into the essence of our very being. I don't use the phrase lightly, but
I would say it's a raping of our spirituality. That is why we find this project
so terribly offensive.

SMITH: This is the heart of the matter. With regards to this dream of
mapping the human gene, and again I speak as a layman, there are major microbiologists who think that it is something of a pipe dream because it assumes the specificity of genes as though they were sort of like
"pellets, like marbles." I'm quoting from memory from an article that
appeared in the *New York Review of Books* by R. C. Lewonton, a respected microbiologist, who is critical, or at least was then, of the whole
genome project. He says the belief that there is a one-to-one relation between a gene and what happens is simply an unproven assumption, in
his words, a pipe dream. Innumerable other factors enter the picture to
determine what happens.

FRICHNER: A pipe dream. Exactly.

THE GREAT WEB

SMITH: Now, let's come to an area that is different from science—the
fullness of the human being. Your people have held on to the conviction
that people are sacred because they have been created by the Great Spirit.
So when science goes in, as you say, "probing," it's not just probing into
pellets of matter. It's probing into the human spirit, into what we are as
human beings. I have a feeling that because your people have retained

the sense of the sacred and the divinity of the human being by virtue of having been created by a divine power, you are more sensitive to that sacred aspect of existence. I know that you have remained very sensitive to the reality of the mutual relatedness in all Creation.

FRICHNER: I think what you are referring to is our perspective of the natural world. The thread that runs through all our discussions about indigenous peoples is that we are part of the natural world. We believe that the natural world is not a resource; the natural world is our relative. We believe we are a part of all those relationships, and the world's sacredness is something we hold very dear. So when you go in and probe on this very deep level into our genetic material, you violate the very tenets of what we believe and hold sacred as far as the natural law is concerned. That is how we see this secret project.

Native American religiousness comes from a profound and astute understanding of the relatedness of all things. The Navajo concept of *hoz'ho*, for example, balances thought and speech, understanding and responsible action.

DUANE CHAMPAGNE, *NATIVE AMERICA: PORTRAIT OF THE PEOPLES*, 1994

SMITH: What comes to my mind is the old belief that God, or the Great Spirit, didn't do it quite right "in the beginning," and now it's up to us to get in there and improve on God's handiwork.

FRICHNER: What I would say, Huston, is that there is a lot of discussion about genetic engineering being able to correct things like diseases (which is why we need to look to science), but we are leaving out the effect of a polluted environment on us as human beings. We are forgetting the effect of poverty on the whole human family. We are not against science. We just believe we cannot be looking at correcting things *only* at a genetic level. Instead, we should be looking at correcting things that are affecting our health every day. These things, we believe, are the result of serious violations of natural law.

For us, it's just common sense. When you violate the natural world, you will pay for it in proportion to your violation. The more you pollute, the harder you will suffer. When you can't drink your water anymore, your people will die. They will succumb because the natural world is very balanced. But we seem to be losing our common sense as people as we go along in looking to science for all the answers.

Now, I'm not a scientist. But I've tried to learn as much as I can about what a human genome is, what a chromosome is, what a gene is. I've asked what it all means in the great scheme of things. It's been a wonderful learning experience for me. But the larger issue has always been to take the information about our genetic makeup into the indigenous communities and explain to them what is going on.

SMITH: The basis for this fundamental disrespect runs very deep. But it seems to me to also reflect a certain obsession with control and a fantasy of ownership that runs amok in some aspects of science.

FRICHNER: Yes, this obsession with control certainly represents disrespect of our peoples. It began in 1492 when the Europeans arrived on this great Turtle Island that the rest of the world calls North and South America. A tradition followed the Europeans to our shores based on fifteenth-century Catholicism. Coming out of that tradition were edicts and papal rules that gave permission to Portugal, in 1455, and Spain in 1493, to conquer—which meant to take away property, and to convert the pagans, the infidels—all those of us who happened to be the indigenous peoples of the Western world.

Catholicism still needs to look at that issue, it needs to look at those edicts, and it needs to reverse them because they represent, for our people, a huge amount of disrespect. This is not impossible. Not too long ago, the pope said the church was sorry for excommunicating Galileo because his scientific findings were against the teaching of the church. His excommunication happened quite a long time ago, but its repercussions have been felt for centuries. That is why we still need to think about the effect of those papal rulings. They were religious doctrines that were adopted by the United States, particularly in Supreme Court decisions, that took this religious language and turned it into a secular language. The courts made it the answer to the Doctrine of Discovery that says indigenous peoples have the right to occupancy but not to title.[3] That right belongs to the U.S. Congress. The foundation of that disrespect came to our shores under the guise of Christianity, and we need to deal with those issues.

At conferences like this Parliament of World Religions, we indigenous peoples can say these things, which is absolutely amazing to me. I am so grateful to the Parliament for inviting us and giving us this platform so we can share with you these thoughts and ideas. It's a great gift.

SMITH: What was the response of your community when you informed them that your tribe was on this kind of "endangered species list"?

FRICHNER: As soon as I heard about the Human Genome Diversity Project, I brought the news back to our Onondaga community and shared the information with our leaders. With that information in hand, the Grand Council of Chiefs sent the chairman of the project a letter very clearly stating why they saw this project as a violation of our human rights. The council also asked me if I would share with the community the information I learned about this project. We chose the annual music and cultural festival on the Onondaga Reservation, where hundreds of people come to have a great time. Non-Indians also come from all over the country to hear people like the singer Joanne Shenandoah, and other members of my community, sing and dance. I was sort of the commercial in between the musicians, but I did my best to inform the audience about the project and what I thought it meant to our people. What I saw was a sea of faces that were suddenly stunned. Their expressions seemed to say, "What is she talking about? Is this true?"

After I finished I was besieged by members of our community and, interestingly enough, by non-Indians as well. Everyone wanted information about this whole business. More than that, they wanted the truth. I was deeply moved by their reaction.

THE DANGER OF PLAYING GOD

SMITH: Still, it seems like your material wishes should not be overlooked. I have another theory about the far-reaching implications of science that I would like to share with you. One of the things that has become apparent in our century is that when there is a major technological breakthrough, it takes on average about thirty-two years before the full consequences of the breakthrough come to life. I'm old enough to remember when DDT came on. You got rid of the pests, and our crops would bloom. Thirty-two years later we have "silent spring."

Here is another example. I happened to be at the University of Chicago as a student, in the 1930s, but we didn't know (because it was hush-hush), that under Stag Stadium scientists were splitting the atom. The consequences of all that released atomic energy was the dropping of the atom bomb on Hiroshima, which I believe was a travesty. At the time the hope was that we wouldn't do that again, and that we had solved our energy problem. Thirty-two years later we have acid rain and all this toxic waste that we don't know what to do with.

So there are different conceptions of the human self and how we should go about living our lives, fitting in, or assuming that we have the wisdom in order to direct history according to our particular ends.

May I go on?

FRICHNER: Well, since you are an elder, I promise I won't interrupt you.

SMITH: Something else has just come over the line and this, of all things, from cognitive scientists. A new theory has appeared from the cognitive science program at MIT. The theory has a strange name for a scientific hypothesis. I don't know whether to call it barbaric or poetic. It goes by the name "mysterianism."

The point of this is that we have known for four hundred years, since the day Vincent Clark drew the map of the brain, that we have brains and we have consciousness. It's impossible to reduce either to the other. We have neuron firings, and we have our subjective experiences. But the thing about this mysterianism hypothesis is that we haven't made an inch of progress—zero progress—in understanding the relationship between these two things, neuron firings and subjective experience. And that may be exactly where it remains, because I never expect to hear scientists say, "What do we think we are? Omniscient?"

We are learning more and more every decade, every year, about how complex, how interrelated, how mysterious, this universe is. Our minds are finite, and we may have bumped up against something, namely, the relation between mind and brain, that is just too big for us.

Now, I think of these recent debates and findings because in probing into the human genome to get our hands on the material things here, we don't understand even the relation between neurons and consciousness.

THE CANARY IN THE MINE

The Indian plays much the same role in our American society that the Jews played in Germany. Like the miner's canary, the Indian marks the shift from fresh air to poison gas in our political atmosphere; and our treatment of Indians, even more than our treatment of other minorities, marks the rise and fall of our democratic faith.

FELIX S. COHEN, INDIAN LAW SCHOLAR AND FATHER OF FEDERAL INDIAN LAW, 1941

Beyond that point lies the sacred and the ultimate. We don't know whether we are closing the shades of the window onto our sense of the sacred, because the relationship between spirit and consciousness and neuron firing is unknown. I bring that in just to underscore your point. I believe this is still a domain of mystery, and really of holiness, because not only does it affect our concept of who we are as human beings, but it also may denature us as fully human beings by virtue of tinkering with the genome.

FRICHNER: Tinkering around with the genome! Yes, into the very essence of our being, the very essence of *who we are*. What will that mean? We don't have any of the answers to that. This is what we keep hearing over and over again: "We will look at this, these are new frontiers."

What I think concerns me the most is that industry and development need to go out and get more resources. You cannot have development without resources, you just cannot do that. But we are depleting the world's resources.

My question is whether industry is moving to the next resource, to the next frontier, to the next Gold Rush, which may be the human genome? But is the gene we carry *who we are,* specifically with regards to indigenous peoples, who may or may not have something unique? The primatologist Jane Goodall says that human beings share 99 percent of their genetic code with chimpanzees. So how much are we really going to be learning as we push the envelope forward?[4]

SMITH: You said that industry is always looking for resources; we haven't even mentioned the patents. At the close of our last session, someone mentioned the issue of property. It raises the Orwellian question of who owns our DNA. Do we own it, or does the government, or does any industry who can buy it or steal it from us?

FRICHNER: That is what patents are. They are property. They are ideas of ownership. What the United States did in the 1980s was to wipe the slate clean by making it possible for patents concerning microorganisms and plant life to be filed. It did say that peoples cannot be patented, but *pieces* of people can be. So tell me what the difference is.

According to the U.S. Supreme Court, the difference is when something is removed from your body it is altered and therefore does not represent you, and you have no ownership of it anymore.[5] If these projects, such as the HGDP, go into our communities asking for blood, hair, and tissue samples, so many things need to be discussed, such as fifty years of the medical profession's appreciation of and respect for "informed consent." Will informed consent exist on every level in a language that indigenous peoples will understand? When our genetic material is taken from us and stored in a storage facility in Maryland, our people think of it as, "Now you have immortalized something."

But we native people believe that when you immortalize something, that immortal human life cannot go back to where it belongs, which is the spiritual home, the spirit world. That sacred circle of life is forever broken, because now you have something outside the sacred circle, which we believe is immortal. And we are not in this particular world to be immortal. So we have all these things to consider and all these things that upset us.

SMITH: This new "Gold Rush," as you deem it, seems to be the latest indignity perpetrated on your people. What can be done to protect your DNA, your "spiritual property," if I may call it that? And is there anything others can do to help your cause?

FRICHNER: I know that UNESCO has been looking at this particular project for indigenous peoples, and indigenous peoples are on every continent. There are millions of us, and we all have different-colored skins. Yesterday, here in South Africa, the indigenous delegation visiting this beautiful country had the privilege of meeting with traditional indigenous elders. The commonality that we shared of our ways of speaking, of our cultures and traditions, has been just incredible and a wonderful experience.

The point of this is that within the United Nations is a forum called the Working Group on Indigenous Populations. It's a little over twenty years old. It's very low on the totem pole within the U.N. structure, but it is the only forum that we have where we can voice our needs and concerns. Out of those twenty years of struggle has come a document called the "Draft Declaration on the Rights of the World's Indigenous Peoples." Indigenous peoples drafted that document themselves. Under article 29 we talk about the protection of our intellectual property and our cultural patrimony, which would keep something like the HGDP out of our communities.

What I would ask the people to do is to go to their governments and ask them to adopt that declaration. Most countries are members of the U.N. Ask your secretaries of state to adopt that declaration as is, without change. It reflects our worldview and our vision, and it is an important way for indigenous peoples to have our rights recognized, for once, in the new millennium. As it stands right now, indigenous peoples do not have human rights. This would move us into the place that we need to be.

I would also like to reiterate what Douglas George said by stating that change begins with obeying your own law. On a domestic level that would certainly improve things for our people. But on an international level you could support the "Draft Declaration on the Rights of the World's Indigenous Peoples." Everything is in there. It talks about protecting our resources, the rights to our land, our intellectual property. It is very thorough. Those of you representing other nation-states should also find out where to make that contact. If you could begin that work for us, that would be wonderful. Let us know that you made contact. That allows us to follow up. It is very important to have that information, because we can use it in a good way.

SMITH: We are coming to the close of our time, and I want to say one more thing about this notion of the very essence of our being. Then I'm going to insist that you have the last word.

In the Abrahamic tradition of Judaism and Christianity, the words for expressing this deep concern are "we were created in the image of God." When I contrast that holy image with that of people just going in to tinker with the foundation of our being, what is that going to do to the image of God, if they change the basic nature of who we are?

Today, here at the Parliament, one of our guests asked about science identifying "junk DNA," which is DNA that they can't identify, and so they declare that it's not useful for anything. I think her question is really, "Can something that comes from the Creator become 'junk DNA'?" But there is no junk. I realize that is simplistic, because that would mean that there is nothing we should do but stay back and fit in, and we know that that's not right. What I'm thinking of is the appendix. It used to be thought of as a junk organ. My understanding is that though it has to be removed if it hurts, it is not a junk organ—it does have its purposes. My impulse is to scrutinize this notion of junk DNA. Well, some people disdain the idea of historical influence on contemporary events, but you believe that the debate has not ended and that we cannot afford to practice anything less than eternal vigilance, do you not?

FRICHNER: Huston, it seems to me that the debate that went on in 1550 has not ended. That debate was about whether indigenous peoples were human beings or not. Whether we had souls. The good news was that Spain supported what Bartolomé de las Casas said: "Yes, indigenous peoples are human beings."[6] That helped defeated his counterpart, the Spanish inquisitor Juan Gines de Sepulveda, who basically said the conquistadors had a right to treat indigenous peoples as beasts of burden and as less than others. The bad news is that once we were identified as human beings we were then capable of being converted to Christianity and made to look like Spaniards so that we would become legitimate and leave behind us all that is Indian.

And this insulting discussion about the humanity, the soul or spirit of indigenous people, is still going on. In particular, this project called the HGDP is looking at us once again as "other," as less than human.

I'm wondering when that debate will stop.

Do we really have to go our Catholic friends and say, "We need you to go the pope to rescind things like papal bulls that in effect said that we were pagans, infidels, Saracens"? Do we have to keep asking the pope and various religious and political authorities to stop treating us like we are people who are less than others?

The tragedy is that when you are considered less than others, the first thing that happens is you lose everything you have. Your property is taken away, your land is taken away, and everything is expropriated in the name of God. That fundamental basis of treatment still seems to be going on today. It has infiltrated court cases, it has infiltrated law, and it has actually become law in North America. When my colleagues talk about the theft of our land as something that we care about and will not stop fighting for, they are not kidding. It's true that we will do that.

We Native Americans have a collective memory. Maybe 1550 sounds like a long time ago, but for us, it's less than thirty grandfathers ago. What's ancient are the rocks we walk on. That mountain overlooking Cape Town with that smooth top, Tabletop Mountain, now, that's ancient. So our collective memory says that 1550 is recent, as is the discussion that began then about whether we were human beings or not.

I would suggest that you people in this room, here at the Parliament, are people of good conscience. You wouldn't be here if you weren't able to take that information with you and think about it. Maybe you and your friends can act as advocates for us and can join us and challenge this old and outdated discussion about whether or not we are human beings. We are taking the debate back to the scientific community and challenging them.

For many reasons, it is still not acceptable for indigenous people to say no to science. Well, now we are saying no. If these things continue to happen, we will prosecute. We are very serious about that. As far as I'm concerned, scientists are not going to take on the responsibility of determining who is an Onondaga, who is a Navajo, and who is Pawnee.

I say that indigenous peoples have the *right* to say no. When that right is not respected, then we also have the right to prosecute, and I think we should do that.

SMITH: I hope you will.

9

THE FIGHT FOR MOUNT GRAHAM

LOOKING FOR THE FINGERPRINTS OF GOD

Anthony Guy Lopez, 2004. Photograph by Yusuf Khan.
Used by permission of Anthony Guy Lopez.

Anthony Guy Lopez, Lakota Sioux, is program director of the American Indian Endangered Species Program, a Thomas J. Watson Fellow, and a specialist on federal Indian law and policy. He is a sacred lands specialist for the Association on American Indian Affairs and coordinator of the Sacred Lands Protection Program for the association. Mr. Lopez also serves as a national coordinator of the Sacred Places Protection Coalition.

In this dialogue at the Parliament of World Religions, Mr. Lopez and Professor Smith explored one of the most hotly disputed sacred land issues in the United States. On the peak of *Dzil Nchaa Sian,* Mount Graham, in southeastern Arizona, where Apaches have gone in search of their visions for countless generations, a consortium of astronomy organizations, including the University of Arizona and the Vatican, has claimed the mountaintop for the construction of a $200 million telescope complex. The representatives of the project believe "everyone is very proud of our achievement," meaning the power of the "Columbus Project," the Large Binocular Telescope, which is ten times greater than the power of the Hubble Space Telescope. But there has been impassioned resistance from the Apache people, the original inhabitants of the area. They believe the worst possible spot was selected for the telescopes, and that scant regard was paid to their belief that the summit of the mountain is a holy place.

As portrayed at the Parliament by Lopez, the Apache struggle has included protests, legal action, and the revival of sacred runs, all in an effort to restore legal access to their ancestral sacred ground. According to Lopez, what also concerns members of the San Carlos Apaches is that their religious vision has been demeaned, and worse, that the Vatican has publicly declared that the Apache religion should be "suppressed." To the dismay of the Apaches, the church dismissed the tribe's claims that the 10,700-foot mountain peak has any religious significance by saying that it could not find any physical evidence, such as a church. This cultural collision suggests two competing forms of vision quests, one using one of the most ancient techniques of the sacred, the eye of the soul, and the other using the lenses of the most advanced telescope technology in history.

The impasse is reminiscent of the prophetic words of Nez Perce Chief

Joseph to missionaries over a century ago: "We don't want churches because they will teach us to quarrel about God." The result is that Apaches now need to obtain a U.S. Forest Service "prayer permit" to visit the summit of their own sacred mountain, resulting in many Apaches being cited for trespassing on their ancestral lands if they don't carry the permit.

For Guy Lopez and the Apache Survival Coalition, the request for a seat at the table means equal representation and respect in the discussion about the future of their ancestral mountain. Despite years of legal and spiritual struggle, the fight for Mount Graham goes on. While granting the church's astronomers respect for their updated theory of "speculative theology," which allows the church huge flexibility in the way it responds to new discoveries, Lopez represents the Indians' desire to be granted the same respect for their beliefs.

In a similar spirit, San Carlos Apache elder Ola Cassadore Davis said at a protest at the University of Arizona, in February 1997, "This Christopher Columbus telescope rider is a double whammy. It reminds us of Christopher Columbus's followers telling Indians their religions and beliefs were wrong and then bringing Indians a plague of European diseases. . . . It's time . . . to restore equality for all American people and to respect our Apache citizens."[1]

For Huston Smith, the dispute is "an exquisite test case" in the centuries-long battle between science and religion, a kind of territorial dispute over the sacred itself. He describes the treatment of the Apache claims as a double standard with its roots in centuries of intolerance toward the indigenous peoples of the world.

This section concludes with Mr. Lopez's poetic reflections on how the remarkable spiritual strength that enabled Nelson Mandela to survive his incarceration can serve as an inspiration for the strength and spirit that Native Americans need to endure and triumph in their own struggles.

There is one God looking down on us all. We are all children
of one God. God is listening to me. The sun, the darkness, the
winds, are all listening to what we now say.

GOYATHLAY, OR GERONIMO (APACHE), 1829–1909

HUSTON SMITH: Let me begin by saying that I see this issue about Mount Graham as an exquisite test case for the most fundamental issue facing the modern world. Alfred North Whitehead, one of the great philosophers of our time, said that the two most powerful forces in human history are science and religion. I think that with a little thought we would agree. That seems pretty clear. But what makes the statement even more interesting is what he added. He said that the future of humanity depends on a single factor—how these two most powerful forces in human history settle into a relationship with one another.

For four hundred years, since the rise of modern science, the relationship has been strained. At first, religion had the power and tried to strangle or impede the development of the new sciences in their cradle. Now the shoe is on the other foot. This is a very important distinction to make. I'm not saying that science or even scientists are not behaving very well. My point is that there has been a tragic misreading that the modern world, and that includes all of us, has slipped into with regard to the understanding of what science is. To make that distinction crystal clear, I'm going to use two words—*science* and *scientism*—because I think the biggest mistake in the modern world is the failure to distinguish between them. Unless we correct the mistake of confusing science and scientism, the consequences will be tremendous.

Now, in my book, science is good. It has changed our world. The scientific method has brought a greater understanding of the natural world. So science is good, but scientism adds two riders, two correlates, to that assumption. The first is that the scientific method is the most, if not the only, reliable method of getting at truth. The second corollary that we tack onto it is that the material world, the things that science deals with, is the most fundamental thing in existence.

I believe those two corollaries turn "science good" into "science bad," which is scientism, because there are no scientific facts that prove the truth of those two corollaries. They are at best philosophical positions, and at worst, they are simply opinions. And yet because of what science has done—the wonders it has brought in our understanding of technological spin-offs of the physical world—it generates in us a kind of momentum to think that scientists have got the window on the truth. We are led to believe that the future of humanity depends on looking out of their window and following their dictates about what is important and the direction we should go in.

Now, I want to emphasize that what I have just said I have not said as a Native American, which I am not. I have given my personal opinion arrived at as an intellectual historian. But I do believe that the failure to distinguish scientism from science is the greatest danger that faces humanity at this point. I'll claim nothing more, though of course I think it's absolutely true.

In this context, tell us about Mount Graham. What is the issue here, as it pertains to the conflict between science, scientism, and the Native American struggle to protect their most sacred lands? Why are you so committed to fighting for your claims to this mountain?

ANTHONY GUY LOPEZ: First, I'd like to say hello and that I'm glad to be here at this conference and glad to be here in South Africa. I want to acknowledge the kind words that have been said to us by the people here.

I'm here to talk about Mount Graham. The issue with Mount Graham is that the powers that be are allowing science and the Vatican to run roughshod over the Apaches and other Native American religious beliefs about sacred lands. The case of Mount Graham merges the power of the Catholic Church and its faith with that of astrophysical science, against the claims of Native Americans for religious freedom.

SMITH: The Apaches claim that it is a sacred mountain and therefore that it is a profanation to put this observatory on the top of it. That's the basic point, am I right?

LOPEZ: Yes, yes it is. First, I'm going to give a little bit of background about the Mount Graham issue. Since 1988 the University of Arizona and its partners, the Vatican observatory, Ohio State University, Notre Dame University, the Research Corporation and Max Planck Institute of Germany, and the Observatory of Florence, Italy, have all teamed up and claimed the top of this beautiful mountain in Arizona. The mountain is approximately eleven thousand feet high. It is a pristine ecological zone. At the top of it is old-growth forest. It's the home of several endangered species of plants and animals. These scientific and theological organizations teamed up and claimed this mountain peak for the building of the "Mount Graham International Observatory." However, this particular location is the aboriginal territory of the San Carlos Apaches, who now live on the San Carlos Apache Reservation. Early on in the 1980s, the Apaches and the environmentalists objected to the claiming of Mount Graham by this international team of astronomers.

SMITH: In my understanding, before it came to light what was going on, those who wanted that observatory had a law passed, in 1988. It was a rider to another bill in Congress, saying that the normal ecological criteria do not apply to Mount Graham because the site is so valuable to science that no other law of the land can impede the building of the telescope. Am I correct?

LOPEZ: Yes, you are. The university's attorneys and their partners asserted that claim in federal court numerous times. Together they claimed an exemption to all U.S. environmental and cultural protection laws. Early on they were deemed to have satisfied the provisions of those laws within the act that gave them permission to begin construction. So we contested the claim they made, which led to a long, drawn-out legal battle with them. Eventually, we were able to halt the observatory construction.

Not long after that the university and its attorneys and allies got together and got another law passed that exempted them again. We realized then that we were outgunned. They had tremendous pull. They had a political machine. If you combine the power of the state of Arizona with one of its major institutions, the University of Arizona, with the Vatican State, the Italian government, the government of Germany, and other universities, you create a public relations machine that was rather difficult for us to compete against.

SMITH: I would add to that equation the climate of opinion in America. It is probably of the order of thinking that if we build a new observatory it means we will know more about the mysteries of the universe. Why? Because science is good. Who cares about a little building up there? The notion of a *sacred* mountain just does not enter into the outlook of most people, since most of them are unfamiliar with native beliefs about the sanctity of the natural world. So the background is in favor of the conglomerate and supports what you are describing here, the victory of the scientists in this matter.

LOPEZ: Unfortunately, the legal context is that the sacred sites of Native Americans are not afforded legal protection. So the University of Arizona and its partners attempted to extend the unfortunate Supreme Court decisions that denied us legal protection for our sacred sites. We were faced with a tremendous political power with unlimited resources and a tremendous pull on the public mind within a context that afforded us no legal protections. But we decided that we had to fight anyway.

The reason we fought and are fighting is that *we can't allow this to happen anymore.*

This land, the Americas, the land I was raised on, is a beautiful place. Sometimes when I'm driving around, walking around, or hiking, I imagine what the states of Arizona, South Dakota, and Colorado once looked like. If you go to these places you can imagine that 150 years ago they were kept in reverence and respect. Look what has happened since. *How* did this happen? What happened to those springs at Pike's Peak, Manatou Springs? What happened to the several dozen limestone pools that were covered up and capped and bottled and are now almost inaccessible to native people? There are so many sacred places like that that have been desecrated and destroyed in this beautiful land.

When we Native Americans walk around we can hear and we can feel the pain that this land is experiencing. We can feel the sorrow of our ancestors that we have to confront as we see our forest, our waters, destroyed, our air polluted. You look around and you wonder, "When is all this going to stop? When are we going to turn this situation around? When are we going to reverse the course of the destruction of this Earth?"

Some of us decided, "So what if it's an observatory?" Let them build it somewhere else. We have every right to stand up for this place. *In fact, it is our duty.*

We had no other choice, especially in light of their marketing theme, which named the observatory after Christopher Columbus. The consortium wanted this observatory to be called the "Columbus Telescope." They said it was going to be the biggest telescope that anyone had ever seen. They claimed it would see into new worlds. That was their theme. They had the Vatican behind it, they had Ohio State University, which happens to be in Columbus, Ohio, and they had the University of Arizona. The main architect of the plan, Charles Polzer, a Jesuit priest, was appointed by [President Ronald] Reagan to the Columbus Commission to help lead the five-hundred-year celebration of Columbus in 1992. Their plan was to inaugurate this telescope on October 12, 1992. We were anticipating that they were going to try and pull something on us, big time.

THE TRANSCENDENT MYSTERY OF MOUNTAINS

As the most dramatic and impressive features of the natural landscape, mountains have the power to awaken an overwhelming sense of the sacred. . . . People throughout the world look up to mountains as sources of blessings, often attributed to the ancestral spirits who dwell within their slopes or upon their heights. . . . As places of power, close to heaven, mountains serve as dramatic sites of revelation or vision, which often transforms the person who receives.

EDWIN BERNBAUM, *SACRED MOUNTAINS OF THE WORLD*, 1998

This was the most expensive monument to Christopher Columbus in the so-called celebrations, so we decided we had to say no.

SMITH: Splendid points. I want to pick up on your phrase "let them build it somewhere else." Again, this is my understanding, and I need you to tell me if I'm right. When this became a public issue, the consortium moved a bill through Congress on a rider that Mount Graham would fall outside environmental laws. They argued that the observatories were so important that the other laws didn't apply. As I understand it, they argued that it was a magnificent, if not incomparable, place for the telescope. But the truth is that in terms of sites on our planet, which are good for seeing into outer space, Mount Graham rates only *thirty-eighth*. That is to say that there are *thirty-seven* better places where the telescopes could have been built. Am I right?

LOPEZ: Yes. But the proximity to Tucson, Arizona, and the University of Arizona reflects something like a juggernaut mentality. It requires a multimillion-dollar endeavor to put a coalition together like that—especially on the kind of foundation that walked all over Native American and environmentalists' concerns. It was arrogance, plain and simple. They decided that they could not stop and that they could not show any weakness. That was the mentality behind this endeavor. This whole struggle with the institutions of higher education—the Vatican, science, astronomy, the state of Arizona—got really crazy because these are foundational interests in society. When the Apache Survival Coalition filed our lawsuit to stop the observatory, they lined up three or four Jesuit priests who submitted claims that Mount Graham in their expert, theological, PhD opinions, wasn't sacred.

SMITH: This sounds like a complete denial of Apache tradition and belief.

LOPEZ: That is exactly what we faced. The powers that be actually denied the validity of Native American people, especially the Apache oral tradition. They demanded proof, archaeological or documentary proof. That's a standard of proof that I have to say they could not give for their religious tenets, the ones that they hold as sacred, their own articles of faith. They don't allow Native American faith-based beliefs any protection. If you look closely at their position, it has to be called hypocrisy. That is what we are dealing with here, incredibly powerful institutions that assert their priorities over anyone they come up against.

Think about it. Look how many Apaches, how many Native Americans, fought Germany, fought Italy in World War II. In contrast, now there are questions raised about the Vatican's involvement, and basically they are turning the other way when it comes to the Holocaust. These questions have been raised publicly. We fought in that war, my grandfather fought in that war. We fought fascism and nazism. Forty or fifty years later, Italy, Germany, and the Vatican have more rights to the public lands of our country than the original peoples of the United States.[2]

THE DOUBLE STANDARD

SMITH: I want to come back to your point about the hidden motivations lurking behind this project, such as the implications for the possible advances of science, and the double standard that native people are still facing in the United States.

LOPEZ: There are a lot of implications. Many people wonder why the Vatican has to build and operate an observatory. What is their interest? Historically their interest was in determining the correct dates of Easter, the liturgical calendar. The Vatican hierarchy begins with the pope, and the pope has direct authority over the Vatican observatory. I think the real reason is that the Vatican realized that they had to keep up with scientific developments regarding the heavens. So we recognize that there is a legitimate connection that they ought to keep up with the times. But I think it's not so much out of scientific interest or curiosity as it is to bolster their institution, because if extraterrestrials did arrive, the Vatican would look pretty silly. Everyone would say, "Why didn't you tell us what was really going on? Can we believe you anymore?"[3]

What's driving them is their belief that they have to be there to interpret and mediate any kind of extraterrestrial encounter so that the stability of society doesn't crumble—or really the stability of the Vatican. What they will try to do if that scenario ever comes to pass is to make it a Christian experience, while it ought to be a *human* experience. I know that this is a really far-out example, but I think the Vatican maintains a belief, and has made public remarks in an article, that every major religion in the world believes in the existence of extraterrestrials in the form of angels.[4] That's true, when you think about it.

What I am told is that Mount Graham is a holy place to the Apaches because it is considered the home of the mountain spirits, who are called the *Ga'an*. As I am told, in the Crown Dancers' tradition, they are beautiful crowns on the heads of the mountain spirits that are very similar to, if not the same as, the image of angels with halos around their heads in many other faiths around the world.

So why is it that the Vatican can't respect that perhaps our tradition is true? The Vatican's tradition says, in their articles of faith, that God's angels or "messengers" have visited them as the Creator's representatives. Why can't they allow the Apaches or other Native Americans that same blessing? Why is it that our faith has to be mediated through the church and verified to be made credible?

SMITH: I know that your organizations have made some progress in containing the construction on the mountain. So tell us about some success in at least limiting this project.

LOPEZ: Originally the university was proposing twenty-seven telescopes. Then they amended it to eighteen, and then they went down to seven, and they were finally given permission to build three. So we had a lot of success there in toning down the impact, the footprint, of the observatory. There has been another success. We were able to get an executive order from President Clinton, which mandates protections within the federal agencies and mandates the procedures that are needed to follow considering Native American interests concerning public lands. Just the public awareness of something that we commonly regard as archaic or ancient, or past history, the fact that we have brought awareness to the role that the church and the state together have played in denying indigenous people's rights, is a success. I think it's an important message. Unless we are able to challenge them effectively, they will continue. But I don't know if they are ready to stop.

SMITH: You haven't named one of your successes, which is that three major scientific institutions have withdrawn from this coalition. The University of Chicago happens to be my alma mater, and I'm proud to say that when the true picture came into focus they withdrew their support. The other two, I think, are Princeton and the National Institute of Science and Technology. They are scientific establishments of the highest order, and the fact that they have withdrawn I take as recognition of the argument on your side.

LOPEZ: The University of Pittsburgh, the University of Toronto, Michigan State University, and the Smithsonian Institution have also been approached, and all have turned down the partnership.

SMITH: Where do things stand? I understand that at present they are generating their own electricity up there on the mountain, but now they want to put up a power line.[5] Is that true?

LOPEZ: That is true.

SMITH: Are you going to be able to stop that?

LOPEZ: We filed a notice of intent to sue, and we will do our best to stop it in court, in the federal court in Arizona.

WHO OWNS SACRED LANDS?

SMITH: The central theme of our symposium at this Parliament of World Religions has been the desire of the indigenous peoples to have "a seat at the table." What would that mean for your struggle? Does it mean getting a voice in determining who owns the land you have dwelled on for centuries?

LOPEZ: Yes, there are larger questions of what is property and of whose property it is. Recently, the White Mountain Apache tribe and also the National Congress of American Indians have both called for Mount Graham to be listed in the register of historic sites. There is a commission that oversees that process, and they make recommendations, as an advisory council, and they have also agreed that it be designated as such, as a culturally protected site. But the university opposes that. That is where we are at right now.

Currently, there are three observatories on Mount Graham. Two of them are completed and are working. The Columbus telescope is the third to be built. At this point they want four more telescopes, at least, to make it a profitable venture. And as far as coming to the table, being granted a seat at *their* table, I think at some point they are going to have to agree to phase out their existing observatories. There has to be at least some recognition, and I think their developments in science and astronomy are such that they are developing better telescopes out there. Some of them are space-based. There are others on other mountains. And instead of placing these telescopes on Mount Graham, they should just recruit somewhere else.

For any Catholics or Jesuits in the room (I know there are probably some), the Apaches and the other Native Americans don't hate you. We don't hate the pope. We don't want to carry that feeling around with us. The call really is for the Catholic Church and the Vatican and the other

institutions involved finally to come to the table and talk and hopefully
to work something out with the Apaches.

> **I don't think I should have a permit. We are the original
> inhabitants of this land. We are not going to vandalize their
> telescopes. They know that for all these (hundreds) of
> years, the Apaches have gone there to pray.**
>
> WENDSLER NOISE, FOUNDER OF APACHES
> FOR CULTURAL PRESERVATION, AUGUST 31, 1998

The Vatican is a megainstitution. It's been around for two thousand years.
It's a church on the one hand and a government on the other. Depend-
ing on what you want and what they want, they can invoke their state's
rights, or they might invoke their papal authority. They are really hard
to pin down. In this case the Vatican State overrode the papal authority.
They overrode the commitment that the pope made to meet with the
Apaches to cancel the meeting. I can't say if the pope knew about it. I
know the secretary of state of the Vatican knew about it. Also the delegation to the United Nations, as well as the bishop of Tucson, I know
they know. At one point several years ago the Apaches were granted an
audience with the pope. At the last minute the delegation was turned
down, even though they were already in Rome.

PERMISSION TO PRAY

SMITH: There is another very important point that hasn't come up, and
that is, as I understand it, that now Apaches or Native Americans must
obtain a permit to go up that mountain to pray. Is that true?

LOPEZ: In a legal sense it is true, if you go by the current law. That is
what the university maintains, that you have to get a permit to go to the
peak of Mount Graham, but Native Americans have a right given by the
Creator to go there anyway. But they have been arrested by the university's security forces, by the Graham county sheriff's department, and
by the U.S. Forest Service rangers and have been put on trial. The cases
have all been dismissed, and the university maintains that they respect

Native American rights, but if you go up there you will be arrested if they see you. In one case a vanload of senior citizens from the San Carlos senior citizens center went up there to pray. They went to the gate and asked if they could get through, and they were denied permission but told to come back later. They went back to their camp, and the next thing you know, a half hour later, six police cars show up. It's that kind of thing. I can't give any credence to the university's claim that they respect Native American rights whatsoever. I have witnessed for myself the policies of the university in action. They would like for us go underground. I think that is their goal. Any time you want to go up on the mountain, the guard will ask you your name. They want your social security number. They want identification—yet they will still deny you access.

It's that kind of thing that can be really hurtful to a person who is going up there humbly; they just want to go up there and pray, and they are told, "Go away." It makes you feel like going underground. It makes you feel like you should never have talked to them, that you should have stayed away or taken another route.

SMITH: In the recent *Chronicle of Higher Education,* a very respected journal that services the university, there appeared a very striking statement. It was so striking that I committed it to memory, and I'm going to quote it because of the light it sheds on this issue.

The sentence reads: "If anything characterizes modernity it is the loss of the sense of transcendence of a being that encompasses and surpasses our quotidian ways." *Quotidian* means "everyday affairs." I find it striking, coming from a university organ that services all the universities, the statement that if *anything* characterizes the modern world it is this loss of transcendence. As you described it, scientists are arrogating the right to require of native people a permit in order to pray. Here is powerful evidence of the notion of transcendence *not* figuring in their consciousness or their view of reality at all.

LOPEZ: If you request a permit to pray, they will want to know the time and the duration of your visit to the summit. They will want to know where you are going. Then when you do go, they follow you around with these Belgian police dogs. They will track you. When you are walking around the observatory parameter, they will be walking around with their police dogs, even though this is public land, a national forest. But there is a public university involved, as well as the Vatican, and the governments of Italy and Germany. We have had to deal with the fact that these institutions are supposed to be humane and respectful, but when it came down to it, they played hardball politics with us. There are some real horror stories about the kinds of serious games they played.

SMITH: Can you give us an example?

LOPEZ: There was one instance, on October 12, 1992, when it turned out that one of their undercover policemen had infiltrated our student demonstration of the observatory. We found out when he was pulling something out of his fanny pack and out dropped a revolver onto the ground. There were hundreds of people around, and everyone gasped. An elder Apache woman, Elder Casitor, went right up to him and said, "Shoot me then. Shoot me." Everyone stood back, and we went up there and confronted him until he pulled out his radio and said, "I'm getting out of here." Then he left. He had been coming to our meetings, to our demonstrations, and all along he was an undercover policeman.

OUR CATHEDRALS, OUR UNIVERSITIES

LOPEZ: We live in the age of billionaires, of incredible wealth, and of incredible disparities between the power of the peoples and their relationship with Mother Earth. The animals are suffering, the waters are suffering. I think about all this. I think about who we native people are in the great scheme of things. And I tell you that our inheritance is greater than that. We have more at stake, and our duty and our responsibility are greater than that of the billionaire families. Our true inheritance is the biodiversity, the equality among ourselves, the justice that we are going to have in our lives with each other. These things are worth far more. In the grand scheme of things, they mean more.

We have cathedrals, huge cathedrals called old-growth forests. We have statues, but they are moving, breathing, flying, growing in our cathedrals. We have beautiful stained-glass windows. We have the sunlight, the moonlight, the starlight that shines through the trees. We have universities where we study and learn. It's the university of our lives, as we contemplate and meditate on what our duties are to the Seven Generations over our lifetime. We ask our professors, our elders, our spiritual people for guidance, for blessings, and they give them to us. They share them with us, they give us stories that we can't forget. We have scientists, people who really know how things work, how to really make things beautiful, we have artists, singers. We have our institutions too.

In the case of Mount Graham we are battling it out. There is no doubt about it. We are asking that these institutions come to recognize us as equals, so that we have something to bring to the table, so that this world might flourish, that we all might flourish together.

So how are we going to proceed in this situation? In the case of Mount Graham, I would like to ask the folks who care about this kind of issue to do *something*. It might be just to study the issue, or it might be to write a letter to the president of the university, or to go visit your local Catholic Church and ask them what they know about it. They will give you a response. They have people employed to do that. But then look deeper, when you get their response, and ask harder questions. Ask for the whole picture. Contact the Apache Survival Coalition in Arizona, or the Mount Graham Coalition in Arizona, and we will give you the whole picture, as personally, and objectively, as we can.

There is something about our native spirituality that I thought about when we visited Nelson Mandela's jail cell on Robben Island. I thought that we Native Americans have to be *so strong* that we can be isolated, removed from all the things that we love, all the things that we know, deprived of sunlight, good food, and the love of our children. We have to be so strong in our spirituality that we can be removed from it for decades—and yet the spirit will still live on within us.

That is how strong we Native Americans have to be, as Nelson Mandela was and is. But in the end we have to have justice, we have to have it mean something so that in the end hopefully we don't just die and go away. Hopefully our sacrifice and our struggle are going to result in our inheritance being recognized and returned to us.

SMITH: Listening to you I have a sense that in one way you have lost the battle but that in another you are winning the war. That you have come out of this particular ordeal more galvanized in your determination in your right to fight for your rights. Do you agree?

SACRED RIGHTS TO SACRED LANDS

I don't want to run over the mountains anymore; I want to make a big treaty. . . . I will keep my words until the stones melt. . . . I can do nothing more, for God made the white man and God made the Apache, and the Apache has just as much right to the country as the white man. I want to make a treaty that will last, so that both can travel over the country and have no trouble.

DELSHAY (TONTO APACHE), OCTOBER 31, 1871

LOPEZ: Ultimately the observatory will not stand; it's just a fact. Time will tell. These institutions that we build are not forever. But the important thing is to work something out that shows mutual respect of people's beliefs. We are not out to destroy the Catholic Church. We are hoping that the Catholic Church will wake up and consider our heartfelt beliefs and convictions, and maybe give us the same kind of consideration that they give one another. We are children of God too.

SMITH: You are, you are.

10

REDEEMING THE FUTURE

THE TRADITIONAL INSTRUCTIONS
OF SPIRITUAL LAW

Chief Oren Lyons, 1991. Photograph by
Toba Tucker. Used by permission of Toba Tucker.

"**F**or hundreds of years," Bill Moyers said in *A World of Ideas,* "the Haudenosaunee people have been talking about democracy, community, and reverence for nature, and Oren Lyons of the Onondaga is helping to continue that conversation . . . by preserving and transmitting the memories and traditions of his people. As director of the Native American Studies Program at the State University of New York of Buffalo, he shares with others the ancient wisdom."[1]

Oren Lyons is the faithkeeper of the Onondaga Nation of the Haudenosaunee. In this conversation, which was recorded in the spring of 2000, in Malibu, California, Lyons explores his vision of a land-based spirituality with his old friend Huston Smith. Here they speak about the deep roots of Indian spiritual law, the Three Instructions given by the ancestors, the power of ceremony and ritual, respect for elders, Indian philosophy, and the wisdom teachings of the "ancient future" for Indian people.

For Oren Lyons, the distinction between religion and spirituality is the difference between commerce and community as the driving forces of life. When asked by Professor Smith what it means to be an Indian, Lyons is characteristically demystifying, saying only that it means helping one another. Lyons also shares his kinetic self-description as "a runner for our nation," one who carries the message of living by natural law around the world and calls for people to practice "interrespect." For Lyons, this means living a life of gratitude and joy and passing on his nation's heritage of the democratic vision.

At his address to the nongovernmental organizations of the United Nations, Geneva, Switzerland, in 1977, Chief Lyons said, "I do not see a delegation for the Four Footed. I see no seat for the Eagles. We forget and we consider ourselves superior. But we are after all a mere part of Creation, and we must consider understanding where we are. We stand somewhere between the mountain and the ant. Somewhere and only there as part and parcel of the Creation."[2]

For Huston Smith, a respected elder in his own right, the conversation was another striking example of his ongoing search for the "winnowed wisdom" of the elders around the world. Smith has come to regard the primal traditions as the embodiment of living by natural law, which doesn't push human beings to the brink of disaster but shows us how to live with respect for balance. That is why, he says, "it's important to the world for their way of life to survive, intact, with full freedoms."

The Creator made it to be this way. An old woman shall be as a child again and her grandchildren shall care for her. For only because she is, they are.

HANDSOME LAKE (SENECA), CA. 1735–1815

HUSTON SMITH: Oren, it is such a pleasure to see you again. It's hard to believe that it's been twenty-five years since we have seen each other, but we haven't been together since I left Syracuse University, which was in 1975. So this meeting gives me a sense of deep satisfaction because it gives me the opportunity to say something that I would not have had the opportunity otherwise, maybe something that you may be totally unaware of. That is the extent to which you have changed my life and my vocation.

If you recall, I went to Syracuse having immersed myself for the first twenty-five years of my life in the field of the historical religions, that is to say, the religions that have cumulative text and written history and are known as the major religions of the world. I had paid no attention to what came before the historical religions, namely, the oral or the primal religions. I did know that the historical religions were just the tip of the iceberg of religious life on this planet. The historical religions are only six thousand years old, whereas the primal religions stretch back to the misty human origins on this planet. I had known that fact, but I'm full of excuses for my ignorance. I was young and impressionable and fresh to the confusions of the world. As I say, I'm full of excuses. But that was the mind-set I took with me from MIT to Syracuse. Many people were surprised that I made that move because MIT was by far the more prestigious institution. But I've come to see that some power up above, unbeknownst to me, engineered this move to increase my education in this important way.

So I came to Syracuse in 1973 benighted and ignorant in the way I have just described. Then it was *you,* because of your visibility in the Onondaga Nation, who introduced me to your nation, your religion, and your people. I must say that in those years of association with you and Chief Leon Shenandoah, those dear names, my regard for the primal religions, yours included, escalated. By the time I left, ten years later, I was seeing them as fully equal in their spiritual profundity and wisdom to anything the historical religions can boast.

So I am just endlessly grateful that I will not go to my grave having omitted that base for the religious life of humanity, and more than any other individual you were the catalyzing factor in this change. I'm happy to have the opportunity to thank you for the profound difference you have made in my life and my understanding.

That said, I want to pass the ball to you. What's on your mind these days? What's of most concern to you at this time? Have we made any progress since you and I last met?

OREN LYONS: It's a little overwhelming to hear that perspective, considering what I know, in my limited understanding of life. I do have a strong belief. I believe implicitly and I feel very strongly about learning and should inform you that today, as we speak, there is a ceremony going on at Onondaga. It has been going on for five or six days. We started our midwinter ceremonies. It will go on until January 23, and it is, as you know, the major event of our ceremonial year.

SMITH: Is this the time when the leaders of the Six Nations come together to rehearse the story of Handsome Lake?

LYONS: No, this is a thanksgiving ceremony where we say we tie the year in a bundle. This is the ceremony where all the people gather and we extend our thanksgiving for what we have. We perform our ceremonies to continue the process, which requires the full community. In each of the Six Nations, in all those territories, a similar event is taking place. But it requires the full involvement of the chiefs, the clan mothers, the faithkeepers, and the people. At the same time it's a ritual of renewal.

SMITH: It haunts me to hear that. It brings to mind a few more vignettes from the first times when we were together, back in the mid-seventies, and may help illuminate our understanding of native ceremony and ritual. I will never forget them.

The first of them concerns the other ceremony that I alluded to. You told me that it was going to happen, and so I came out to the reservation because I thought it would give me the opportunity to meet the chiefs of the other nations. We were out there in the warm sun, having our coffee, when the dramatic moment for me came. You stood up and said, "Huston, you know that we regard you and recognize you as a friend, but it's now 11:00 A.M., and we are going into the longhouse and you are not."

What interests me to this day about this rather shocking moment is that rather than hearing your words as a rebuff I just felt a charge of . . . *elation.* I was elated to discover that there are still people on this planet who believe their traditions are so precious that it would profane those traditions if they fell on alien ears. I found the moment thrilling, and I still do. Christianity used to have that depth of numinous power, that confidence in ritual, that belief in the sacred as being divided from the profane. At least it did in its first three centuries. The early Christians ushered to the doors those who had not been initiated in the mysteries of the faith. I believe Christianity lost that, around 1700. But that sense of reverence for ritual and ceremony survives in Indian country.

That's just one moment.

Another profound one for me was when I was in your house and my eyes fell on your passport. That was the first time I'd seen a Six Nations passport. I said, "What are you doing getting into trinkets?"

You said, "Look, this took me all the way to Geneva and back."

That confidence astonished me. I asked, "With no trouble?"

You replied, "All kinds of trouble—but none that we couldn't handle."

That was another numinous moment and a real eye-opener about honoring one's religion.

The third memorable moment was when you were telling me about the time you were negotiating over certain issues with members of Congress, and at the end of the afternoon they would take you to their lounge for their happy hour. They asked you what you wanted to drink, and you answered, "Orange juice would be nice." They thought you meant a screwdriver. As you were drinking your orange juice they were having more and more hard liquor, and you could see their eyes glazing over and their bodies rocking back and forth. You thought, "History is being created now. The shoe is on the other foot. Now *they're* getting drunk and I'm staying sober." That's an interesting twist on the sordid history of the introduction of alcohol into the world of Native Americans and is the kind of thing that sparkles in my memory.

LYONS: For the sake of public discourse, so people understand our ceremonies, our way of life, the way we live is a very, very old way. We are not sure how old it is. We do know our first message was about how to live. Our people were able to survive on that for many years. Our second message came as the Great Law of Peace for the Six Nations. That was about a thousand years ago, and the messenger, this spiritual being, came and brought this message of peace and a process of government, which was democratic in nature. That vision established a process to help us continue to exist. He said to our leaders, whom he had raised and established, that our first duty was to see that the ceremonies were carried on at the proper time, and in the proper way, and in the proper places. Your second duty, he said, is to sit in council for the welfare of the people. So primary then, in our government, is the spiritual law. That is what guides us. We were told that when we are weak, as human beings often are, when our spines are weak, as often happens, it will be spiritual law that will be our strength, like the great pine.

THE VISION FOR SEVEN GENERATIONS

SMITH: That's a beautiful vision, but will it, can it, continue? You are here, but you are advancing in age. Are you confident that a new generation of leaders is coming up that will replace the present generation?

LYONS: The messenger expressed a lot in the way of instruction. He instructed the leaders on the process and procedure. He warned us about certain things. He prepared the leaders for things that we wouldn't understand at the moment they occurred but would become clear as we became more experienced.

What he actually said was, "You must have skin seven spans thick, like seven spans of a tree, to withstand the abuse that you are going to receive in your position. You must be tolerant and must not respond in kind, but you must understand and be prepared to absorb all of that because it is not going to be coming from your enemies, it is going to be coming from your friends and your families. This you can expect."

SMITH: The wisdom of those words makes me think of Reuben Snake, the great Winnebago leader. But he is gone. Is there a new generation learning this point?

LYONS: Yes. I think of the other spiritual instruction the messenger gave us. He said that when you sit in your council you should sit for the welfare of the people. You should think not of yourself, or of your family, or even of your generation. He said when you make your decisions you should make your decisions on behalf of the Seventh Generation coming after you. See their faces. Think of them. Make your decisions on their behalf so that they may enjoy what you have today. If you do this then you yourself will have peace.

So peace was the fundamental principle of the Great Law, the Great Law of Peace. Around a thousand years ago there was a government, a spiritual law for our subsistence, for our benefit and for that of the future, because they are always looking ahead to this responsibility of leadership, of adult people doing adult things. The question was asked, just as you asked it. One of the women spoke up and asked him, "How long will this last?" He said, "That's up to you. Everything is always up to you."

So we know that each generation has its own responsibilities. You can't live another generation's life for them. They must sustain themselves, and so they must have principles, they must have ideas, and what you are talking about is the sustainability of this whole process. That is the event we are preparing for, the "Great Condolence."

The genius of this process is just amazing. It's quite profound how it operates. There are no elections, and yet it is democratic. It is by consensus. Women are very much responsible. Women choose the leaders. Women are our life. The Earth itself is female. Without the female there is no life. Fundamentally women carry that long life. Men seem to have problems with it all the time; they seem to be challenged by it. We learned a long time ago that men and women must work in full partnership, because that is what it takes. That is why everything is in twos: day and night, life and death, man and woman. It's all in twos.

SMITH: Years ago, I remember your telling me that from the outside your religion looks like it's male dominated because the chiefs are all men. But what the outsiders do not see is the inner workings of your religion. Namely, that the women are the power behind the throne. In a sense they name their "front men."

LYONS: There is a clan mother, a chief and subchief, and two faith-keepers, male and female. That is who is operational in each clan. But it's the clan mother who has the responsibility to choose all the leaders. Her choice must be ratified by consensus, by the clan, by the nation, by the whole Six Nations. It's a long process but extremely democratic. She also has the power of recall. It is her duty to remove a chief if he is not performing correctly. She has a great deal of responsibility. But there has to be balance between male and female. Instead, what I often see today is this great lack of respect for women and a great misunderstanding, a lack of the kind of balance that only comes from working with women.

What you will find with most traditional and indigenous peoples is that they have this common understanding and balance because they work together as partners. We couldn't survive if just the males were here or just the females. It takes two.

> **Sooner or later we all will remember to do the duties we were instructed to do. Sooner is better. Later brings the suffering that will cause us to remember the Creator. The decision as to when it will be is always up to each person. In the end everybody will be doing the same thing, and that is remembering. . . . These are our times and responsibilities. Every human being has a sacred duty to protect the welfare of our Mother Earth, from whom all life comes. In order to do this we must recognize the enemy—the one within us. We must begin with ourselves. We must live in harmony with the Natural World and recognize that excessive exploitation can only lead to our own destruction. We cannot trade the welfare of our future generations for profit now. We must abide by the Natural Law or be victims of its ultimate reality.**
>
> CHIEF LEON SHENANDOAH (ONONDAGA),
> 1915–1996, *TO BECOME A HUMAN BEING*, 2001

As for the question of how long it will last, well, it's always in the hearts of the people. It will last as long as the people want it to last. I think looking ahead and seeing the great interest in our nations today and among the young people, it will go beyond us. Chief Leon Shenandoah worried and talked a lot about that. He had a great perspective. I learned from those old leaders, our elders. But I've seen many of these men and women die.

THE ROLE OF ELDERS

SMITH: In my experience with religious groups around the world I've found it important to name and recognize one's elders. Would you like to name some of the ones on your horizon?

LYONS: Yes, yes. I'd like to begin with my grandmother, who was a clan mother and a leader. She was extremely instructive, and she was the sister of Chief Leon Shenandoah, and Rica Lyons, who is my aunt and became my clan mother and Mrs. Peters. She married a chief from Six Nations in Oswegan, Canada. He came with us and stayed until his death. She was very direct; she was tremendous. A wonderful woman. Great perspective. Very simple. I learned a lot from her.

But, Huston, I am not really versed in everything I should be. I'm lacking a great deal in terms of language and understanding. I find that I'm getting old now. There is a great pressure to continue the language. The language is at greatest risk now, not only here, but around the world. It's the process of homogenization, which is going to be terrible in the face of diversity. You call it biodiversity, but you have to include human cultures as well. I again take great instruction from my aunt and her amazing inquisitiveness and interest in other peoples, in other nations, in other places where she traveled. She was all over the world. She was always so interested in what was going on. She reminded me of a field of wild flowers where the colors are all different. People are the same way, colorful but different.

SMITH: Your botanical comparison reminds me of another powerful moment for me at the reservation. On your table there was a photograph of flowers, and you told me that members of the botany department at the university had come out because there were some species of plants on your reservation that they could not identify. The flowers were taken to them, and they took photographs, and then they came back with the developed film. You reported to me that members of your nation could tell the scientists the name and certain facts about the plant but also the time of day that the picture was taken. This came as a revelation and a verification to me of the extent to which your people are in touch with the land, and they're in touch in such a precise way.

LYONS: Yes, there was a real clear example of that in Navajo country, where some scientists came and talked to a native woman who spoke no English. They asked her if she could identify a flower in a black-and-white photograph, and she said yes. Then they asked her the name of the flower. She asked, "What part?" They came to find out that this so-called uneducated person could name more parts of the plant than they could.

So yes, native people were also native scientists. Everybody understood everything about the natural world. *Everybody* knew because they were all educated about the Creator's world. They understood the connections. I think that the discussion we are having here is similar to the message that I know was delivered by native people and other world leaders at the Third Parliament of World Religions, in South Africa. I understand that they were trying to come together, trying to find peace among themselves.

But as old as religions are, the Parliament was only the *third* such gathering where different people from around the world made an attempt to sit down in peace. All because of the old rivalries between religions.

We know because when all the different preachers would come by the reservation carrying the same book but with a different message, each one would say, "Who was that that just left here?" "Oh, well, I think he was an Anglican." "Oh, don't listen to him. He doesn't know anything."

I think it was Red Jacket who was asked if he was coming to the local church and said, "I don't think so. First of all, I get embarrassed if I have nothing to put in your box when it comes around, and I feel bad about that. We are to observe the conduct of your people, and I think that we will wait until the conduct of your people matches your speech. When what they say matches what they do, then maybe we will join you, but until that time we will be over here."

SMITH: That reminds me of the old expression I learned from my missionary parents: "Your actions speak so loudly that I can't hear what you say."

LYONS: In America, the conquests, as they call it, of the native peoples here and the conquest of our lands was a fundamental process that was established from the beginning. It was Christian in nature. The countries that were involved in colonization of the New World were great nations like England, the Netherlands, Spain, Portugal, Germany, and France. The strongest power at that time was the Catholic Church, which ruled almost the whole domain of Europe. When they ran into each other, they understood that this was a common discovery, so they established a process known as "the Law of Nations."

They said, "Look, we keep bumping into each other, so let's make some rules here."

So they decided among themselves that if you were Christian and you were there first, then that would be respected by the other Christian nations. They said that in claiming the land (which is what they did when they came here) they were planting flags. Well, while the colonists were

planting flags our people were planting corn. Our people were not thinking in terms of flags and claiming land. So it was uneven competition
from the beginning.

But when they established the Law of Nations, it was the Christians
who developed and refined it into what they called *terra nullis,* the theory of "empty lands." If the people were pagan, were heathens, were not
Christians, then the land was declared empty. That process took almost
all of Africa; Australia; North, Central, and South America; and even
parts of Asia. The Asians fought harder, they were more versed in the
Art of War, which arose, I think, in the oldest civilization, China, in terms
of longevity. They understood.

At the time of colonization we native people were caught unawares.
We were thinking in one set of rules, and the colonists were thinking in
another. We would say that your word is your bond, in honor of your
nation. The leaders of the colonists would say, "Get it in writing."

In other words, it didn't matter what you said; it mattered what you
wrote.

We didn't know that. Interestingly enough, in 1951 there was a legal
case in the United States called *Petition vs. the U.S.,* which was a lawsuit
for land. The U.S. Supreme Court denied the petition for land because
they said they were instructed by the Law of Nations that, in fact, native people only had *use* of land, they couldn't *own* it. That prevailed
into the 1950s, which is not very long ago, unless you think of when it
started, which was in 1496.

But then in 1991 the Gettson Indians petitioned for the same rights in
British Columbia, and they were also denied, on the basis of the Law of
Nations. So right up to this very moment, this Christian racist doctrine
that calls us pagans still prevails.

SMITH: That's illuminating, because the general opinion is that colonialism officially ended with World War II. That may be true for most of
Asia, Indonesia, and India, who have won their independence from the
colonizers. But in the case of North and South America, two continents
of indigenous people, the Europeans just came and took the land, and
that is still where it stands today.

GOD, GOLD, AND GLORY

LYONS: I think that it may have been the quest for gold that brought
the Europeans here in the first place. It was also about God, about glory,

and it was about gold. This quest for gold still seems to be the driving force in the world today.[3]

The question comes back around to what the Peacemaker told us. He said we should look after the coming generations and be responsible. Today the quest is much more sophisticated, but nonetheless it is driven by the same emotion and the same drive. The consequences and the damage that style of thinking will bring to the future—the Seventh Generation—is what this whole discussion is about. We're really talking about the responsibility of leadership and the accountability of leaders to people and the principles of leadership. I think today those principles have been abdicated by international leadership and by great economic forces and the corporate states that abound.

I believe it was Lester Brown who said that of the one hundred most powerful and richest entities in the world today, fifty-one are corporations and forty-one are countries. The balance is tipped already in terms of corporations—and it's moving and tipping faster and faster. The questions that arise are really about leadership. Are economic wealth and personal wealth going to be the sole driving forces for people? Or is there going to be some responsibility to culture, language, health, and, above all, community?

SMITH: This brings me back to your earlier point about the danger that comes with the homogenization of the people of the world. You were referring earlier to this trend of homogenizing the world into a single culture or outlook. You were deploring that, and I couldn't agree with you more, but I want to ask you, *why* do you feel that it is important that your nation and the Native American peoples as a whole resist this? Is it because you don't like the way that homogenized outlook is going and so you don't want to be swept up into it? Or do you think that retaining your own identity and your unique outlook on the world is important, especially for those who already have been homogenized? Is it because you believe it's important to convey to young people that there is another way of looking at things, which may have values that the majority has overlooked?

LYONS: You have opened up a varied subject that relates back to the question of how we think and what our beliefs are. I have a very strong belief in the Creation and the Creator. All Indian nations, as far as I know, have this profound understanding of and belief in the Creation. We believe that the Creation was perfect, and the Creation was profoundly diverse, from the smallest creatures to the varieties of bugs, the varieties of plants, the varieties of fish, the varieties of trees, and the varieties of peoples. They were all different, and they were all interconnected, and they were all related.

In fact, what you had was community. You had a world community of life. A life that really existed in what I would call the Great Law of Regeneration. The greatest natural law is the law of regeneration, the ability to regenerate endlessly as long as you maintain the rules of the law, which is variety. So if you tamper with variety then you are challenging the laws of regeneration, which of course means that it's the human beings who are doing it. Absolutely the only ones who are doing it. They are challenging the process of life itself. They put themselves in jeopardy now because in our understanding and in our belief, you can *never* challenge these laws. You can only abide by them. You can only understand them.

For example, I guess the nature of our oldest ceremonies was thanksgiving. Our ancestors were being grateful. Those were the two instructions we had: "Be thankful" and "Enjoy life." We built nations around those instructions. We built ceremonies around those instructions. As for the Earth itself, Huston, you mentioned earlier, "Well, we don't have all the time in the world." But the *world* has all the time in the world. Whether or not we are here doesn't matter to the world at all. The natural law, as far as we know, is merciless. All it demands is loyalty. All it demands is that you abide. As long as you do you will survive. But if you challenge natural law and think you are going to change it, then eventually you are going to come to that crisis point where life is *not* regenerating itself anymore.

One of our Indian leaders said, "Only after you cut the last tree, and only after you've caught the last fish, and only after there is nothing left; only then will you realize that you can't eat coal."

Only after.

As you mentioned earlier, I told you outside the longhouse, "Huston, we are going into the ceremony and you are *not* going to be in there." The reason you were barred from our ceremonies was that at one time they were open to outsiders, but it reached the point where we couldn't get into our own longhouse. Indian people, being who they are, set the time for the ceremonies and said, "Tomorrow we will start in the morning when all the people get here." So there was no real time for beginning the ceremony. If you arrive late, then you have time to chat, and if you arrive early you have time to chat, and nobody pays any mind. In the ceremony, Indians come when they come, and nobody questions why. There are no rules. So what happens? Suddenly we find that the place was filled up with non-Indians and the Indians who came could not get in. That meant that the ceremony couldn't be carried on. The elders said we have to do something about this.

In the discussion that followed they concluded that the ceremonies were fundamental to our way of life, the most important thing that had to be taken care of. That was our sacred duty and what we knew how to do. Rather than offend anybody we knew we had to either open it to everyone or to close it to outsiders. No exceptions. We closed it because the ceremony has got to be performed.

Then they added that the ceremonies were inclusive at any rate. When we have our ceremonies, we don't have our ceremonies for the Onondaga Nation, or the Bear Clan, or the Beaver Clan. We have ceremonies for the whole. Since it's inclusive, people don't have to be there. In our territories we have all kinds of medicine societies. When we meet all we have to do is call these societies. They go out, and if you are invited and you become part of that society, all's well and good. The rest of the people are not curious. They don't have to be there. What they do know is that the societies are performing their business.

SMITH: I understand that very well. I hope and pray it was clear that I respect that. I respect the fact that boundaries are very important. There is a kind of leakage if these boundaries are not kept clean. But as you say the individual and the inclusive world need not be totally in opposition. Both sides can be present in different ways.

LYONS: I appreciate your comment on the possibility for us to hang on to those principles.

SMITH: I look at my own church, the Methodist Church, and can tell you there are no boundaries at all. If anyone wants to join in, they can. It just gets watered down. I deeply value what you are trying to do there.

LYONS: Well, we maintain it. I think each generation does. It's up to each generation. I can look into our community now, and I can see the leaders coming. At one time, I didn't.

SMITH: Speaking of strong young leaders, I just had the chance to see Douglas George, who was my student at Syracuse. What a splendid human being and leader he has become.

LYONS: I think that my concern really is about this lack of will in national and international leadership when it comes to challenging these economic forces.

SMITH: Are you speaking of your people?

LYONS: No. I'm talking about the world as a whole. We think in those terms. We're just a small part. We keep our things going, and we know that the people in this country keep their things going, and we are very grateful for all these differences that continue. We want to promote that in bringing up our children. We promote individuality, what some people call "style." "We like this kid's style. Hasn't he got a different style?" Every one of the kids does. So we promote those idiosyncrasies and support each child to be that way. What happens at the end of the day when you have a major problem is that you throw it out to the people and see what will come back. Out there in the community you have all these individuals, and somebody is going to be thinking of a creative solution somewhere. Each individual is diverse. That's why it's important to have diversity in thought and being. If you carry them to their utmost limit of their individuality, it will strengthen your nation and your people.

THREE MESSAGES FROM INDIAN COUNTRY

SMITH: When I think about your people and their individuality, as compared to the dominant culture, I see three messages or three fundamental clues that this homogenized culture of ours is not seeing or not adhering to.

The first message is diversity. All these companies merge and become more alike, including in their insensitivity to the importance of diversity. The second message is indifference to the principle of sustainability or regeneration, a program that promotes regeneration. The third is thanksgiving. The sense of gravity (which lends itself to gratitude) is one of the qualities that comes through so clearly to me in indigenous cultures.

If we look at our mainstream culture today, which is secular and prompted by modern science, it only extracts the material components of the Earth and can't deal with the other way of sustainability and regeneration. So *what* and *who* is there to be thankful to? Where is the Great Spirit in that? What I'm hearing from you is that you are retaining your boundaries and your individuality as a kind of warning signal to the dominant culture. If you lose hold of these three truths, what lies ahead for humanity?

LYONS: The homogenization of humanity is the product of commerce. It's the direction and the end result. It's much easier for the market force today to sell a product to a large group of people who think the same way. Flattening out and getting rid of all these differences—that's what makes these corporations successful. They are able to reach a larger and larger market that thinks alike. So homogenization makes them much more pliable. It's all based on consumerism; it's based on profit. But the question is, profit for whom? As we see now, fewer and fewer are becoming richer and richer.

SMITH: More profit for the profiteers.

LYONS: The religion of Christ teaches that he threw people out of the temple for only professing to be religious. I should say that there is a distinction between spirituality and religion. Indian nations and indigenous people have a spiritual law. Religions are not necessarily spiritual. Religions have become more businesslike, and they have lost their spiritual strength, and so they have lost people. But that has not been directly their fault. It's a major agreement internationally on the fundamental importance of commerce. The driving force today is not spiritual law. The driving force today is commerce, the market and the marketplace. Nobody has any boundaries on that because it is too powerful and too emotional.

All the great civilizations and societies and communities have rules. The first rule they have is to deal with greed and jealously—to keep these forces in check—because they are so destructive and they abide in every human being. But how do you maintain that control? Here comes the philosophy of personal wealth that promotes that. Now that the genie is out of the bottle, you're not going to get him back him.

SMITH: Sometimes I wonder where it is all going to end. As one of the vaunted wisdomkeepers of your people, do you have any wisdom to share with us?

LYONS: I don't know where the end is. We are going to have to depend on the strength and will of the next generation. These next two generations are coming to save and to readjust and to get what you would say is the course chartered by humanity back on course to a regenerated style of life that will continue. Right now that regeneration law is being challenged by industry. They're cutting down the trees, and at the rate they are going they are going to cut all the trees. They are catching all the fish. Right now there are problems in every body of fishing water in the world. And yet do you see them standing back and setting laws and saying, "We must have a greater principle of survival?" No, they say, "I'm fishing because he's fishing. If he's gonna fish, I'm gonna fish."

As our messenger envisioned, we must think about the future. So we must ask, "What about the Seventh Generation?" This means we must ask, "What's downstream?" Nothing. Nothing is downstream. This idea that science is going to find a solution is so stupid. Science isn't what drives a nation or a community; it's principles and leadership. If you lose those principles there is nothing that science can do about it, except probably to accelerate the process.

And then there is this other idea that people have: "Well, there is a whole universe, so we'll all just fly to another planet." That is even stupider, because who has the money? Who is going to fly? If anybody is, it will be Bill Gates. It certainly isn't going to be anybody walking down the street here in Malibu or anywhere else. It is going to be the people who have the money. That is what I'm afraid of now. Is that consolidation of wealth? No, it's the consolidated power that's controlling thought now, and it's controlling principles and international leadership. Presidents and prime ministers have abdicated the responsibility of leadership that can help with the Seventh Generation coming.

SMITH: I want to change the direction a little bit and come back to this notion of cultural boundaries and the colonialism of culture. What's your feeling about Anglos using the icons of your traditional societies such as taking a name for a football team, like the Washington Redskins[4] or selling kachina dolls in the Southwest as trinkets?

LYONS: It is very difficult to pilfer something that's ten thousand years old. There is no way you can appropriate three or ten thousand years of culture. Oh, sure, you can try, but there is really no way you can steal or destroy it. It's just something that is so profoundly involved in the culture, and it's part of the spectrum, part of the mosaic that comes together to make this beautiful blanket of color, of cultures, of thanksgivings, of ways to continue as a community interacting on a very large scale. You can't really appropriate it.

Without making light of it, I would say that I've seen many of these New Age people who are very sincere in the way that they're looking for some spiritual strength. They are searching *so hard*. But I'm afraid they see that the last thing left for the Indians is their religion, and now they are coming after that. But you can't take that eagle feather and carry it around and suddenly have the same understanding between that bird and the nation that works with it.

SMITH: I see that point very clearly. If you pilfer something, it cannot mean to you a fraction of what it meant to its original owner. That's fair.

But beyond that, is it a desecration? Let's switch from kachina dolls to shamanism. Now, shamanism is a very important tradition among your people because of its powers of healing and divination and the like. When Anglos set up workshops on teaching people the shamanic technique, their students are not going to get 2 percent of what shamanism really is. But should we go beyond the usual responses of anger or resentment or mockery and say, "Stop it"? Should you come right out and say to these people that you think this is cultural theft or trivialization of your old ways, or at least that it waters down what the reality really was? Is it time to shout "hands off"?

LYONS: This question really goes to the problem of the lack of spiritual resources and spiritual sources at large, which are natural. But the New Agers don't have them. They haven't stolen them; they can't. We believe that every human is a spiritual being. We believe in the Creation, and if we believe in the Creation, then we believe that the Creator put that person there. No matter what color that person is. Therefore I must automatically respect what I see. What we say to people who may be violating our traditions is that they have their own traditions, their own spiritual resources. We tell them, "Go home and find it. It doesn't help you to be over here."

Every now and then there are great exceptions. Exceptional people do change. It's happened, but it's not a common thing. The more I think about it the more I believe that people really need to get back to their spiritual origins, their own needs, and develop them. This begins with the simple word *respect*. If there was a law among the old Indian nations and Indian people, it was respect. Everything immediately begins to prosper; everything begins to change if you respect the land, if you respect the water, and if you respect the people. Respect begets respect, and that begets peace. Then you have community. Community is the interaction and the support of one person, and we have a large human community. Human beings are really one people with a lot of different cultures and a lot of different ways.

You know, I learned so much from the old guys who have gone by, like Thomas Banyacka and Mina Lanza from the Hopi nation, a great spiritual leader and a great woman. There is Phillip Deere, from the Muskogee, a wonderful man, a great spiritual man. A lot of these guys like Austin Two Moons, a Northern Cheyenne, were hell-raisers when they were young. Oh, man, they raised hell. Austin was a broncobuster and did all that crazy stuff. They all drank, but they became great spiritual

men. It takes time. The Onondaga Chief Leon Shenandoah: all those
people had this fundamental understanding of simplicity. It's not complicated, but it's hard to simplify your own thinking.

I'm merely a runner for our nation. I do a lot of running and a lot of
presenting and a lot of speaking. They say, "You speak English well, so
you talk to them." But I don't have this great wealth of wisdom; it's the
nation; it's the chiefs before me. I'm still learning, but I'm way behind.

On the other hand, we all do what we can. That's what makes the
community. That is why it's important to have it. You know we believe
each individual has a gift, and some have many more than one. But everybody has to hone that gift to its best and then *share* it. That's what creates strength, the sharing of what you have, which is such a contrast to
the market idea. The sharing and the market—they don't work, they
don't mix.

SMITH: I see it as a bulwark in this effort to create a nation within a
larger nation. What does that come down to? What does it mean, and
how do you go about it?

LYONS: It ain't easy.

SMITH: Do you have a philosophy of how that should work—or is it
sort of improvising as you go along?

LYONS: No, the principles that we function by are very old. *Peace* is
the number one principle. The second is *power,* but it isn't that, it's the
combination of the good minds that gives you strength. Put your minds
together as one, and you get this unity of strength. Then you have *justice,* equality. They work together, and then there's *health.* Health is very
important. The chiefs always talk about health. When we give our greeting they answer, *"Nyawenha skanonh,"* which means: "Thank you for
being well." That's our fundamental greeting: "Thank you for being well."
Our other response is, "Yes, it's true." This lays down the principle of
how we think: *Thank you for being well.* It reflects how we always think
about the other person. We are always in concert and agreement.

Indian nations were never wealthy; they never acquired a lot of things.
They shared; there was an *ethic* of sharing, which profoundly antago-
nized the American government. They were always trying to break our
idea of common land. They said that was not right: "You have to learn
how to look after yourself. You have to grow up and understand about
being an *individual.*" Well, we have great individuality, but we have a

different perspective. Our perspective is responsibility, responsibility to the family, responsibility to the public, responsibility to your future.

Chief Louis Farmer told me a long time ago, "It's not easy being an Indian. Do you know what it means to be an Indian? It means: *When someone comes along and asks for help, you put down what you are doing and you help them.* That's what it means to be an Indian."

SMITH: This relates to something now going on over the adjudication of land rights in upstate New York and other places, and my understanding is that your nation, the Onondaga, is taking a different position on this issue than some of the other Indian nations. Correct me if I am not right in thinking that when it comes to the land over which, it turns out, you have jurisdiction, the treaty wasn't honored but at the moment the courts are supporting you.

But if you get jurisdiction over a wider range of land it will not be to divide it up into personal property, as some nations that have adopted the ways of the dominant culture seemed to be approaching it. Your attitude is, "No, we are not going to parcel it out so much for each person and so on. That is not our way because the land to be held is for everybody. To think about selling land would be like selling the air. Who owns the air?"

So it wouldn't go the route of the dominant culture of private property at all. It would dig in on the principle that this land is sacred and people have a divine trust to take care of the land. If we get the jurisdiction what we want to do is to kick off the industries that are desecrating the land, let's say, by restoring Lake Onondaga, one of the most polluted lakes in the world, restoring the sanctity and integrity and rights of the land itself, rather than looking to parcel it out into private hands. Do I have it right?

LYONS: That's pretty good, Huston. We will have to get you on our council.

SMITH: It would be a great honor.

LYONS: Essentially its responsibility is to the future. Obviously when the chiefs talk about environment being *us,* that doesn't just mean us right here and we are just part of it. We *are* the environment. So is society. When the environment is sick, the people are sick. Everything suffers. Yes, we would like to bring cleaner water and the process of regeneration—that's one of the major things we put to the U.N., in 1994, the first project for the Decade of the Indigenous Peoples. They gave us a decade, and we brought in a project that was to regenerate and revitalize the lands of the Six Nations, which we presented and called "The Blue Book to the United Nations."

We never got one supportive response about that project, which essentially lays out our vision. We think that is important as a responsibility to the future. It works in complete syncretism with our law and our responsibility as chiefs. When they stand you out there, they tell you we are going to put into your hands the responsibility for all life. That is what they lay in the hands of the chiefs. When they talk about all life, they are not talking about cousins, and aunts, and nations, and people: they are talking about everything.

And so it is a very inclusive phrase. We think and talk about that all the time, and we think that maybe with this land claim, we are finding equity and justice and trying to bring peace, which the Americans have to do. The United States must fulfill its obligations and right all the injustices that they visited on the original people here before we can collectively move on to the next step that is regeneration and a fruitful future.

We have to come to terms with the future. The United States has to clean its own house. It can't be speaking in terms of human rights to the rest of the world. It can't be speaking in terms of justice. It can't be doing all that with its very own people in its midst, while the original people here have suffered so. Fundamentally, I think "The Blue Book to the United Nations" will give us an opportunity.

SMITH: I know some philosophers and other commentators who believe that religion should center on the search for social justice. Is that the kind of change you are seeking?

LYONS: Everyone wants to be first. But instead of an electronic wire, there is a stone wall. A solid wall. You are racing toward that wall. I don't see any of you pulling your horses up. Now, can I ask you why?

If we take another aspect of racing, car racing, a yellow flag means there is an accident, and so everybody slows down. Then they maintain their position and can figure out a way to clean out the wreckage, continue the race, and nobody loses their spot. How come? Where is your concept here? Can anybody answer why you are going into challenging every definition of continuing your life heading for that stone wall?

During a meeting I was attending as a consultant a man said, "I'm a CEO and I'll tell you quite frankly that if I don't show a profit for my corporation I will be fired. That's the nature of it. I must show an advance."

"Well, who is going to fire you?"

He said that it was the stockholders, and he pointed at me.

I said, "You're blaming me? It's the stockholders who demand that. Let me ask you another question. Do you have children?" He said yes. And I said, "Do you have grandchildren?" He said, "Yes, one, he's about eight years old."

At that time I had one about the same age, and so I said, "Isn't that interesting? I have a grandson who is about eight years old too. Let me ask you, 'When do you cease to be a CEO and become a grandfather?'"

There was no answer. That was the moral question. He didn't answer. It got kind of uncomfortable in there. So he makes a joke and says, "Well, I've heard about these Indian prophecies. Can you tell us a prophecy?"

I said, "I'm an Indian, and of course I will tell you a prophecy. This one will be a *guaranteed* prophecy. You will meet next year, and nothing will have changed."

That's how we left the committee. So I would say that what the world is looking at today is the moral question and the understanding of spiritual law. If people do not abide, or do not understand it, or ignore it, then I do not see much hope for the Seventh Generation.

Then again, our first message was "How You Live." The second message was the "Great Law." The third message was the "Good Word" brought by Skananiateriio, or Handsome Lake. In 1799 he was shown in a vision for the Six Nations what was coming, and those were the prophecies that those men on the committee were asking about.

I don't talk about prophecies because they are not mine. They belong to the Six Nations. It's the Six Nations' responsibility to say okay now, let's talk about it. You hear it every now and then. But after being shown what was coming, Skananiateriio said to these four spiritual beings, "If that's the case, then what's the use?" And this was in 1799! He was shown what was going to happen. They said to him, "You tell your people that the generation that allows this to happen will suffer beyond all comprehension. You tell them just don't let it be your generation."

So then it was put back into the hands of the people. It's like the question the woman asked of the Peacemaker: "How long will this last?"

"That's up to you," he said.

How long will this Earth last, and how long will life last?

That's up to us and no one else.

11

THE HEALING OF INDIAN COUNTRY

KINSHIP, CUSTOM, CEREMONY, AND ORATORY

The Buffalo Shield. Painting by Billy Mack Steele.
Used by permission of Billy Mack Steele.

As the legendary San Francisco newspaper columnist Herb Caen once said, "Some remember, some care, some still fight." In that spirit of creative resistance the second half of the conversation between Huston Smith and Vine Deloria Jr. explores several profound themes at the heart of the Indian struggle for religious freedom.

For Deloria one of the central issues still facing Indian people in North America is the great divide between indigenous and Western religious thinking. "The first and great difference between primitive religious thought," he writes, "and the world religions . . . is that primitive peoples maintain a sense of mystery through their bond with nature; the world religions sever the relationship and attempt to establish a new, more comprehensible one."[1]

The final chapter of this book concerns the numerous creative efforts at healing the great divide between indigenous peoples and the colonizing powers whose influence is still felt. This conversation between Deloria and Smith furthers their earlier exploration of the meaning of the "Red Road," the native spiritual path that involves the community, the traditions, and the sacred.

In the spirit of the elders who believed in living with respect for the Seven Generations of the past and the Seven Generations of the future, Deloria calls for a return to ceremonies, a revival of kinship relationships, the teaching of native language, and clan responsibility. Other topics include the role of ancestral spirits, the difference between individually based and communally based religions, the revival of ceremonial life, the influence of Christian missionaries on the reservations, the pros and cons of using native icons in mainstream American life, and Deloria's unique vision of an interfaith future.

When Professor Smith asked what changes might bring about healing in Indian country, Deloria responded by sounding a tocsin call for native people to return to a "disciplined" practice of ceremony and oratory and for the outside world to realize that "indigenous peoples may misunderstand but do not 'misexperience.'"

This concluding dialogue revives the spirit evoked by the words of the great Winnebago leader Reuben Snake: "We are all on this road of life together, and the best we can do is offer our brothers and sisters our arm to lean on."

You must speak straight so that your words will go as sunlight to our hearts.

COCHISE (APACHE), 1866

HUSTON SMITH: I've heard some remarkable accounts of the Eskimo Indians about their utter lack of a fear of death. When it looked as though there was not enough food to carry the whole family through the winter, the elders would slip away at night and just bury themselves in the snow. They just accepted that their act was a part of the circle of life and death.

VINE DELORIA: There's a lot of information coming out now about how much a belief in reincarnation was involved with some of those things. That's why there was no fear of death for our ancestors. If you knew you were going to die you sang your death song and you went out with some dignity. But then Christianity comes along and promises eternal life, which is what makes Christians scared to death of death. So then you have to have insurance companies.

Now, the anti-Indian people have taken that information and said, "You Indians used to abandon your elders." All we can say in response to that is that in the environment our ancestors were in, where tribes were warring against each other, sometimes there weren't enough adult males to protect the whole community. Sometimes the tribe had to travel fast. When they didn't have enough food the elders recognized what needed to be done to ensure the survival of the entire tribe. The elders weren't left on the ground screaming, "No!" Instead they said, "I've lived a good life and I'm ready to go, so I'll stay behind."

There's a great story about an Osage, the son of an elderly Indian, who is accused of murder. The officials want to hang him, so his father goes out and says, "If you have to take a life, take mine. My son has just started his life and he was following the rules of our tribe. That's why he killed this person. I'm ready to go. Put me in his place."

Oren Lyons has probably told you about the infamous Iroquois incident in which five Frenchmen killed an Iroquois. The French held a trial, and the five Frenchmen were convicted. The French were going to shoot them, so the Iroquois could see that justice had been done. The Iroquois went to the French for justice and said, "No, no, no. We just lost one person. Don't kill five people because of the one." The French said, "No, they are all guilty." The Iroquois said again that their group had lost only one guy, and they tried to buy the freedom of those four people, and the French wouldn't relent. So there you see entirely different ideas of what justice is.

SMITH: But the search for justice is meaningless if you believe that the universe itself has no meaning. Isn't this the metaphysical quandary we are in right now?

DELORIA: I'm thinking about what you've said about meaning and meaninglessness, Huston. In a way it's strange, but in another way it's completely logical. When human beings—and I'm talking about those in the modern West—believe they are the only repository of meaning in this universe and that they are in charge of the future, then they've lost control over history. So it can seem like we're on an escalating course with extinction. You probably have heard the physicist Steven Weinberg say that the more intelligible the universe becomes, the more meaningless it seems. I suppose that's true if you bring it down only to mathematical equations. Sometimes they talk about the *beauty* of these equations, but if that's all there is out there—just equations—then meaning just shrivels. *We* know that's not true!

SMITH: I love the confidence with which you say that! You are absolutely right, *we* know there is more out there than just equations. But I wish that it could be expanded to our whole ethos. Yes, I think the indigenous people have avoided this metaphysical trap. But if you say in the *New York Times* that we know this is not the right or adequate view of things, of course it would never get printed.

DELORIA: No, but newspapers don't do us any good as far as news goes. They're all propaganda sheets. We don't do the right kind of research, ask the right questions. We have to get back to all kinds of fundamentals; we have to really look at things. Look at all the people who are on death row who are innocent. Yet we haven't phrased the question right about the death penalty. You've got anti–death penalty people and pro–death penalty people, and they just scream at each other. We haven't done the *middle work* of researching and identifying issues.

SMITH: Not only do they scream at each other, but each party, in a way, is inconsistent because the people who press most for antiabortion laws on the grounds that life is sacred are often the ones who vote for the death penalty.

DELORIA: And they're the same ones who cut appropriations to feed children; they're the ones who promote homelessness.

SMITH: Right, so right.

SYMBOLISM, METAPHOR, AND LITERALISM

DELORIA: There's one thing that I've always wanted to say in front of a camera. I hope I can say it right. One of the problems you have with Indian religion is that you're always caught in a Western epistemology. If you look at the ceremonies we're doing, they show you why sacred places are sacred. You start the ceremony, and you say we have the sacred pipe and the bowl, and that this bowl represents the universe. We hold it up to the four directions, and the powers of these directions come in. Now, that's a very sophisticated thing, because in the universe as we think we know it today, the center can be anywhere. So what they're really doing there is standing there *creating a moment*. When you find a sacred place that's had all those moments, then you enhance the thing. When Indians say the bowl represents the universe, they don't mean it in the Western sense of being a surrogate for "me." This is not a symbolic thing here: *It really is the universe.*

Now, you see so many New Agers who say, "The eagle feather represents this, and that represents that," and they appropriate those things. Well, they can appropriate them and go through the motions and feel emotionally cleansed. But when the *medicine men* are doing it they're not saying this crow feather symbolizes the birds or something. *They're saying the crow actually is here with all the birds.*

The majority of our ceremonies consist of nontangible entities doing things. That's how you can do healing, and that's how you can do the prophecies. You see, the idea of "represents" is symbolic in the non-Indian context, but it's a very concrete thing in the Indian context. You can say Mount Graham represents this, but Mount Graham actually *is* these things. It's *not* symbolic.

SMITH: This is so important that I want to restate it to see if I've got it. When used in a ceremony the bowl *is* the universe, while in Western epistemologies scholars assume that the bowl is simply a "metaphor" for the universe.

DELORIA: Right!

SMITH: That's where your point about epistemology comes in. The Native American views the bowl *literally* as being the universe. That's what literalism is. When we think about the universe in terms of 15 billion light years, Indian people say, "That's the metaphor." Wow, that's something, a complete reversal. I thought I knew a few things about epistemology, but that's a new way to put a bite into the concept. I thank you for that insight!

DELORIA: If you're going to reform your society, examine our Indian concepts. If you move them into Christianity, this point of view could change the way you see and do things. Take ancestral spirits. Christians believe that they should take the Communion of Saints seriously—that they should revere them and try to live up to their examples. But if you were to move our view of ancestral spirits over into your notion of the Communion of Saints, you would see that you are already a part of that Communion, and you would start acting as if you were. It would make a real difference in your behavior.

We've got to realize that if we stand in historical tradition we have to live up to higher ideals than we have today. Today is just a moment passing.

If you say this bowl literally *is* the universe, then you have to go over here and say this literally has to be the "Mass," and you take them away from a symbolic universe that requires nothing from them and you put responsibility on them.

SMITH: That's profound. My mind goes back to where we started, namely, that the *force* of Indian religion focuses on the community, which includes the land. Now, I want to relate that to religious studies and people who are reading about religion. In the last century there may been no religious book other than the Bible that has had a larger readership than William James's *The Varieties of Religious Experience*. For a century that may have been the most used textbook in religious studies. When I used it I didn't find any flaws in it. But recently someone pointed out that it's a very individualistic book. It is devoted entirely to accounts of the religious experiences of individuals and overlooks the communal aspect of Christianity—the Church, or metaphorically, the body of Christ. *The Varieties of Religious Experience* is a durable book; it has lasted for a century because something is right about it. This critique was an

The White House, Canyon de Chelly, Arizona, pilgrimage site for
Navajo and Hopi for the past thousand years. Photograph by Phil
Cousineau. Used by permission of Phil Cousineau.

eye-opener. I now see that there's something wrong with it too, its neglect
of the communal aspect of religion. Am I right in thinking that Indian
religion doesn't make that mistake?

DELORIA: I think that's an invalid criticism. The contrast isn't so absolute. We have our tribal traditions in which individuals go off by themselves
and do vision quests and are gone for a long time. Individuals have dreams,

and individuals do ceremony. But it is true that these visions and dreams are reported back to the community, first to a senior medicine man or an elder. Individuals always get advice from the community. There are times in our ceremonies when an elder will say, "Well, one of us had this dream or vision. What do we make of it? How do we handle it? Let's have one of our young men do such-and-such a ritual or ceremony and open himself to us, then let's see what happens." The Acomas might tell about how they didn't know what to eat when they were created. This woman was walking along, and this plant spoke to her, and it said, "I am a camus root and this is how you prepare me." That vision feeds into the communal life.

To come back to William James's anecdotal book, what's the difference between that and the scientific method where you choose the number of trials you are going to play with? You see, all evidence is particular and specific. It's the generalizations you make once you see the pattern, and the kinds of patterns you see that make the difference.

THE SEARCH FOR THE PATTERN

SMITH: But who has the patterns? In our society it's the elite scientists who have patterns they are trying to fill in, but that's not necessarily all the patterns possible.

DELORIA: Over many generations in the Indian community you pass down this wisdom that whatever you decide is relevant. When the Sioux were forced onto the reservation they wanted to continue the Buffalo Dance, but of course there were no buffalo left. The hunters had killed them all. So they debated and debated a long time, and they said, "What animal should we use if we're going to continue this dance?" Now, if you talk to the average anthropologist familiar with Indian country, he would say they probably took cattle because cattle had horns like buffalo and they were big. Actually, after much debate the Sioux chose *sheep* because they said the wool of the sheep up around the neck reminded them of the buffalo. For the time when the Sioux did the Buffalo Dance the sheep became a surrogate for the buffalo. The dance long ago passed out of existence; they knew they had to have the buffalo there.

Ceremonies are there forever in a lot of religions, but in Indian religions the ceremonies are there only for a period of time. When the world ends you get new ceremonies. Some carry over; some don't. So you get new prophecies.

SMITH: Let me see if I have this straight. I began by mentioning a criticism of William James's *Varieties of Religious Experience*. You responded by defending him, whereas the criticism clicked with me. Now, this is my explanation of our differences. The first epigraph in your book *God Is Red* says that the community that includes nature is fundamental. Since that is solidly in place, then you can validate what William James did in reporting only individual testimonies. As you say, in vision quests and dreams, individual testimonies are very important. I was speaking out of the individualism that shapes white culture. I can't take community for granted. Therefore, when I heard the critique that James's book leaves out the communal, I responded, "Yes, yes, it certainly does." So we put what the critic was saying into a different context because of the different traditions we come from.

DELORIA: And you end up creating communities for yourselves so you can retain the experiences in question. That's why you have Spiritualism and all these New Age religions. But you've got to have a community that's in time. That's the Seven Generations concept. There has to be enough similarity and continuity between one and seven so that you don't lose your identity.

SMITH: Of course, I come out of a splintering Protestant tradition. Roger Williams started his own religion because he couldn't agree with the other factions, and then having started it he thought, well they don't have it right, and he ended up with a new religion that had three people, himself, his wife, and one other member. Now, that's individualism gone haywire. You're protected from that. Now, *that's* a great blessing.

DELORIA: I rely a little bit on Wilcomb E. Washburn's *Red Man's Land, White Man's Law*. I think he did a good job of explaining the 1493 papal bull. You can take it beyond Washburn's analysis, but his is the first effort to come up with some kind of terms to define international law. It leads to Hugh Grotius's "natural law" and other theories. The basic idea is that if you can find the source of authority in one institution, then that institution has the power to affect everything else. What it does, however, is to place Indians outside the realm of humans with rights. That's continuing in American jurisprudence with the Doctrine of Discovery. It comes down to the point that Indians are not and never will be capable of making their own decisions. Therefore, someone has to do it for them. If that is true, then historically there would have been no treaties. You sign treaties with people who are capable of making their own decisions.

You come down to the present day that's still anchored back in the papal bull, when the pope sets himself up as the solitary authority by pretending to mediate between Spain and Portugal. Look at medieval Catholicism. The pope was always trying to gain secular power under the guise of exercising religious power.

SMITH: This Doctrine of Discovery has been the basis of international law ever since. It has excluded most of humanity. Today it translates into the economics of the haves and the have-nots. It's a very pernicious doctrine; there's no question about that. But in trying to root it out we have to attack more than law. Politics enters. President George W. Bush is acting against everything we have been talking about. But now that we are getting the hell kicked out of us, I think it's actually a hopeful time, for I think that the tide is turning in favor of the viable Indian way.

DELORIA: If you force any religion down to one ceremony, when you've really got all these other ceremonies, that's unequal treatment. You have hymn sings, and you have counseling. All these other religions in the larger culture get to have their full spectrum of ceremonies. But Indian religions are not allowed to do theirs.

INDIANS AND CHRISTIANITY

SMITH: Vine, I'm very well aware of the fact that your people have suffered at the hands of Christians, and behind that suffering has been the Christian religion. At the same time we have reservations filled with Indians who blend elements of Christianity with their own Indian practices. How do you see that situation? Is there something positive in this religion of the oppressors that crosses the bridge between the whites and the natives for those people who do incorporate the best of the two worlds? If the true goal is to bring people closer to God's infinite reality, then we need to develop a religious sense that speaks to the timelessness within us. Traditional peoples have always known how to weave the vast world of nature in a seamless way right into their spiritual lives. Is that how Indians incorporated Christianity without losing their own identity?

DELORIA: When tribes were confined to reservations, about the only people who spoke up for them were the missionaries. In fact, my grandfather was a chief of the Yanktons who converted to Christianity and became a well-known priest. You have to look from about 1870 in a lot of tribes, and from around 1880 in others, clear into the Depression years in the late 1920s, early '30s, when Indian ceremonies were suppressed. You've got to realize that about three generations of Indians were brought up in this Christian context, and they looked at churches as they looked at traditional counsels. That's why they wanted the churches to provide them with education; they wanted them to help them make a living; they wanted them to offer all kinds of comfort in times of grief; they wanted them to endorse marriages. So it was simply a matter of taking in this new Christian context and making that teaching your vehicle to express your sense of community.

Remember, the reservations used to have gigantic, four-strand barbed-wire fences to keep Indians in. The only ones who were allowed out were those who were going to participate in the Buffalo Bill Wild West Shows and those going to church services. And so the Episcopal Church in South Dakota became popular by inspiring Indians to get off the reservation once in a while. So they adopted the outward forms of Christianity, and I'm sure people were very sincere in their belief that this was a religion. But they never gave up kinship. They never gave up burial practices. They never gave up songs. They didn't give up a lot of things. They couldn't do public ceremonies and everything else. When I was growing up all those elders said, "No, you don't do that." They followed all those kinship customs, which were the heart of Indian religion. It was the community. They just translated those customs over. They loved Christian hymns! They were translated into Sioux languages. People would go to meetings, and they'd say, "Let's sing some hymns," and they'd sing until two o'clock in the morning.

But deep down Indians never changed their allegiance to the view of the native universe that they'd always had. When Congress took the lid off the ban on Indian ceremonies in the 1930s the social dances started up again. By the 1950s it began to be more popular to do more traditional Indian things. During the 1960s you had Sun Dances, and rumor has it there were some Ghost Dances. So Indians were trying to bring these things forward all along. I'd say at least half the Indians in the country, if not more, are nominally Christian, but no more Christian and no less Christian than whites of the same economic status.

Personally, I've been trying to push support for traditional religion because I think that brings the community together. The most devout Christian who gets into a crisis will go right back to that Indian religion anyway. There are good Presbyterian elders. I had a lot of Roman Catholics on the Standing Rock Reservation who were just totally traumatized.

They called me one time when somebody was going to have a Sun Dance who wasn't authorized to have one. Now, why would good Roman Catholics be worried about that? Underneath that Roman Catholicism was the traditional religion. In America, you're a Broncos fan or a Raiders fan or you're a Republican or you're a Democrat or you're an environmentalist. You can adopt tags—but that's not who you *really* are.

SMITH: Can you tell us your parable of the cemetery? I find it to be illustrative of the notion of "myth as other people's religion."

DELORIA: It's a great story. I was on the executive council of the Episcopal Church, and this notice came to us from Fort Hall. They were having a terrible time with the Indians. They had the church, and the Indians wanted the cemetery about a mile away. These people said, "We're not going to do this because we'd have to move the church." They said, "It's just an Indian superstition." I said, "That's right. The Shoshones say that when they go to night services they're bothered by the ghosts in the cemetery. If they're going to go to that service they want the church moved so they're not near those spirits." They said, "We can't do that!" I said, "Do you know why that church is by the cemetery? The reason is because in the Middle Ages your people thought the Devil was going to steal their souls unless they were close to the reserve sacrament. That's why the cemeteries are right outside the windows of the church." I said, "If all we're talking about is superstition, why should we accept your superstition rather than ours?"

SMITH: Oh, that's wonderful.

DELORIA: If we're talking about both groups being able to apprehend the presence of spirits, then you have got to let each group solve it in its own way. So we got the church moved! These were third-generation Episcopalians, but they still had that Indian belief, see?

INDIAN ICONS

SMITH: Let me change to a different subject. What are your feelings regarding Europeans appropriating icons from your people? The obvious example is the Washington Redskins, and I guess the kachina dolls, which have sort of become tourist trinkets. What do you think? Is this a desecration, a profanation of sacred symbols?

DELORIA: I'm one of the Indians who sued the Redskins.

SMITH: I didn't know that. Maybe that's why I intuitively raised that example.

DELORIA: I don't think that's racism and derogatory, per se. You move to other things, and I think it's a toss-up. You can't obliterate all references to Indians in every place. Sure, there are derogatory stereotypes, but there are good stereotypes too. One of the problems today is we take the differences and accentuate them and get very sensitive about these things. I've had women curse me for opening the door for them when I was just being polite. I do that for anybody behind me. The big fuss about all these names and everything should be cooled a little bit. Now, there are a lot of young people out there who are just becoming aware of the nature of discrimination. So when something like the issue of icons hits them, they react like I did in my youth and probably you did in your youth—they're damn mad about it! I think you've got to moderate those things back and forth. But what are you going to do with Sioux Bee Honey? I mean, so what?

What I don't like is when people react to *positive* images of Indians and say, "I'm going to tear that down!" Just like what those "Stepin Fetchit" Indians and some of these overly earnest ecologist people are doing now. That's just political propaganda. I think that there has to be a broad latitude in a diverse society. We tell intertribal jokes all the time, but then you start to go outside the group and say, "I don't want you white people saying bad things about us." Every group has to become more aware of itself and relax a little bit. You know, that's the way I would solve a lot of things.

But I mean, c'mon, the "Redskins"? From the word go that was derogatory. Every dictionary says it's derogatory. In newspaper articles they're saying we want a total extermination of the Redskins, see? That's a call for total genocide.

When you get to the word *chief*, though, what are you really saying? You could argue that "chief" is a political office or whatever. When we first raised the Redskin issue, all the sportswriters said, "Oh, my God, then the Lions and Tigers will want a change." Now *that's* downright racist. It's like saying Indians are a group of animals. Then they eased up a little bit and said, well, we have Vikings and Cowboys, and we have to remind them that Vikings and Cowboys always had a positive image. See? The Redskins *never* did.

Actually, what I object to more are Indians who are trying to put Christianity and traditional Indian religion together and are using the symbols of each of them. You go to a Mass, and they want to burn sweet-grass and have a pipe in there. You go to a Sun Dance, and they want to have Communion. I think that's blurring the traditions too much. I've come under criticism for saying that, but that's what I think. It's the wrong kind of syncretism, you see, because you're not being true to either tradition. You're saying, "I'm just going to merge everything together." You're no better than a New Ager, as far as I can see.

So you have to keep the integrity of ceremonies going. There's nothing stupider than an Episcopal bishop with a war bonnet on! When old traditional Christians and old traditional Indians saw that, they didn't like it. The new generation thought, "This is great, the bishop is sympathetic to us." This is just American politics: you say the right word and everybody says, hey, he's a good guy. It's just so superficial.

SMITH: My mind goes to a medical analogy. We have now organ transplants. But my understanding is that the medical profession is also bumping into the integrity of the organism, and it will withstand certain transplants, but it's a very precarious situation.

DELORIA: They are going to transplant arms, and somebody is going to be caught in a crime and claim that the arm wasn't his! They'll claim it had a mind of its own—that's why it shoplifted! So we're raising problem areas where nobody is going to know what's happening!

SMITH: You were saying that on this issue there has to be an overlap between the traditional and the modern. You can't just have a clean-cut separation. I wonder how many of the names of our fifty states are Indian? I don't ask you to do the calculation now, but I believe it's a very large number.

DELORIA: Oh, yes, and almost all the rivers are named after Indians.

ENVISIONING THE ANCIENT FUTURE

SMITH: I hadn't thought of that. I want to come back to a kind of global question. For better or worse, we're saddled with this interfaith between two civilizations, and looking at it from your side, let me just push it back to say that if you were twenty years old and looking at the future, what would be the most important thing that your people could contribute to bring us out of the mess that history has saddled us with?

DELORIA: I would emphasize two things. One is a determined disciplined return of kinship and clan responsibilities. The other is a return and redevelopment of Indian oratory.

SMITH: Oratory! Oh, I'm so glad you mentioned that. I haven't heard that word mentioned for some time. I knew William Arrowsmith, who made his name as a classicist, and when asked why he went into that sort of backwater, he said it was just their language that he fell in love with, that Greek oratory. But you know the story. In the end he switched from the Greek to the Native American, and for the same reason, not for any political reason or anything like that. It was on the grounds of language. Can you sort of flesh that out a little bit?

DELORIA: N. Scott Momaday is the expert on that. He really is good there. I've been reading transcripts of treaty proceedings, and you see chief after chief giving eloquent speeches trying to get the U.S. side to recognize what they're doing. They really came away from those treaty meetings believing that because they made those eloquent speeches that the whites understood them and were going to live up to what was said in the speeches. Then these great chiefs go to Washington and get into these horrible situations where they learn that Article 12 says this or that or whatever. The old Indian orators are just incredible.

Here's a little anecdote to show you the difference. This man from church headquarters came out, and we were at this Episcopal convocation. My dad was speaking to the men's group. Indians were sitting like this, some of them were sitting like that, others like this. Nobody was looking at him.

After he finished the speech, this guy from New York came up and said, "Aren't you terribly distressed when your audience acts like that?" He said, "No, no, no. They're listening. They're blocking out everything except what I'm saying."

He said, "You go and speak to a white audience, and you'll see that

---

INDIAN ORATORY

Shall we, without a struggle, give up our homes, our country bequeathed to us by the Great Spirit, the graves of our dead and everything that is dear and sacred to us? I know you will cry with me, Never! Never! That people will continue longest in the enjoyment of peace who timely prepare to vindicate themselves and manifest a determination to protect themselves whenever they are wronged.

TECUMSEH (SHAWNEE), 1811

---

all the faces are looking like they're just waiting to interrupt you and give their story instead of yours." And he said, "Those Indians have learned to listen, and other people don't."

SMITH: You are so right. Our people don't learn to listen. I remember what Senator Daniel Inouye, chair of the Senate Commission on Indian Affairs, said in Portland, Oregon, in 1993, about Indian treaties that didn't please him. He said that out of over eight hundred treaties the United States had shelved 430. They just didn't act on their commitment, while insisting that the Indians acted on theirs. Of the other 370 treaties that they did act on, they violated their agreement in every one of them. So we live in a time when oratory doesn't have the effect that it did in Chief Seattle's time.

DELORIA: But we could get it back!

SMITH: Oh, wonderful! You've almost done it with your writing and teaching. This morning is at least a good step forward. If we did bring oratory back, perhaps "we could be brothers yet." That line just ricocheted in my mind. Chief Seattle, wasn't it? I mean, what a wonderful blessing it would be. *We could be brothers yet!*

AFTERWORD

HUSTON SMITH

> We shall live again.
> We shall live again.
> **COMANCHE CHANT**

As I let the extraordinary days with these wonderful native leaders wash over my mind, my reactions fall into two categories. The first is very personal. As I look across these tables I see the faces of eight new friends. I am going to just recite their first names to drill them into my memory, because I hope to remember them for a long time: Tonya, Frank, Walter, Guy, Winona, Doug, Lenny, and Charlotte. I will always be happy that we had this week together in Cape Town, South Africa.

Having expressed that personal note, let me turn to the second category, which may sound very abstract. I've been trying to distill what has been running through all our conversations to lift out what is fundamental to them all. This is how I find myself putting that point to myself, so that I might remember the essence of our time together.

The crisis that the world finds itself in today is deeper than the way in which we structure our political and economic institutions. Those who live in the North and South, East and West, in their various ways, are all experiencing a common crisis. That crisis is the spiritual condition of the modern world. It's a strange situation and yet ultimately quite logical. The moment of crisis began as soon as human beings came to regard themselves as the repositories of the highest meaning in the world. That is when meaning began to drain from the world and human stature began to diminish. Having taking control of the modern world through their aspirations, the human race has suddenly discovered that it has lost control of where it is going.

We live in a time of great skepticism, the first skeptical civilization that has ever appeared in human history. It remains for human history to tell us whether a civilization as skeptical as ours has any survival value. There is a great danger today that this skepticism may spiral into cynicism and ultimately into despair. This brings me back to the Native American component of this Third Parliament of World Religions. At the root level I find the leaders with whom I have been in conversation reminding us of this basic crisis that we are in and making efforts to reverse it. They have a vision and determination that inspires my own vision and determination.

I will close by coming back to the personal.

I have been asking myself, "Why do I feel so happy with these people?" I feel far happier than I do at gatherings of the American Academy of Religion, my professional organization, or even at the university, where I have taught for the past fifty years. This feeling of happiness is like the one I often get when I am traveling in the other India, on the other side of the planet, where the poverty is almost intolerable and disease is rampant. Yet I always find myself happy there, too. I think the reason is that the name of God is in the air in India, as it is whenever I spend time with Native Americans, but not on Wall Street or on the streets of San Francisco.

With that I want to express my enormous happiness, and I want to testify that you have done this for me and that I'm leaving very happily.

MESSAGE FROM THE HOPI ELDERS

You have been telling the people that this is the Eleventh Hour.
Now you must go back and tell the people that this is the Hour.
And there are things to be considered:
Where are you living?
What are you doing?
What are your relationships?
Are you in right relation?
Where is your water?
Know your garden.
It is time to speak your Truth.
Create your community.
Be good to each other.
And do not look outside yourself for the leader.
This could be a good time!
There is a river flowing now very fast.
It is so great and swift that there are those who will be afraid.
They will try to hold onto the shore.
They will feel they are being torn apart and they will suffer greatly.
Know the river has its destination.
The elders say we must let go of the shore,
push off into the middle of the river,
keep our eyes open and our heads above the water.
See who is in there with you and celebrate.
At this time in history, we are to take nothing personally.
Least of all, ourselves.
For the moment that we do,
our spiritual growth and journey come to a halt.
The time of the lone wolf is over.
Gather yourselves!
Banish the word struggle
from your attitude and your vocabulary.
All that we do now must be done
in a sacred manner and in celebration.
We are the ones we've been waiting for.

NOTES

PREFACE

1. Jim Kenney, for the Council for a Parliament of the World newsletter (Fall 1999): 1.

2. Luther Standing Bear, *The Living Spirit of the Indian,* available at www .indigenouspeople.net/standbea.htm.

3. Arlene Hirschfelder and Martha Kreipe de Montano, *The Native American Almanac: A Portrait of Native America Today* (New York: Prentice-Hall, 1993), 36. For the first half of the twentieth century, scholars estimated the pre-Columbian population of North America to be between 900,000 and 2 million. In 1966 anthropologist Henry Dobyns challenged demographers to consider the question of pre-Columbian population using different methods. Dobyns estimated that there were between 9.8 and 12 million native North Americans before 1492. Russell Thornton, a historical demographer at the University of California at Berkeley, estimated in 1978 that the aboriginal population of the conterminous United States area was more than 5 million before contact. By 1890 the population of American Indians in the coterminous United States was reduced to 250,000, a decline of at least 95 percent, based on Thornton's estimate.

4. Editorial, *New York Times,* 26 September 2004.

5. Richard Erdoes and Lame Deer (John Fire), *Lame Deer, Seeker of Visions* (New York: Washington Square Press, 1994), 29; Charles Alexander Eastman

(Ohiyesa), *The Soul of the Indian: An Interpretation* (1911; repr., Lincoln: University of Nebraska Press, 1980), 14–15.

6. Quoted in John Neihardt, trans. and transcr., *Black Elk Speaks: Being the Life Story of a Holy Man of the Oglala Sioux* (New York: Washington Square Press, 1959), 29.

7. Thomas Hayden, "By the People," *Smithsonian* 35, no. 6 (September 2004): 53.

1. THE SPIRITUAL MALAISE IN AMERICA

1. Vine Deloria, *God Is Red: A Native View of Religion,* 2d ed. (Golden, CO: North American Press, 1992), 292.

2. Huston Smith, *The World's Religions,* rev. ed. (San Francisco: HarperCollins, 1989), 380.

3. Vine Deloria, "Native American Spirituality," in *For This Land: Writings on Religion in America* (New York: Routledge, 1999), 132.

2. FIVE HUNDRED NATIONS WITHIN ONE

1. Elizabeth A. Fenn, "The Great Smallpox Epidemic of 1775–82," *History Today* 53 (August 2003). Smallpox was already a weapon of war before the 1770s: "In 1763, British officials at Fort Pitt gave smallpox-infected blankets to Delaware Indians in an attempt to quell the uprising known as Pontiac's Rebellion. Unaware that his subordinates had already done this, General Jeffery Amherst also proposed that the Indians might be infected 'by means of Blankets'" (16).

2. The American Indian Ritual Object Repatriation Organization, founded by Elizabeth Sackler, also worked to educate private collectors and to return sacred objects and human remains.

3. ECOLOGY AND SPIRITUALITY

1. Jay Walljasper, "Celebrating Hellraisers: Winona LaDuke," interview with Winona LaDuke, *Mother Jones* (January/February 1996): 65.

2. Luther Standing Bear, *Land of the Spotted Eagle* (Boston: Houghton Mifflin, 1932), 248.

3. From Huston Smith, *The Illustrated World's Religions* (San Francisco: HarperCollins, 1994), 138.

4. Gerald Hausman, *Turtle Island Alphabet: A Lexicon of Native American Symbols and Culture* (New York: St. Martins Press), 1991. "Among some Native American tribes, the word *medicine* is synonymous with the word *mystery.* And so, a medicine man is a mystery man. Generally speaking, medicine in Indian culture means two things: plant, vegetal, herbal cures; and what we might call, for lack of a better term, psychic healing" (71).

5. The severe inequality of income is surpassed by the even greater concentration of the nation's wealth. Based on research by Edward N. Wolff, a leading

expert on wealth in the United States, holdings of the wealthy have grown steeply during the past three decades. In 1976 the richest 10 percent of families held 50 percent of the country's wealth, and by 1995 they held 70 percent of all wealth. In 1995 the top 20 percent of families owned 83 percent of wealth, with the remaining 80 percent of families holding only 17 percent. Compared to the distribution of income, here is the picture: the top 20 percent of families had about 50 percent of income; the remaining 50 percent was shared by the other 80 percent. Americans for Democratic Action and the Americans for Democratic Action Fund, "Income and Inequality: Millions Left Behind" (February 2004), available at www.adaction.org/income2004.htm.

4. THE HOMELANDS OF RELIGION

1. As reported by Charlotte Black Elk to *High Country Times,* 26 May 1997.
2. The Uluru people in Australia also claim this distinction for Ayers Rock.
3. Gerald Hausman, *Turtle Island Alphabet: A Lexicon of Native American Symbols and Culture* (New York: St. Martins Press, 1991), 123. The first historical mention of the sacred pipe was in 1724 when a French explorer described the *calumet,* or pipe, as the altar of sacrifice when native people prayed to the sun.

5. NATIVE LANGUAGE, NATIVE SPIRITUALITY

1. Rosemarie Ostler, "More Than Words," *Whole Earth* (Spring 2000): 4.
2. David Crystal, "Vanishing Landscapes," *Civilization* (February/March 1997): 41.
3. Rosemarie Ostler, "Disappearing Languages," *The Futurist* (August/September 1999): 16. *Ethnologue* lists 7,200 languages spoken worldwide, 440 of them within a generation or two of extinction. Most linguists accept rough projections that without sustained conservation efforts, half or more of the languages currently spoken will fall out of use by the end of the century. Raymond G. Gordon Jr., ed., *Ethnologue: Languages of the World,* 15th ed. (Dallas: SIL International, 2005).
4. UNESCO's Endangered Language Project, the Foundation for Endangered Languages (established in the UK in 1995), and the Linguistic Society of America's Committee on Endangered Languages and Their Preservation are fostering research into the status of minority languages: "The Native American Languages Act of 1990 (PL 101-477, October 30, 1990) recognizing the language rights of American Indians, Alaska Natives, Native Hawaiians, and Pacific Islanders was quietly enacted in the waning hours of the 101st Congress. Sponsored by Senator Daniel Inouye, Democrat of Hawaii, the bill passed on a voice vote in both House and Senate without hearings or vocal opposition. It authorizes no new programs for Native Americans, nor additional funding for existing ones, but is expected to facilitate efforts to preserve indigenous languages." Douglas George-Kanentiio, in an email to the editor, 13 January 2005.
5. One estimate is that some 250,000 native children were seized or "adopted," to use the parlance of the time, by white parents.

6. THE TRIUMPH OF THE NATIVE AMERICAN CHURCH

1. Quoted in Weston La Barre, *The Peyote Cult,* 2d ed. (New York: Schocken Books, 1969), 96, 166.

2. Huston Smith with Reuben Snake, *One Nation under God: The Triumph of the Native American Church* (Santa Fe, NM: Clear Light Publishers, 1996), 9.

3. The language used to describe this ancient spiritual practice testifies to its sacred and intimate nature. Peyote is variously referred to as "Grandfather," the "medicine," and the "sacrament." Its practice is described variously as the "peyote road" or the "way of the teepee," and its gatherings as "prayer meetings."

4. The relationship between the Religious Freedom Restoration Act Coalition (RFRA Coalition) and the Native American Church needs some clarification. By late 1990 the RFRA Coalition had formed. As Professor Smith says, it was historic in that never before had such a broad group of diverse religions united around a single goal. That goal was to enact a law requiring courts once again to apply the "compelling state interest test" to questions of religious freedom. The Native American Church wanted to support that goal but knew that simply doing so would not restore its lawful status, because in a concurring opinion in the *Smith* case, Justice Sandra Day O'Connor said that she thought the Court should keep the venerable old "compelling state interest test" and simply rule that the Indians had flunked the test. When the church approached the RFRA Coalition for mutual support, it asked if an additional sentence could be added to the proposed RFRA legislation that would expressly protect the use of peyote in Indian religious practices. The leadership of the RFRA Coalition apologetically declined. They said the sole unifying element of this most diverse coalition was precisely the restoration of the compelling state interest standard, and that adding anything else could easily cause the coalition to disintegrate. The Native American Church strongly believed in the goal of the RFRA Coalition, so it did nevertheless join the coalition. However, it also went about the business of forming its own coalition called the American Indian Religious Freedom Act Coalition (AIRFA Coalition) to pursue companion legislation that would specifically protect the sacramental use of peyote in Indian religious practices. Interestingly, many of the denominations in the RFRA Coalition also joined the AIRFA Coalition.

5. The case referred to is the 1997 *City of Boerne v. Flores,* in which the U.S. Supreme Court ruled on the scope of the restoration of the "compelling state interest test" to religious freedom questions generally. The generic Religious Freedom Restoration Act of 1993 instructed both state and federal courts to apply the "compelling state interest test," but in this case the Supreme Court ruled that the legislation was overbroad and that Congress could not tell the various state courts what standard they had to apply to cases. The Court did not strike down the law's applicability to the federal courts.

7. THE FIGHT FOR NATIVE AMERICAN PRISONERS' RIGHTS

1. Victor Turner, *From Ritual to Theater: The Human Seriousness of Play* (New York: Performing Arts Journal Publications, 1982).

2. On 25 June 1975, a tragic shootout took place between FBI agents and

Native Americans on the Pine Ridge Reservation, near Oglala, South Dakota. Two federal agents and one Indian were killed. Four members of AIM, the American Indian Movement, were arrested. Of those who went to trial only Leonard Peltier was convicted. He is in a federal prison serving a life sentence; his case is still under appeal. See Peter Matthiessen's magnificent book *In the Spirit of Crazy Horse* (New York: Penguin Books, 1992) for the most detailed reexamination of the case.

3. In 2000 7,000 native people were incarcerated in American prisons.

8. STEALING OUR SPIRIT

1. Sharon Begley, "Decoding the Human Body," *Newsweek* 135, no. 15 (April 2000): "For biologists and the genome it was far from love at first sight. Critics pointed out that some 97 percent of the human genome—3.1 billion of the 3.2 billion A's, T's, C's and G's—does not spell out a gene. Why bother sequencing this 'junk' DNA, whose presence no one can explain, especially when there was no know way to tell what was junk and what was a gene?" (53–54).

2. Editorial, *El Pais,* 27 June 2000.

3. Steve Newcomb (Shawnee/Legape), "Five Hundred Years of Injustice: The Legacy of Fifteenth Century Religious Prejudice": "When Christopher Columbus first set foot on the white sands of Guanahani Island, he performed a ceremony to 'take possession' of the land for the king and queen of Spain, acting under the international laws of Western Christendom. Although the story of Columbus' 'discovery' has taken on mythological proportions in most of the Western world, few people are aware that his act of 'possession' was based on a religious doctrine now known in history as the Doctrine of Discovery. Even fewer people realize that today—five centuries later—the United States government still uses this archaic Judeo-Christian doctrine to deny the rights of Native American Indians." Available at http://ile.nativeweb.org/sdrm_art.html.

4. Jane Goodall, "Fifi Fights Back: Lessons from Gombe, Tanzania," *National Geographic* (April 2003). "Perhaps the most important thing we've learned at Gombe is how similar we are to these creatures, with whom we share between 95 and 98 percent of our DNA. As we watch their numbers dwindle and their numbers fall, their legacy becomes as clear as a Gombe stream: As they go, one day, so may we" (80).

5. Supreme Court Decision, No. 79-136: *Diamond, Commissioner of Patents and Trademarks v. Chakrabarty* (1980).

6. In 1504 the Dominican priest Bartolomé de las Casas (1474–1566) arrived in the New World as a missionary carrying the "word of salvation" but left as a staunch defender of Indians. Over many decades he wrote luminous papers, letters, and theses in their defense from his diocese in Chiapas, the heart of the Lacandon region of the Maya.

But his fame rests on his 1542 eyewitness account, which was published under the title *The Tears of the Indians: Being an Historical and True Account of the Cruel Massacres and Slaughters Committed by the Spaniards in the Islands of the West Indies, Mexico, Peru, Etc.* It first appeared in English in London, in 1656, in a translation by John Phillips, from the French, and became a noteworthy defense of the "simple nobility of Indian people." The book helped defeat the rapacious charges of one of the leaders of the Spanish Inquisition, the Cordovan theologian Juan Gines de Sepulveda.

9. THE FIGHT FOR MOUNT GRAHAM

1. As reported in *Indian Country Today,* 7 March 1996.

2. Lyric Wallwork Winik, "There's a New Generation with a Different Attitude," *Parade* (July 1999): "Nearly 190,000 Indians are military veterans. American Indians have the highest record of service per capita of any ethnic group in the U.S." (7).

3. In 1997 the *London Times* reported: "Father Chris Connolly, an English Jesuit who is the observatory's deputy director, said: 'If civilization were to be found on other planets and if it were feasible to communicate, then we would want to send missionaries to save them, just as we did in the past when new lands were discovered.'" Jonathan Lenke, "Pope Builds Telescope to Find God," *London Times,* 14 December 1997.

4. Steve Yozwiak, "Could I See Your Permit to Pray?" *High Country News,* 31 August 1998.

5. According to Guy Lopez, since the 1999 Parliament a swath of trees has been cut down and power cables laid. Personal correspondence, March 2005.

10. REDEEMING THE FUTURE

1. "Oren Lyons: The Faithkeeper with Bill Moyers," Public Affairs Television, 3 July 1991.

2. Quoted in Akwesasne Notes, ed., *A Basic Call to Consciousness* (Summertown, TN: Book Publishing Company, 1995).

3. There were two fundamentally opposed ways of viewing gold: spiritually and economically. The Lakota medicine man Little Bear said, "The Black Hills are the house of gold for our Indians. We watch it to grow rich." In contrast was the trumpeting headline in the *Californian* on 17 May 1848: "Considerable excitement exists in our midst which bids fair to become quite a gold fever." On 20 May, it followed up: "A terrible visitant we have had of late, a FEVER which has well nigh depopulated our town, a town hard pressing upon a thousand souls. And this is the GOLD FEVER." J. S. Holliday, *Rush to Riches* (Berkeley and Los Angeles: University of California Press, 1999), 67.

4. Gerald Hausman speculates that the term *redskin* may derive from the French *peau-rouge. Turtle Island Alphabet: A Lexicon of Native American Symbols and Culture* (New York: St. Martins Press, 1991), 71.

11. THE HEALING OF INDIAN COUNTRY

1. As reported in *North Beach Journal* 5, no. 11 (December 2004): 8.

BIBLIOGRAPHY

RECOMMENDED READING

Aberle, David Friend. *The Peyote Religion among the Navajo*. Norman: University of Oklahoma Press, 1991.

Allen, Paula Gunn. *Life Is a Fatal Disease: Collected Poems: 1962–1995*. Albuquerque: West End Press, 1997.

Barney, Gerald O., with Jane Blewett and Kristen R. Barney. *Threshold 2000: Critical Issues and Spiritual Values for a Global Age*. For the Parliament of World Religions, Cape Town, 1999. Arlington, VA: Millennium Institute, 2000.

Berkhofer, Robert F., Jr. *The White Man's Indian: Images of the American Indian from Columbus to the Present*. New York: Vintage Books, 1978.

Brown, Dee. *Bury My Heart at Wounded Knee: An Indian History of the American West*. New York: Bantam, 1971.

Brown, Joseph Epes, ed. *The Sacred Pipe: Black Elk's Account of the Seven Rites of the Oglala Sioux*. Baltimore: Penguin, 1971.

Catlin, George. *North American Indian Portfolio*. London: George Catlin, 1844.

Champagne, Duane. *Native America: Portrait of the Peoples*. Foreword by Dennis Banks. Detroit: Visible Ink Press, 1994.

Coltelli, Laura. *Winged Words: American Indian Writers Speak*. Lincoln: University of Nebraska Press, 1990.

Cousineau, Phil. *The Art of Pilgrimage: The Seeker's Guide to Making Travel Sacred*. Berkeley: Conari Press, 1998.

Day, A. Grove, ed. *The Sky Clears: Poetry of the American Indians*. New York: Bison Books, 1951.

De las Casas, Bartolomé. *The Tears of the Indians: Being an Historical and True Account of the Cruel Masters and Slaughters in the Islands of the West Indies, Mexico, Peru, Etc*. Translated by John Phillips. 1656. Revised edition with an introduction by Colin Steele. Oxford: Bodleian Library and Oriole Chapbooks, 1972.

Deloria, Philip J. *Playing Indian*. New Haven: Yale University Press, 1998.

Deloria, Vine, Jr. *Custer Died for Your Sins: An Indian Manifesto*. New York: Avon, 1969.

———. *God Is Red: A Native View of Religion*. 2d ed. Golden, CO: North American Press, 1992.

———. *For This Land: Writings on Religion in America*. New York: Routledge, 1999.

———. *Spirit and Reason: The Vine Deloria, Jr. Reader*. Golden, CO: Fulcrum Publishing, 1999.

Drinnon, Richard. *Facing West: The Metaphysics of Indian-Hating and Empire-Building*. New York: New American Library, 1980.

Eastman, Charles Alexander (Ohiyesa). *The Soul of the Indian: An Interpretation*. 1911. Reprint, Lincoln: University of Nebraska Press, 1980.

Echo-Hawk, Roger C., and Walter R. Echo-Hawk. *Battlefields and Burial Grounds: The Indian Struggle to Protect Ancestral Graves in the United States*. Minneapolis: Lerner Publications, 1994.

Edmunds, R. David, ed. *American Indian Leaders: Studies in Diversity*. Lincoln: University of Nebraska Press, 1980.

Eldredge, Niles. *Time Frames: The Re-Thinking of Darwinian Evolution and the Theory of Punctuated Equilibria*. New York: Simon & Schuster, 1985.

Eliot, T. S. *Four Quartets*. London: Faber & Faber, 1961.

Erdoes, Richard, and Lame Deer (John Fire). *Lame Deer, Seeker of Visions*. New York: Washington Square Press, 1994.

Ewen, Alexander, ed. *Voice of Indigenous Peoples: Native People Address the United Nations*. Santa Fe, NM: Clear Light Publishers, 1994.

Farb, Peter. *Man's Rise to Civilization: As Shown by the Indians of North America from Primeval Times to the Coming of the Industrial State*. New York: Avon, 1968.

George-Kanentiio, Doug. *Iroquois Culture & Commentary*. Santa Fe, NM: Clear Light Publishers, 2000.

Geronimo: His Own Life: The Autobiography of a Great Patriot Warrior. As told to S. M. Barrett. 1906. Revised and edited by Frederick Turner. New York and London: Penguin, 1970.

Glover, Vic. *Keeping Heart on Pine Ridge: Family Ties, Warrior Culture, Commodity Foods, Rez Dogs and the Sacred*. Summertown, TN: Vic Glover Book Publishing, 2004.

Hausman, Gerald. Foreword by N. Scott Momaday. *Turtle Island Alphabet: A*

Lexicon of Native American Symbols and Culture. New York: St. Martins Press, 1991.

Hirschfelder, Arlene, and Martha Kreipe de Montaño. *The Native American Almanac: A Portrait of Native America Today.* New York: Prentice-Hall, 1993.

Horgan, John. *The End of Science: Facing the Limits of Knowledge in the Twilight of the Scientific Age.* Reading, MA: Addison-Wesley, 1996.

Josephy, Alvin F., Jr. *The Indian Heritage of America.* New York: Bantam, 1968.

———. *The Patriot Chiefs: A Chronicle of American Indian Resistance.* New York: Penguin, 1969.

Jung, Carl G. *Memories, Dreams, Reflections.* Recorded and edited by Aniela Jaffe. Translated from the German by Richard and Clare Winston. New York: Vintage Books, 1961.

La Barre, Weston. *The Peyote Cult.* 2d ed. New York: Schocken Books, 1969.

LaDuke, Winona. *All My Relations: Native Struggles for Land and Life.* Cambridge, MA: South End Press, 1999.

Lincoln, Kenneth, and Al Logan Slagle. *The Good Red Road: Passages into Native America.* New York: HarperCollins, 1989.

Matthiessen, Peter. *Indian Country.* New York: Penguin, 1984.

Momaday, N. Scott. *House Made of Dawn.* New York: Harper & Row, 1966.

———. *The Way to Rainy Mountain.* Albuquerque: University of New Mexico Press, 1969.

Moyers, Bill. *A World of Ideas.* New York: Doubleday, 1990.

Nabakov, Peter. *Indian Running.* Santa Barbara: Capra Press, 1981.

Neihardt, John, trans. and transcr. *Black Elk Speaks: Being the Life Story of a Holy Man of the Oglala Sioux.* New York: Washington Square Press, 1959.

Ortiz, Simon. *A Good Journey.* Berkeley: Turtle Island Press, 1977.

Page, Jake. *In the Hands of the Great Spirit: The 20,000-Year History of American Indians.* New York: Free Press, 2003.

Peltier, Leonard. *Prison Writings: My Life Is a Sun Dance.* Edited by Harvey Arden. New York: St. Martins, 2000.

Reuben Snake, Your Humble Serpent: Indian Visionary and Activist. As told to Jay Fikes. Foreword by James Botsford. Afterword by Walter R. Echo-Hawk. Santa Fe, NM: Clear Light Publishers, 1996.

Rhine, Gary, and Phil Cousineau, *The Peyote Road.* Malibu, CA: DreamCatchers Productions, 1993. Videotape.

———. *The Red Road to Sobriety.* Malibu, CA: DreamCatchers Productions, 1995. Videotape.

———. *Your Humble Serpent: The Life of Reuben Snake.* Malibu, CA: DreamCatchers Productions, 1996. Videotape.

Rothenberg, Jerome, edited with commentaries. *Technicians of the Sacred: A Range of Poetries from Africa, America, Asia, Europe & Oceania.* Berkeley and Los Angeles: University of California Press, 1968.

———. *Shaking the Pumpkin: Traditional Poetry of the Indian North Americas.* Revised edition. New York: Alfred van der Marck, 1986.

Silko, Leslie Marmon. *Ceremonies.* New York: Viking, 1977.

Slotkin, J. S. *The Peyote Religion: A Study in Indian-White Relations*. Glencoe, IL: Free Press, 1956.

Smith, Huston. *The World's Religions*. Revised edition. San Francisco: Harper-Collins, 1989.

———. *Why Religion Matters*. New York: HarperCollins, 2001.

———, comp. and ed. with Reuben Snake. *One Nation under God: The Triumph of the Native American Church*. Santa Fe, NM: Clear Light Publishers, 1996.

Sullivan, Lawrence E., ed. *Native American Religions: North America: Religion, History, and Culture Selections from the Encyclopedia of Religion*. New York: Macmillan, 1987.

Thorpe, Dagmar. *People of the Seventh Fire: Returning Lifeways of Native America*. Ithaca, NY: Akwekon Press, Cornell University American Indian Program, 1977.

Underhill, Ruth. *Singing for Power: The Song Magic of the Papago Indians of Southern Arizona*. Berkeley and Los Angeles: University of California Press, 1968.

Utter, Jack. *American Indians: Answers to Today's Questions*. Lake Ann, MI: National Woodlands Publishing, 1993.

Vanderwerth, W. C., comp. *Indian Oratory: Famous Speeches by Noted Indian Chiefs*. Norman: University of Oklahoma Press, 1971.

Washburn, Wilcomb E. *Red Man's Land, White Man's Law: Past and Present Status of the American Indian*. 2d ed. Norman: University of Oklahoma Press, 1995.

Waters, Frank. *Book of the Hopi*. New York: Viking Press, 1980.

Wellman, Paul I. *Death on the Prairie: The Thirty Years' Struggle for the Western Plains*. 1934. Reprint, Lincoln: University of Nebraska Press, 1987.

RECOMMENDED WEB LINKS

American Indian Law Alliance: www.ailanyc.org.

American Indian Ritual Object Repatriation Foundation: www.repatriation foundation.org.

Cultural Conservancy: www.nativeland.org.

Dating the Iroquois Confederacy: www.ratical.org/many_worlds/6Nations/ DatingIC.html.

Draft Declaration on the Rights of Indigenous Peoples: www.iwgia.org/sw248.as .The Great Law of Peace: http://sixnations.buffnet.net/Great_Law_of_Peace.

Draft Declaration on the Rights of Indigenous Peoples: www/usask.ca/nativelaw/ ddir.html.

Dreamcatchers Film Productions: www.dreamcatchers.org.

Honor the Earth (Winona LaDuke): www.honorearth.org.

Human Genome Diversity Project: www.6nations.org.

Human Genome Diversity Project: www.nativenet.uthscsa.edu/archive/nl/hgdp .html.

Human Genome Diversity Project: www.stanford.edu/group/morrinst/hgdp.html.

Indian Burial and Sacred Grounds Watch: www.ibsgwatch.indigenous.imagedjinn .com.

Indian language statistics: www-rcf.usc.edu/~cmmr/Native_American.html.

Indian languages spoken today: www.indians.org/welker/americas.htm.

Indian Law Resource Center: www.indianlaw.org.

Indigenous Environmental Network: www.ienearth.org.

Indigenous Peoples Council on Biocolonialism: www.ipcb.org.

Indigenous Peoples Council on Biocolonialism—Human Genetics: www.ipcb
.org/issues/human_genetics/index.html.

Indigenous Women's Network: www/welrp.org.

International Work Group for Indigenous Affairs: www.iwgia.org.

Iroquois Confederacy: www.ratical.org/many_worlds/6Nations/DatingIC.html.

Iroquois opening prayer: www.tyedinaga.net/ohenton.

Joanne Shenandoah: www.joanneshenandoah.com.

MAPS: Languages of the USA: www.ethnologue.com/show_map.asp?name =
USA.

Mount Graham Coalition and the Apache Survival Coalition: www.mountgraham
.org.

National Congress of American Indians: www.ncai.org.

Native American Authors Project: www.ipl.org/div/natam/bin/browse.pl/A31.

Native American Church: www.well.com/user/dpd/nachurch.html.

Native American Rights Fund: www.narf.org.

Native Land Organization: www.nativeland.org.

Native Languages of the Americas: www.native-languages.org.

Nisqually Tribe: www.ohwy.com/wa/n/nisqintb.htm.

Oren Lyons on the World Bank, October 3, 1995, Ethics and Spiritual Values
and the Promotion of Environmentally Sustainable Development "50 Years
of the World Bank, Over 50 Tribes Devastated": http://fraktali.849pm.com/
text/lyons/worldbank.html.

Oren Lyons, Haudenosaunee Faithkeeper, addressing delegates to the United Nations Organization, opened "The Year of the Indigenous Peoples" (1993) in
the United Nations General Assembly Auditorium, United Nations Plaza, New
York City, December 10, 1992: www.ratical.org/many_worlds/6Nations/
OLatUNin92.html.

Parliament of World Religions: www.cpwr.org.

Plastic Medicine Man: users.pandora.be/gohiyuhi/articles/art00039.htm.

Regarding the Human Genome Diversity Project: www.indians.org/welker/
genome.htm.

Repatriation Laws: www.cr.nps.gov/nagpra.

Resolution to Oppose the Human Genome Diversity Project: www.ipcb.org/
resolutions/htmls/model_resolution_hgdp.html.

Seventh Generation Fund: www.7genfund.org/environmental.html.

Six Nations Home Page: www.sixnations.org.

Society for the Study of Indigenous Languages of the Americas: www.ssila.org.

United Nations Working Group on Indigenous Populations: www.unhchr.ch/
indigenous/groups-01.htm.

White Earth Land Recovery Project and Native Harvest Online Catalog: www
.welrp.org.

ACKNOWLEDGMENTS

As I learned long ago from an old friend and one of my favorite teachers, the Winnebago wise man Reuben Snake, who learned from an old medicine man before him, life is a journey during which we must learn to help one another. This book and the film on which it is based have been one such journey. Over the past six years the project has stretched halfway around the world and involved dozens of stouthearted and long-visioned people in South Africa, Canada, the Six Nations, the Southwest, northern Mexico, and California.

First and foremost is my brother Gary Rhine, tireless champion of indigenous rights and the main motivation behind *A Seat at the Table,* and his kind and generous wife, Irene Romero, without whom we would not have been able to stay the course these last several years. My tremendous respect for Gary continues to grow; he was an invaluable resource for many of the painstaking details that needed to be verified, in honor of our Indian friends. My deep gratitude also to James Botsford, an Indian rights lawyer, and poetic defender of human rights, who was an invaluable guide through the maze of legal details and who helped write some of the footnotes that have helped to clarify those points.

I also owe an immeasurable debt to Huston Smith, longtime friend, mentor, and honorary godfather to my son, Jack, who agreed to endure the long flight to Cape Town to lead the forums at the Parliament of World Religions in 1999. He has kept a faithful vigil ever since by calmly agreeing to several post-Parliament interviews and manuscript reviews. His much-vaunted compassion graced this project each time he was asked to help: "We want to get it right to honor our friends."

By "our friends" he was referring to the ten leaders from Indian country who agreed to share their lives, ideas, philosophies, and spiritual beliefs over the course of these six years. I would like to formally thank them here for their patience and time and courage: Charlotte Black Elk, Frank Dayish Jr., Vine Deloria Jr., Walter Echo-Hawk, Lenny Foster, Tonya Gonnella Frichner, Douglas George-Kanentiio, Winona LaDuke, Anthony Guy Lopez, and Oren Lyons. We are honored to play a small part in their ceaseless struggle for religious freedom. Thanks, too, to those who supplied us with photographs and artwork, including George Braziller, Inc., Don Doll, S.J., the Minnesota Historical Society, the Parliament of World Religions, Billy Mack Steele, and Toba Taylor. To all of you, a hearty *Aho!*

And to all those at the University of California Press in Berkeley, my deep appreciation for believing in this book, especially to my editor, Reed Malcolm, for his faith in the power of conversations, Suzanne Knott for her guidance through production, and Mimi Kusch for her superb manuscript editing. I am also deeply grateful to my agent, Thomas Grady, who made this project possible.

Finally, I want to thank my partner, Jo Beaton, and our son, Jack, for patiently walking down the Red Road with me over the past several years; you both deserve credit in the creation of this book.

INDEX

Ochwiay Biano (Mountain Lake), 15
Oglala Sioux: Charlotte Black Elk, xiv,
58–74, 58*illus.;* Blaska, 61; Crazy
Horse, v, 67–68; Red Cloud, 73;
Standing Bear, xiv, xviii, 41–42, 65.
See also Black Elk, Nicholas
Ohio State University, Columbus, Ohio,
150, 152
Ohiyesa (Charles Alexander Eastman),
xvii
Ojibway: Copway, 87; Creators, 44–46;
language, 44–46, 56–57; medicine,
43–44; Peltier, 115, 116, 128–29,
209n2(ch7); sturgeon, 45, 46, 48.
See also Lakota Sioux
Oklahoma, Native American Church,
101, 102
Oneidas, 76, 78
One Nation Under God (Huston Smith
and Snake), 99
Onondagas, 78, 85; Chief Leon Shenandoah, 3, 165, 169, 170, 180; endangered species, 135–36, 139; Frichner,
xiv, 130–45, 130*illus.;* midwinter
ceremonies, 165; Onondaga Nation,
135–36, 139, 164–65; Onondaga
Reservation (New York)/Huston
Smith visits, 2–3, 5, 165–66, 174.
See also Lyons, Oren
oral traditions, 2, 30, 109, 164; Apache,
153; archeology, 4; Iroquois, 76, 83,
84, 86, 87, 89–90; land in, 50; and
language loss, 76, 83, 84, 86; laws,
87; memory devices, 43; oratory, xiv,
198–99; as religious education, 86;
science verifying, 59, 60. *See also*
indigenous religions; languages;
songs; storytelling
oratory, xiv, 198–99
Oregon: *Employment Division of
Oregon v. Smith* (1990), 12–13,
32, 99, 102–8, 208n4; Senate Select
Committee on Indian Affairs hearings in Portland, 105, 199
Organization of American States, Declaration on the Rights of Indigenous
Peoples, 131
orthopraxis, 12
Ortiz, Simon (Navajo), xii–xiii, xix,
132–33
Osage, 186
Ostler, Rosemarie, 76
The Outline of History (Wells), 70
ozone layer, 50

paintings, Sun Dance, 69*illus.,* 184*illus.*
El Pais, Madrid, 132

Paiute, Sarah Winnemucca, 122
Palestine, Mount Tabor/Mount of
Transfiguration, 70
parable, cemetery, 195
Parker, Quanah (Comanche chief and
Road Man), 98–99
Parliament of World Religions: First
(1893), xv, 26, 27*illus.;* Second
(1994), 26–27. *See also* Third
Parliament of World Religions
(1999), Cape Town, South Africa
past, concern with, 47–48
patents, on genes, 131, 141
patterns, 191–93
Pawnee, 28; Pawnee Nation as isolates of
historic interest, 135–36; war song,
26. *See also* Echo-Hawk, Walter
(Pawnee)
peace: Great Law of Peace, 87–88, 167–
69; Parliaments of World Religions,
171; peacemaking process, 117,
127; prayer, 73; principle of, 180
Peacemaker, 87–88, 167–69, 173,
183
Peltier, Leonard (Lakota/Ojibway), 115,
116, 128–29, 209n2(ch7)
Permanent Forum on Indigenous Issues,
131
permits, for sacred sites, 66, 148,
157–58
personal God, 20
Petition vs. the U.S. (1951), 172
peyote, sacrament of, 12–13, 32, 35,
98–110, 208nn3,4
The Peyote Road film, 105
pilgrimage, 64, 70–71, 190*illus.*
pilgrims, to America, 31
Pillsbury family, 54
Pima Indian Nation, Derrick Gerlaugh,
123–25
Pine Ridge Indian Reservation, South
Dakota, 59, 209n2(ch7)
pipe. *See* sacred pipe
Pipestone, 66
Pokagon, Simon (Potawatomie), 34
politics, 33, 55–56, 196; Iroquois, 84–
85; Mount Graham, 151, 158–59;
and religion, xiii, 12, 36, 40; right
wing, 12. *See also* rights; seat at the
table; U.S. laws
pollution, 22, 50–52, 137–38, 152, 181;
pollution credits, 46, 51
Polzer, Charles, 152
Pontiac's Rebellion, 206n1(ch2)
pope, 193; and Mount Graham, 154,
156–57; rulings, 138, 144,
192–93